Kingston Frontenac Public Library

P9-CRU-715

DEC - - 2014

INDESTRUCTIBLE HULK

S.M.A.S.H. TIME

VOLUME 03

INDESTRUCTIBLE HULK VOL. 0: S.M.A.S.H. TIME. Contains material originally published in magazine form as INDESTRUCTIBLE HULK #11-15. First printing 2014. ISBN# 978-0-7851-8884-1. Published by MARVEL WORLDWIDE, INC., a subsidiary of MARVEL ENTERTAINMENT, LLC. OFFICE OF PUBLICATION: 135 West 50th Street, New York, NY 10020. Copyright © 2010 and 2011 Marvel Characters, Inc. All rights reserved. All characters featured in this issue and the distinctive names and likenesses thereof, and all related indicia are trademarks of Marvel Characters, Inc. No similarity between any of the names, characters, persons, and/or institutions in this magazine with those of any living or dead person or institution is intended, and any such similarity which may exist is purely coincidental. Printed in the U.S.A. ALAN FINE, EVP - Office of the President, Marvel Worldwide, Inc. and EVP & CMO Marvel Characters B.V.; DAN BUCKLEY, Publisher & President - Print, Animation & Digital Divisions; JOE QUESADA, Chief Creative Officer; TOM BREVOORT, SVP of Publishing; DAVID BOGART, SVP of Operations & Procurement, Publishing; C.B. CEBULSKI, SVP of Creator & Content Development; DAVID GABRIEL, SVP of Print & Digital Publishing Sales; JIM O'KEEFE, VP of Operations & Logistics; DAN CARR, Executive Director of Publishing Technology; SUSAN CRESPI, Editorial Operations Manager; ALEX MORALES, Publishing Operations Manager; STAN LEE, Chairman Emeritus. For information regarding advertising in Marvel Comics or on Marvel.com, please contact Niza Disla, Director of Marvel Partnerships, at ndisla@marvel.com. For Marvel subscription inquiries, please call 800-217-9158. Manufactured between 11/22/2013 and 1/6/2014 by R.R. DONNELLEY, INC., SALEM, VA, USA.

LEGO AND THE MINIFIGURE FIGURINE ARE TRADEMARKS OR COPYRIGHTS OF THE LEGO GROUP OF COMPANIES. ©2013 THE LEGO GROUP. CHARACTERS FEATURED IN PARTICULAR DECORATIONS ARE NOT COMMERCIAL PRODUCTS AND MIGHT NOT BE AVAILABLE FOR PURCHASE.

10 9 8 7 6 5 4 3 2 1

WRITER
MARK WAID
ARTISTS
MATTEO SCALERA (#11-13)
KIM JACINTO (#13-15) WITH MAHMUD ASRAR (#14)
COLOR ARTIST
VAL STAPLES WITH LEE LOUGHRIDGE (#15)
LETTERERS
CHRIS ELIOPOULOS (#11-13) & VC'S CORY PETIT (#14-15)
COVER ARTIST
MUKESH SINGH
ASSISTANT EDITOR
EMILY SHAW
EDITOR
MARK PANICCIA

COLLECTION EDITOR
CORY LEVINE
ASSISTANT EDITORS
ALEX STARBUCK
NELSON RIBEIRO
EDITORS, SPECIAL PROJECTS
JENNIFER GRÜNWALD
MARK D. BEAZLEY

SENIOR EDITOR,
SPECIAL PROJECTS
JEFF YOUNGQUIST
SVP OF PRINT & DIGITAL
PUBLISHING SALES
DAVID GABRIEL
BOOK DESIGN
JEFF POWELL & CORY LEVINE

EDITOR IN CHIEF
AXEL ALONSO
CHIEF CREATIVE OFFICER
JOE QUESADA
PUBLISHER
DAN BUCKLEY
EXECUTIVE PRODUCER
ALAN FINE

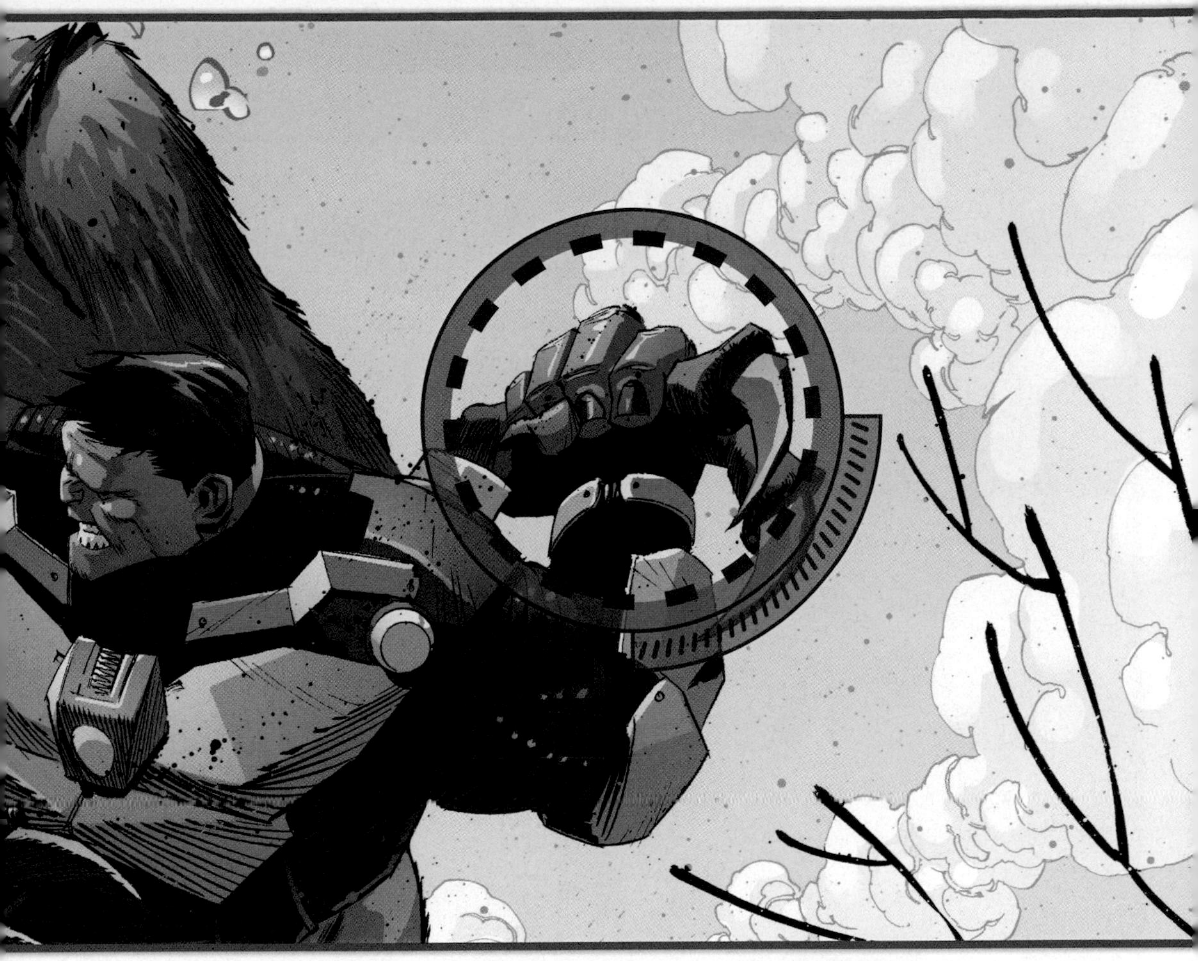

THE HULK WILL ALWAYS BE A PART OF DR. BRUCE BANNER, BUT BANNER WANTS TO BE REMEMBERED FOR HIS CONTRIBUTIONS TO SCIENCE AND NOT FOR TURNING INTO A BIG, GREEN FORCE OF RAGE AND DESTRUCTION. TO ACHIEVE THAT GOAL, BANNER HAS STRUCK A MUTUALLY BENEFICIAL DEAL WITH MARIA HILL, THE DIRECTOR OF S.H.I.E.L.D. SHE PROVIDES BANNER WITH A LAB, STAFF, EQUIPMENT AND ALL OF THE RESOURCES HE NEEDS TO BETTER MANKIND, AND BANNER PROVIDES S.H.I.E.L.D. WITH THE HULK FOR ANY MISSIONS THAT MIGHT NEED THAT EXTRA MUSCLE.

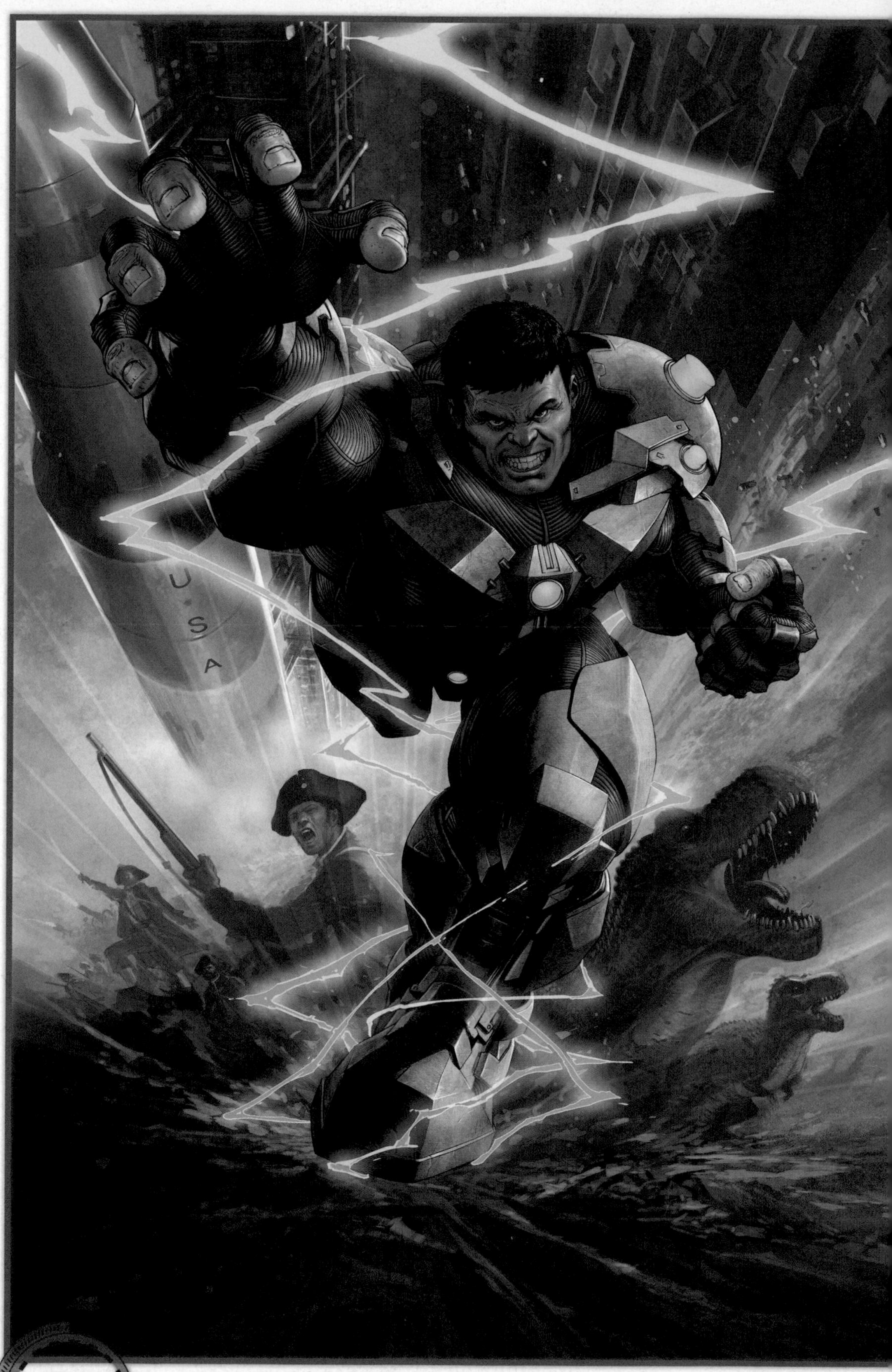
USA

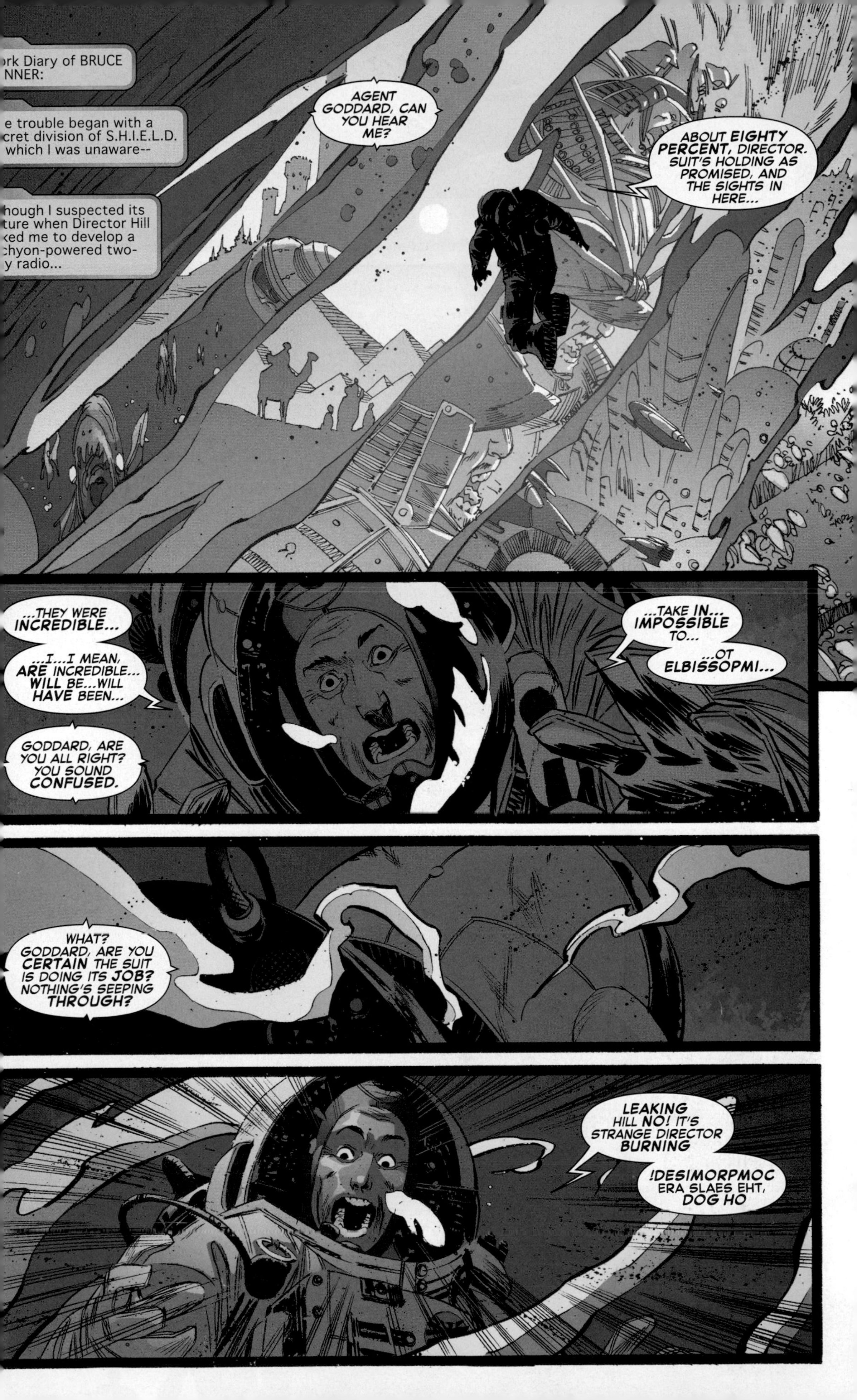

ork Diary of BRUCE
NNER:
e trouble began with a
cret division of S.H.I.E.L.D.
which I was unaware--
hough I suspected its
ture when Director Hill
ked me to develop a
chyon-powered two-
y radio...
AGENT GODDARD, CAN YOU HEAR ME?
ABOUT EIGHTY PERCENT, DIRECTOR. SUIT'S HOLDING AS PROMISED, AND THE SIGHTS IN HERE...
...THEY WERE INCREDIBLE...
...I...I MEAN, ARE INCREDIBLE... WILL BE...WILL HAVE BEEN...
...TAKE IN... IMPOSSIBLE TO...
...OT ELBISSOPMI...
GODDARD, ARE YOU ALL RIGHT? YOU SOUND CONFUSED.
WHAT? GODDARD, ARE YOU CERTAIN THE SUIT IS DOING ITS JOB? NOTHING'S SEEPING THROUGH?
LEAKING HILL NO! IT'S STRANGE DIRECTOR BURNING
!DESIMORPMOC ERA SLAES EHT, DOG HO

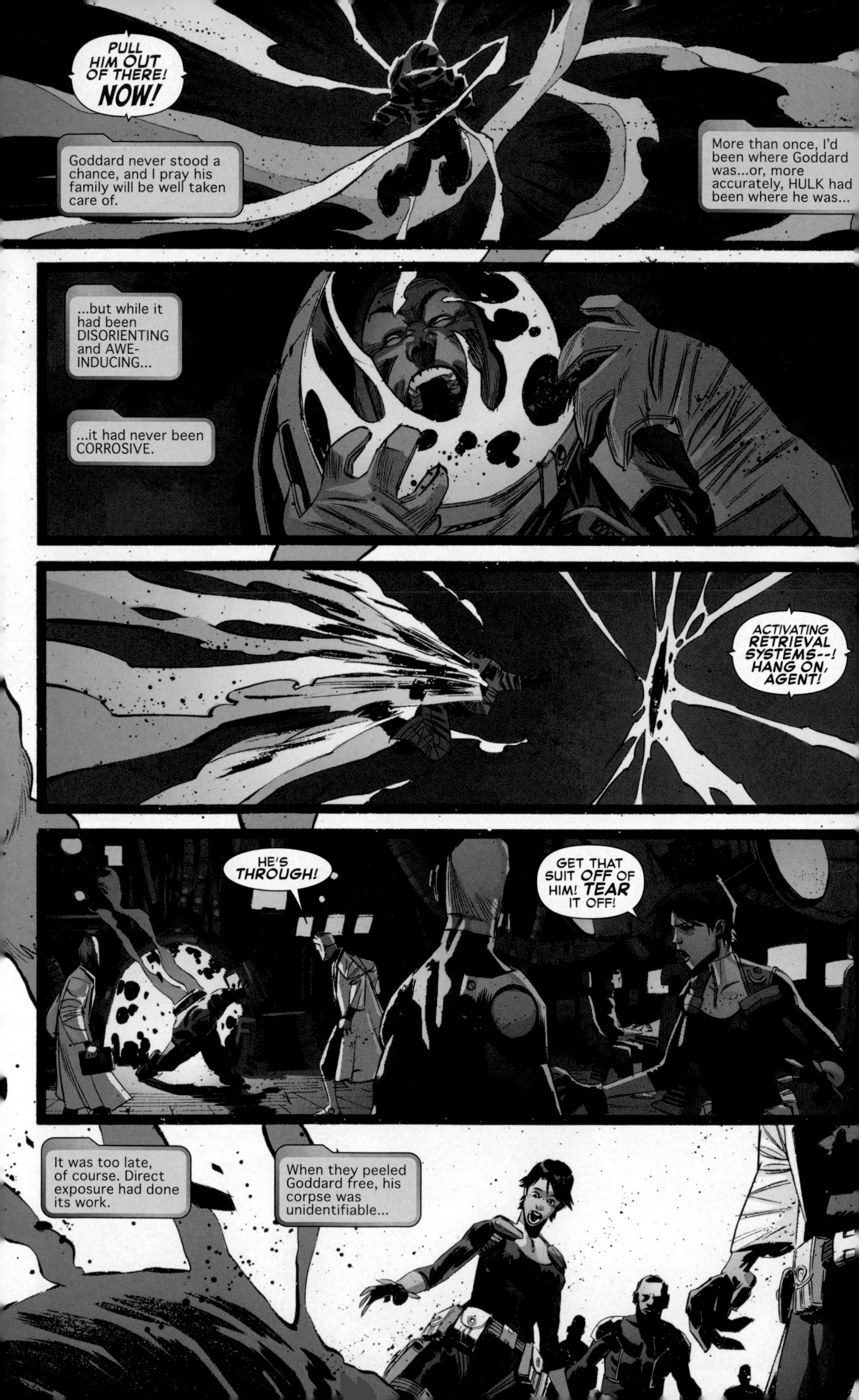

PULL HIM OUT OF THERE! NOW!
Goddard never stood a chance, and I pray his family will be well taken care of.
More than once, I'd been where Goddard was...or, more accurately, HULK had been where he was...
...but while it had been DISORIENTING and AWE-INDUCING...
...it had never been CORROSIVE.
ACTIVATING RETRIEVAL SYSTEMS--! HANG ON, AGENT!
HE'S THROUGH!
GET THAT SUIT OFF OF HIM! TEAR IT OFF!
It was too late, of course. Direct exposure had done its work.
When they peeled Goddard free, his corpse was unidentifiable...

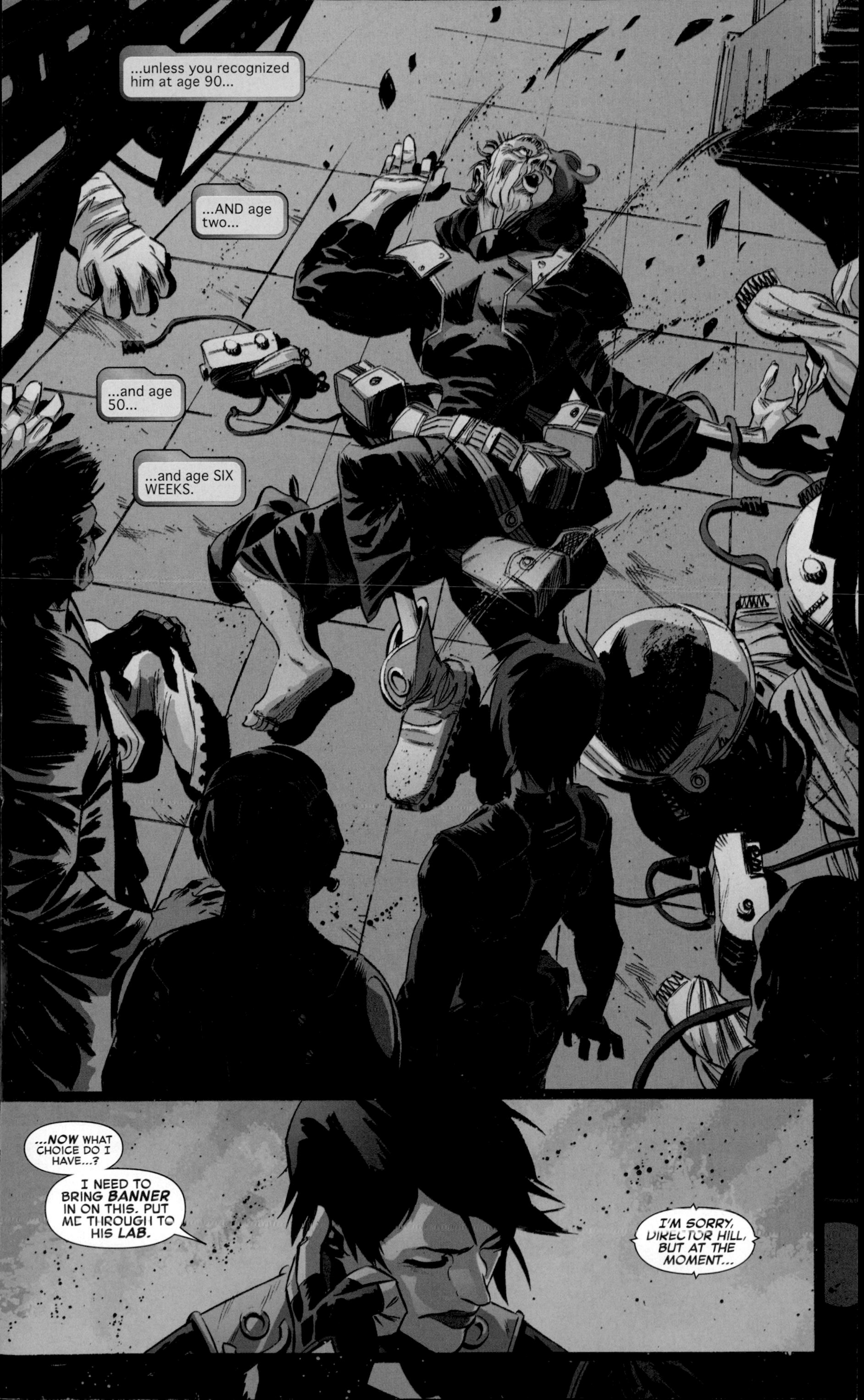
...unless you recognized him at age 90...
...AND age two...
...and age 50...
...and age SIX WEEKS.
...NOW WHAT CHOICE DO I HAVE...?
I NEED TO BRING BANNER IN ON THIS. PUT ME THROUGH TO HIS LAB.
I'M SORRY, DIRECTOR HILL, BUT AT THE MOMENT...

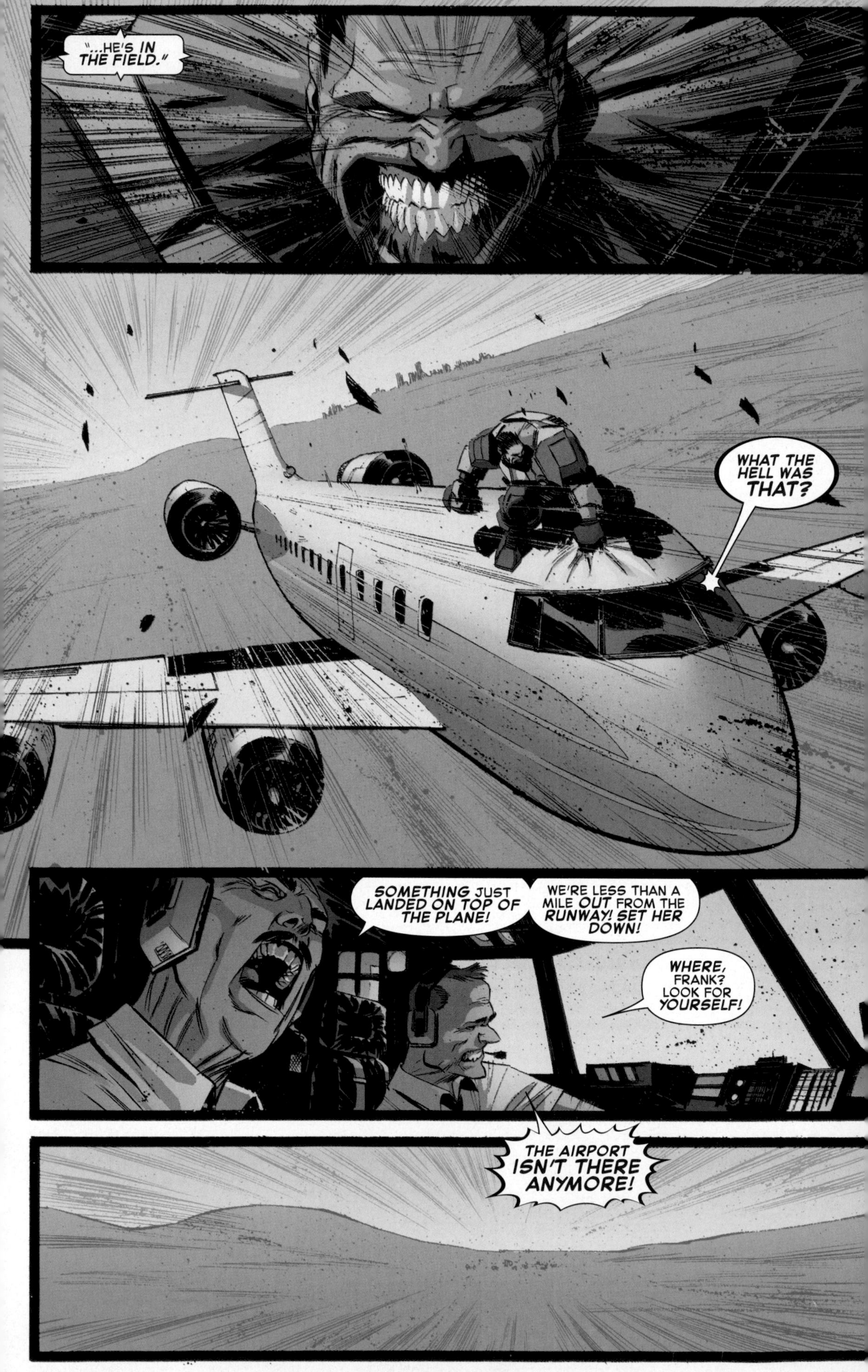
"...HE'S IN THE FIELD."
WHAT THE HELL WAS THAT?
SOMETHING JUST LANDED ON TOP OF THE PLANE!
WE'RE LESS THAN A MILE OUT FROM THE RUNWAY! SET HER DOWN!
WHERE, FRANK? LOOK FOR YOURSELF!
THE AIRPORT ISN'T THERE ANYMORE!

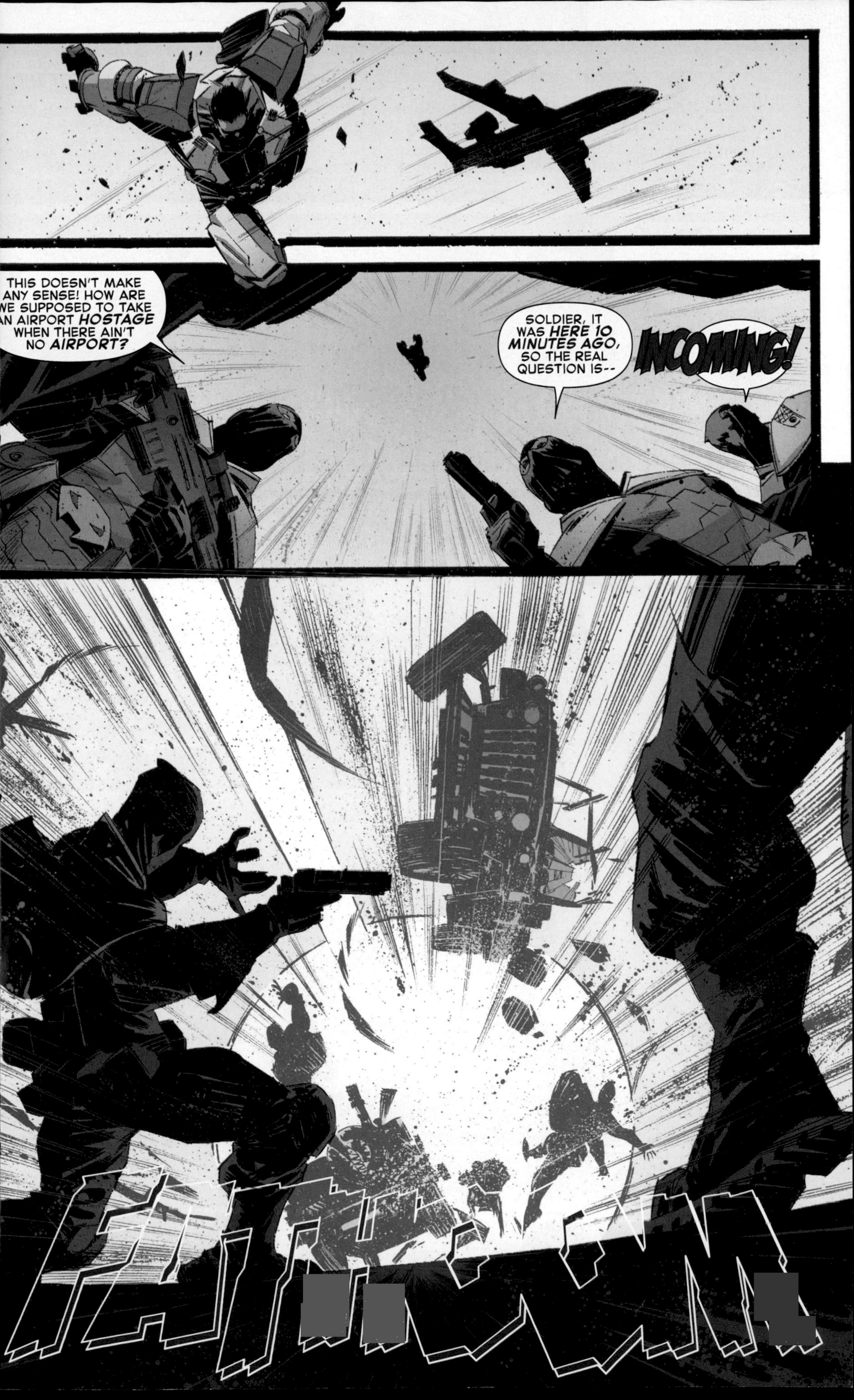
THIS DOESN'T MAKE ANY SENSE! HOW ARE WE SUPPOSED TO TAKE AN AIRPORT *HOSTAGE* WHEN THERE AIN'T NO *AIRPORT*?
SOLDIER, IT WAS *HERE 10 MINUTES AGO*, SO THE REAL QUESTION IS--
INCOMING!

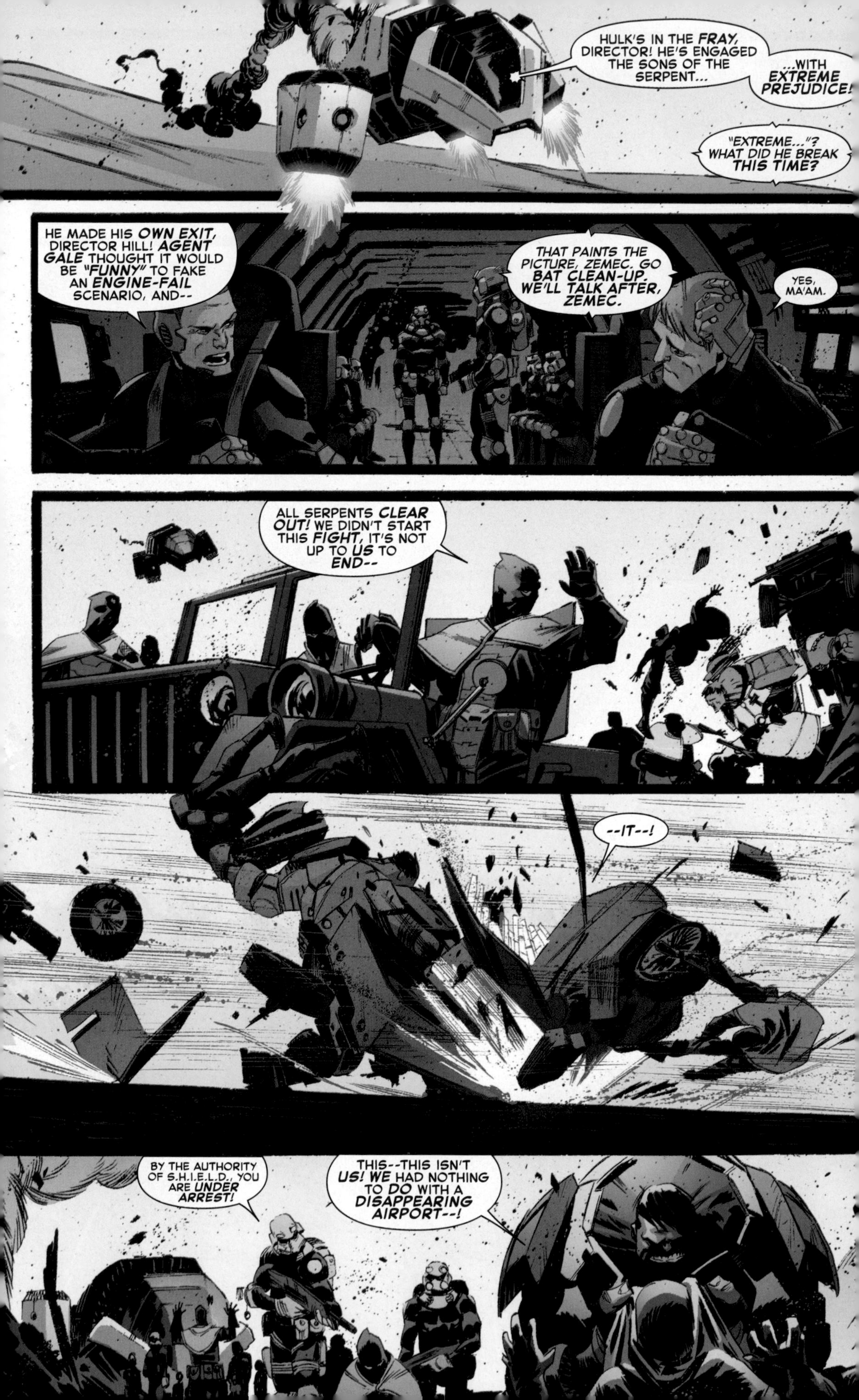
HULK'S IN THE FRAY, DIRECTOR! HE'S ENGAGED THE SONS OF THE SERPENT...
...WITH EXTREME PREJUDICE!
"EXTREME..."? WHAT DID HE BREAK THIS TIME?
HE MADE HIS OWN EXIT, DIRECTOR HILL! AGENT GALE THOUGHT IT WOULD BE "FUNNY" TO FAKE AN ENGINE-FAIL SCENARIO, AND--
THAT PAINTS THE PICTURE, ZEMEC. GO BAT CLEAN-UP. WE'LL TALK AFTER, ZEMEC.
YES, MA'AM.
ALL SERPENTS CLEAR OUT! WE DIDN'T START THIS FIGHT, IT'S NOT UP TO US TO END--
--IT--!
BY THE AUTHORITY OF S.H.I.E.L.D., YOU ARE UNDER ARREST!
THIS--THIS ISN'T US! WE HAD NOTHING TO DO WITH A DISAPPEARING AIRPORT--!

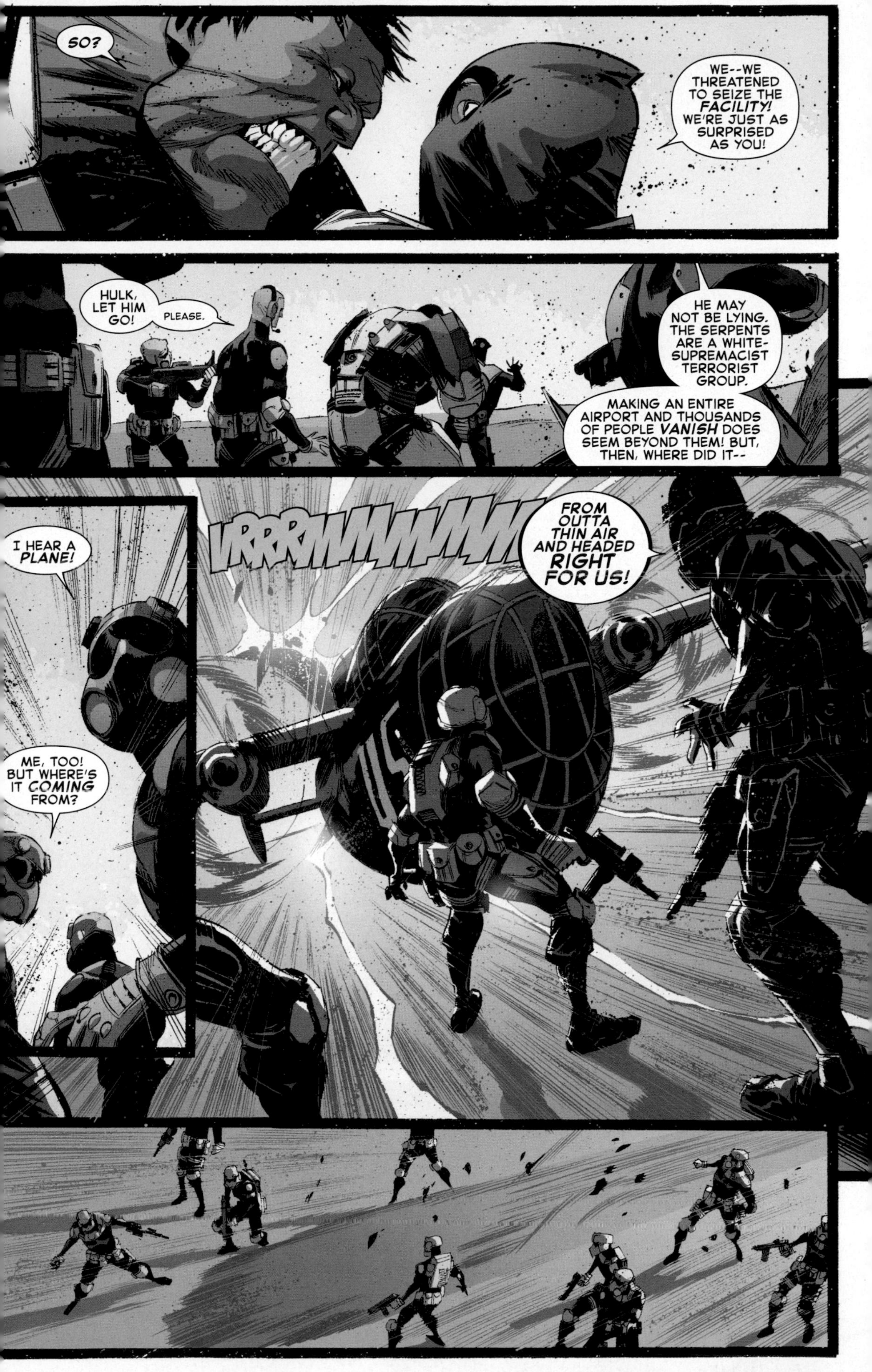

SO?
WE--WE THREATENED TO SEIZE THE FACILITY! WE'RE JUST AS SURPRISED AS YOU!
HULK, LET HIM GO!
PLEASE.
HE MAY NOT BE LYING. THE SERPENTS ARE A WHITE-SUPREMACIST TERRORIST GROUP.
MAKING AN ENTIRE AIRPORT AND THOUSANDS OF PEOPLE VANISH DOES SEEM BEYOND THEM! BUT, THEN, WHERE DID IT--
I HEAR A PLANE!
ME, TOO! BUT WHERE'S IT COMING FROM?
VRRRMMMMMM
FROM OUTTA THIN AIR AND HEADED RIGHT FOR US!

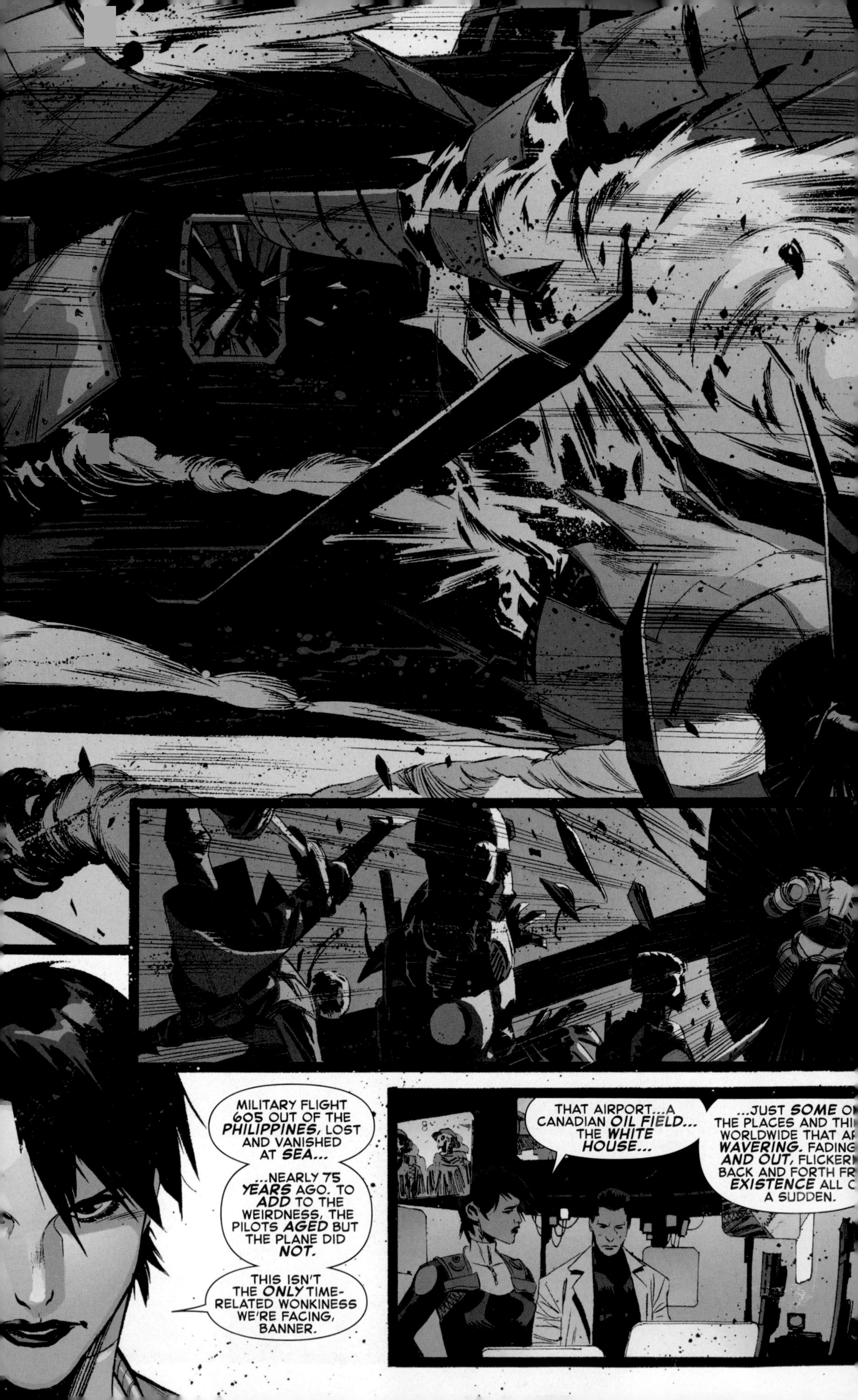
MILITARY FLIGHT 605 OUT OF THE PHILIPPINES, LOST AND VANISHED AT SEA...
...NEARLY 75 YEARS AGO. TO ADD TO THE WEIRDNESS, THE PILOTS AGED BUT THE PLANE DID NOT.
THIS ISN'T THE ONLY TIME-RELATED WONKINESS WE'RE FACING, BANNER.
THAT AIRPORT...A CANADIAN OIL FIELD... THE WHITE HOUSE...
...JUST SOME O THE PLACES AND THI WORLDWIDE THAT A WAVERING. FADING AND OUT, FLICKER BACK AND FORTH FR EXISTENCE ALL C A SUDDEN.

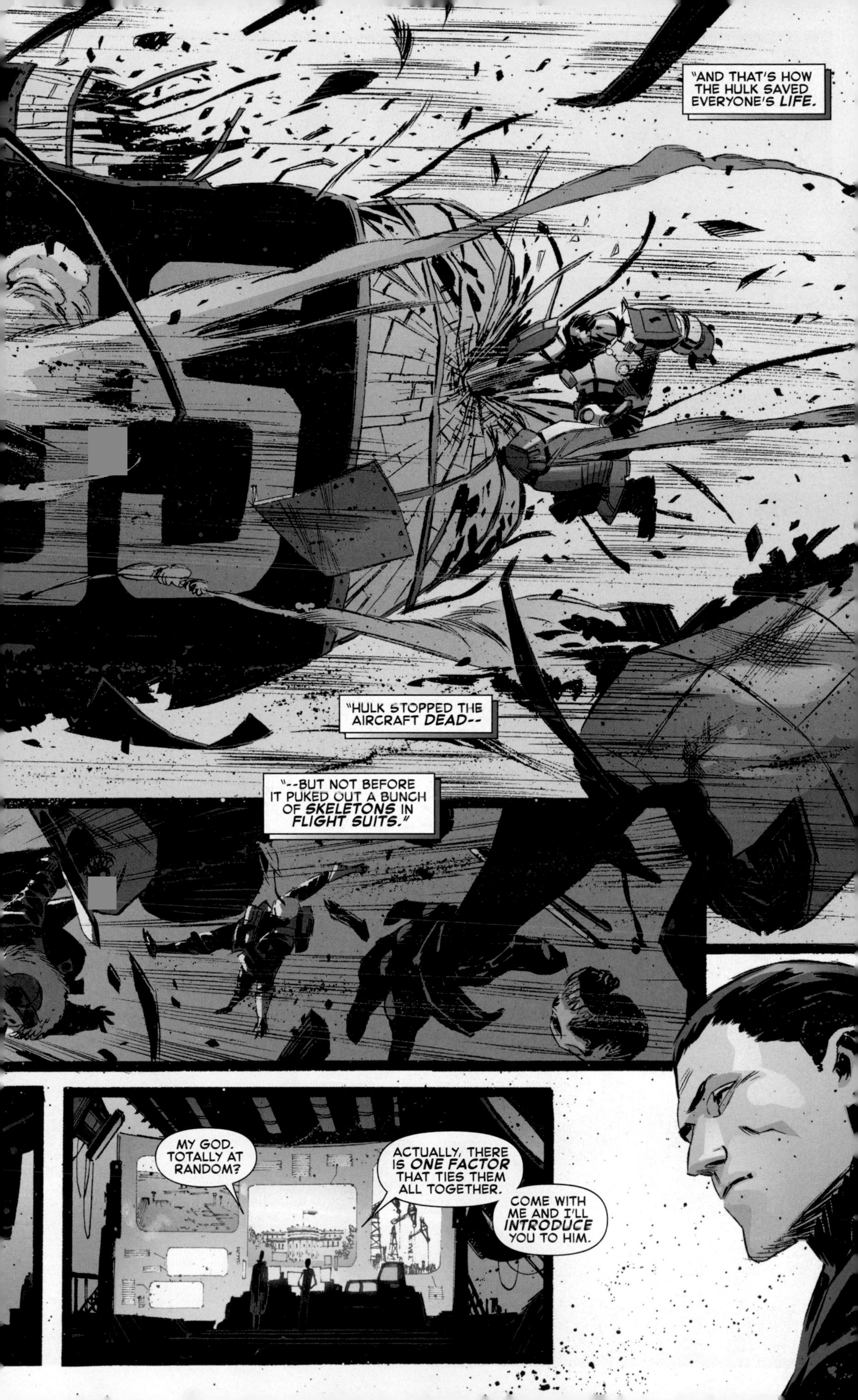
"AND THAT'S HOW THE HULK SAVED EVERYONE'S LIFE.
"HULK STOPPED THE AIRCRAFT DEAD--
"--BUT NOT BEFORE IT PUKED OUT A BUNCH OF SKELETONS IN FLIGHT SUITS."
MY GOD. TOTALLY AT RANDOM?
ACTUALLY, THERE IS ONE FACTOR THAT TIES THEM ALL TOGETHER.
COME WITH ME AND I'LL INTRODUCE YOU TO HIM.

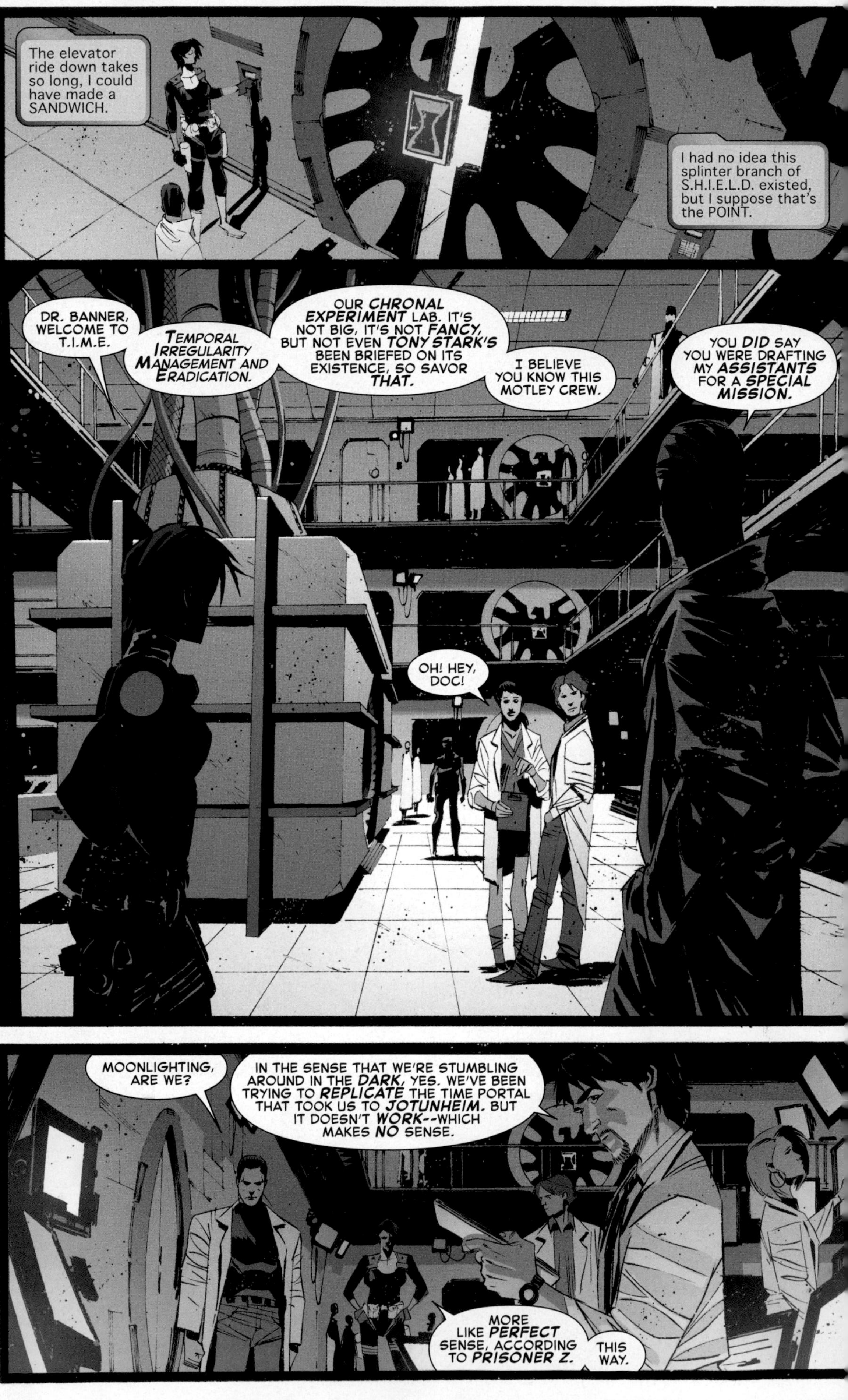
The elevator ride down takes so long, I could have made a SANDWICH.
I had no idea this splinter branch of S.H.I.E.L.D. existed, but I suppose that's the POINT.
DR. BANNER, WELCOME TO T.I.M.E.
TEMPORAL IRREGULARITY MANAGEMENT AND ERADICATION.
OUR CHRONAL EXPERIMENT LAB. IT'S NOT BIG, IT'S NOT FANCY, BUT NOT EVEN TONY STARK'S BEEN BRIEFED ON ITS EXISTENCE, SO SAVOR THAT.
I BELIEVE YOU KNOW THIS MOTLEY CREW.
YOU DID SAY YOU WERE DRAFTING MY ASSISTANTS FOR A SPECIAL MISSION.
OH! HEY, DOC!
MOONLIGHTING, ARE WE?
IN THE SENSE THAT WE'RE STUMBLING AROUND IN THE DARK, YES. WE'VE BEEN TRYING TO REPLICATE THE TIME PORTAL THAT TOOK US TO JOTUNHEIM. BUT IT DOESN'T WORK--WHICH MAKES NO SENSE.
MORE LIKE PERFECT SENSE, ACCORDING TO PRISONER Z.
THIS WAY.

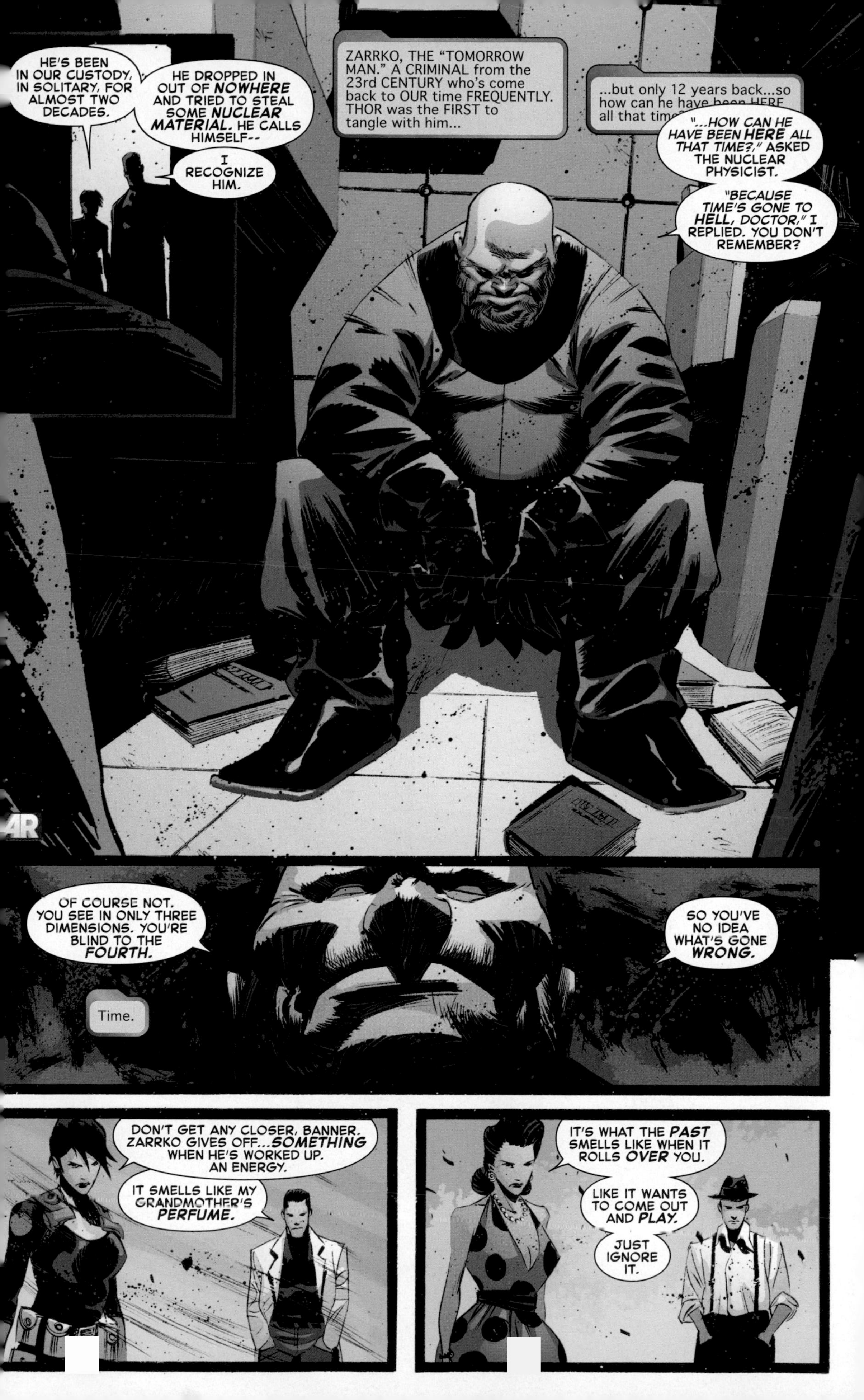
HE'S BEEN IN OUR CUSTODY, IN SOLITARY, FOR ALMOST TWO DECADES.
HE DROPPED IN OUT OF NOWHERE AND TRIED TO STEAL SOME NUCLEAR MATERIAL. HE CALLS HIMSELF--
I RECOGNIZE HIM.
ZARRKO, THE "TOMORROW MAN." A CRIMINAL from the 23rd CENTURY who's come back to OUR time FREQUENTLY. THOR was the FIRST to tangle with him...
...but only 12 years back...so how can he have
"...HOW CAN HE HAVE BEEN HERE ALL THAT TIME?," ASKED THE NUCLEAR PHYSICIST.
"BECAUSE TIME'S GONE TO HELL, DOCTOR," I REPLIED. YOU DON'T REMEMBER?
OF COURSE NOT. YOU SEE IN ONLY THREE DIMENSIONS. YOU'RE BLIND TO THE FOURTH.
Time.
SO YOU'VE NO IDEA WHAT'S GONE WRONG.
DON'T GET ANY CLOSER, BANNER. ZARRKO GIVES OFF...SOMETHING WHEN HE'S WORKED UP. AN ENERGY.
IT SMELLS LIKE MY GRANDMOTHER'S PERFUME.
IT'S WHAT THE PAST SMELLS LIKE WHEN IT ROLLS OVER YOU.
LIKE IT WANTS TO COME OUT AND PLAY.
JUST IGNORE IT.

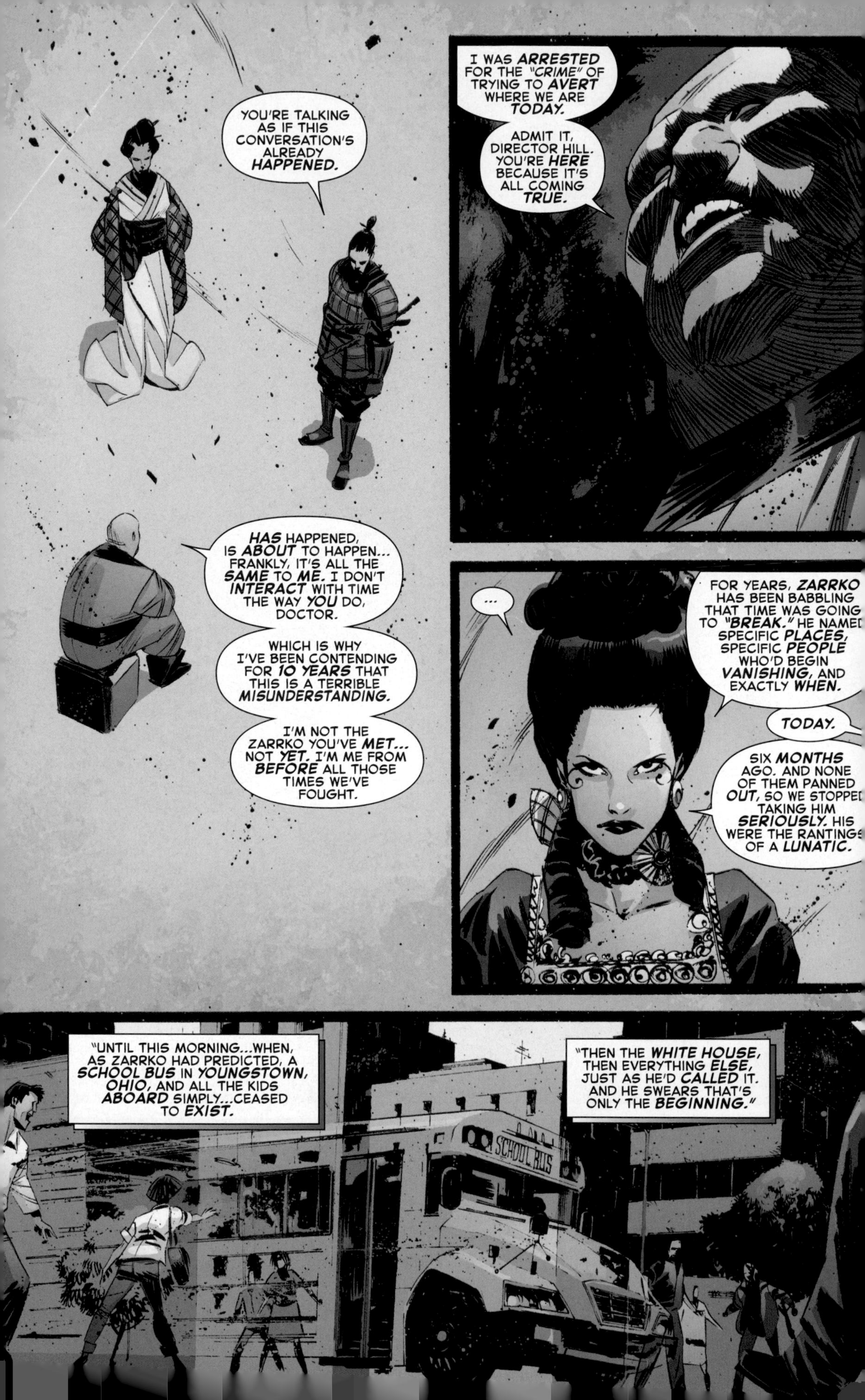
YOU'RE TALKING AS IF THIS CONVERSATION'S ALREADY HAPPENED.
HAS HAPPENED, IS ABOUT TO HAPPEN... FRANKLY, IT'S ALL THE SAME TO ME. I DON'T INTERACT WITH TIME THE WAY YOU DO, DOCTOR.
WHICH IS WHY I'VE BEEN CONTENDING FOR 10 YEARS THAT THIS IS A TERRIBLE MISUNDERSTANDING.
I'M NOT THE ZARRKO YOU'VE MET... NOT YET. I'M ME FROM BEFORE ALL THOSE TIMES WE'VE FOUGHT.
I WAS ARRESTED FOR THE "CRIME" OF TRYING TO AVERT WHERE WE ARE TODAY.
ADMIT IT, DIRECTOR HILL. YOU'RE HERE BECAUSE IT'S ALL COMING TRUE.
...
FOR YEARS, ZARRKO HAS BEEN BABBLING THAT TIME WAS GOING TO "BREAK." HE NAMED SPECIFIC PLACES, SPECIFIC PEOPLE WHO'D BEGIN VANISHING, AND EXACTLY WHEN.
TODAY.
SIX MONTHS AGO. AND NONE OF THEM PANNED OUT, SO WE STOPPED TAKING HIM SERIOUSLY. HIS WERE THE RANTINGS OF A LUNATIC.
"UNTIL THIS MORNING...WHEN, AS ZARRKO HAD PREDICTED, A SCHOOL BUS IN YOUNGSTOWN, OHIO, AND ALL THE KIDS ABOARD SIMPLY...CEASED TO EXIST.
"THEN THE WHITE HOUSE, THEN EVERYTHING ELSE, JUST AS HE'D CALLED IT. AND HE SWEARS THAT'S ONLY THE BEGINNING."
SCHOOL BUS

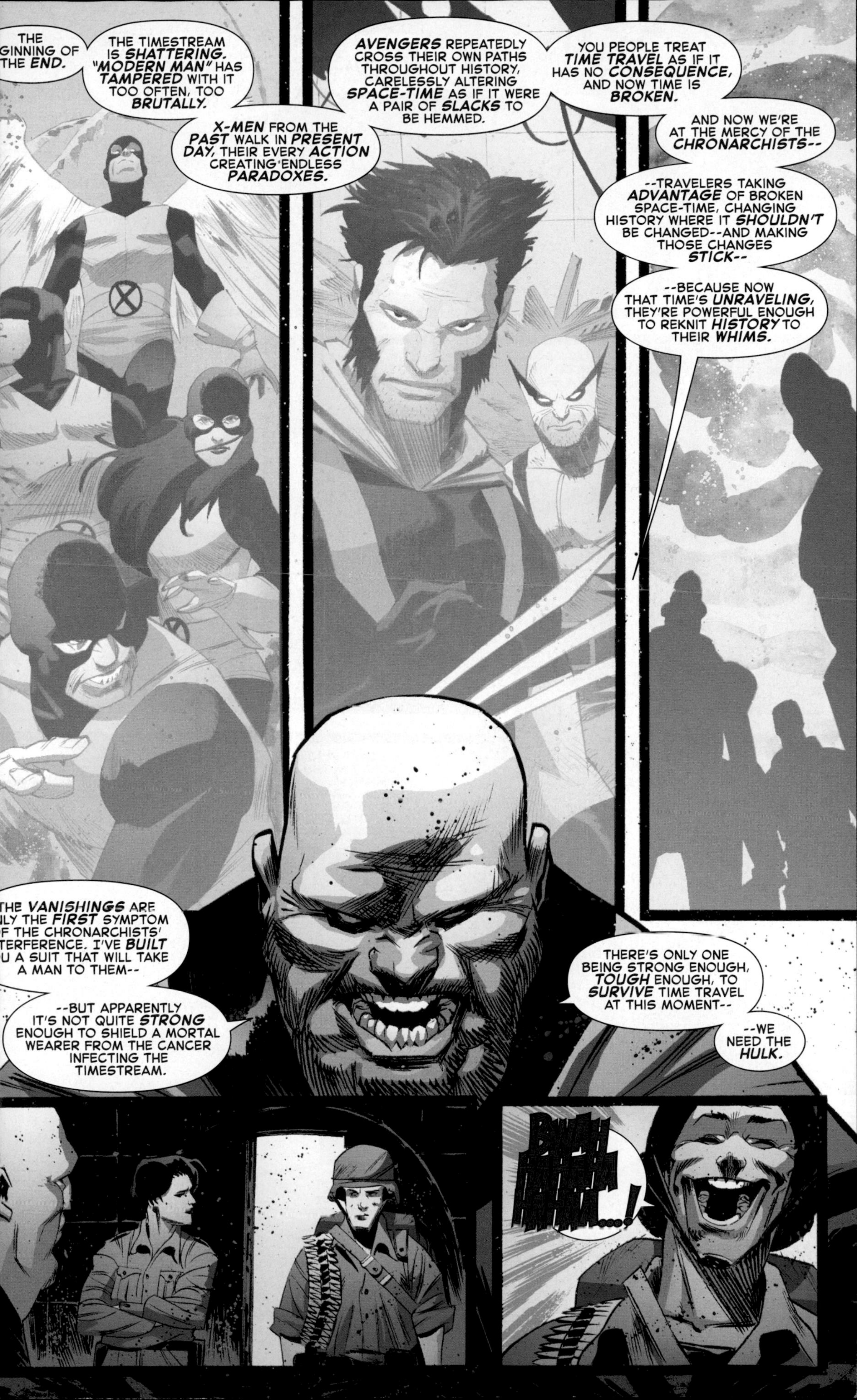
THE GINNING OF THE END.
THE TIMESTREAM IS SHATTERING. "MODERN MAN" HAS TAMPERED WITH IT TOO OFTEN, TOO BRUTALLY.
X-MEN FROM THE PAST WALK IN PRESENT DAY, THEIR EVERY ACTION CREATING ENDLESS PARADOXES.
AVENGERS REPEATEDLY CROSS THEIR OWN PATHS THROUGHOUT HISTORY, CARELESSLY ALTERING SPACE-TIME AS IF IT WERE A PAIR OF SLACKS TO BE HEMMED.
YOU PEOPLE TREAT TIME TRAVEL AS IF IT HAS NO CONSEQUENCE, AND NOW TIME IS BROKEN.
AND NOW WE'RE AT THE MERCY OF THE CHRONARCHISTS--
--TRAVELERS TAKING ADVANTAGE OF BROKEN SPACE-TIME, CHANGING HISTORY WHERE IT SHOULDN'T BE CHANGED--AND MAKING THOSE CHANGES STICK--
--BECAUSE NOW THAT TIME'S UNRAVELING, THEY'RE POWERFUL ENOUGH TO REKNIT HISTORY TO THEIR WHIMS.
THE VANISHINGS ARE ILY THE FIRST SYMPTOM F THE CHRONARCHISTS' TERFERENCE. I'VE BUILT U A SUIT THAT WILL TAKE A MAN TO THEM--
--BUT APPARENTLY IT'S NOT QUITE STRONG ENOUGH TO SHIELD A MORTAL WEARER FROM THE CANCER INFECTING THE TIMESTREAM.
THERE'S ONLY ONE BEING STRONG ENOUGH, TOUGH ENOUGH, TO SURVIVE TIME TRAVEL AT THIS MOMENT--
--WE NEED THE HULK.

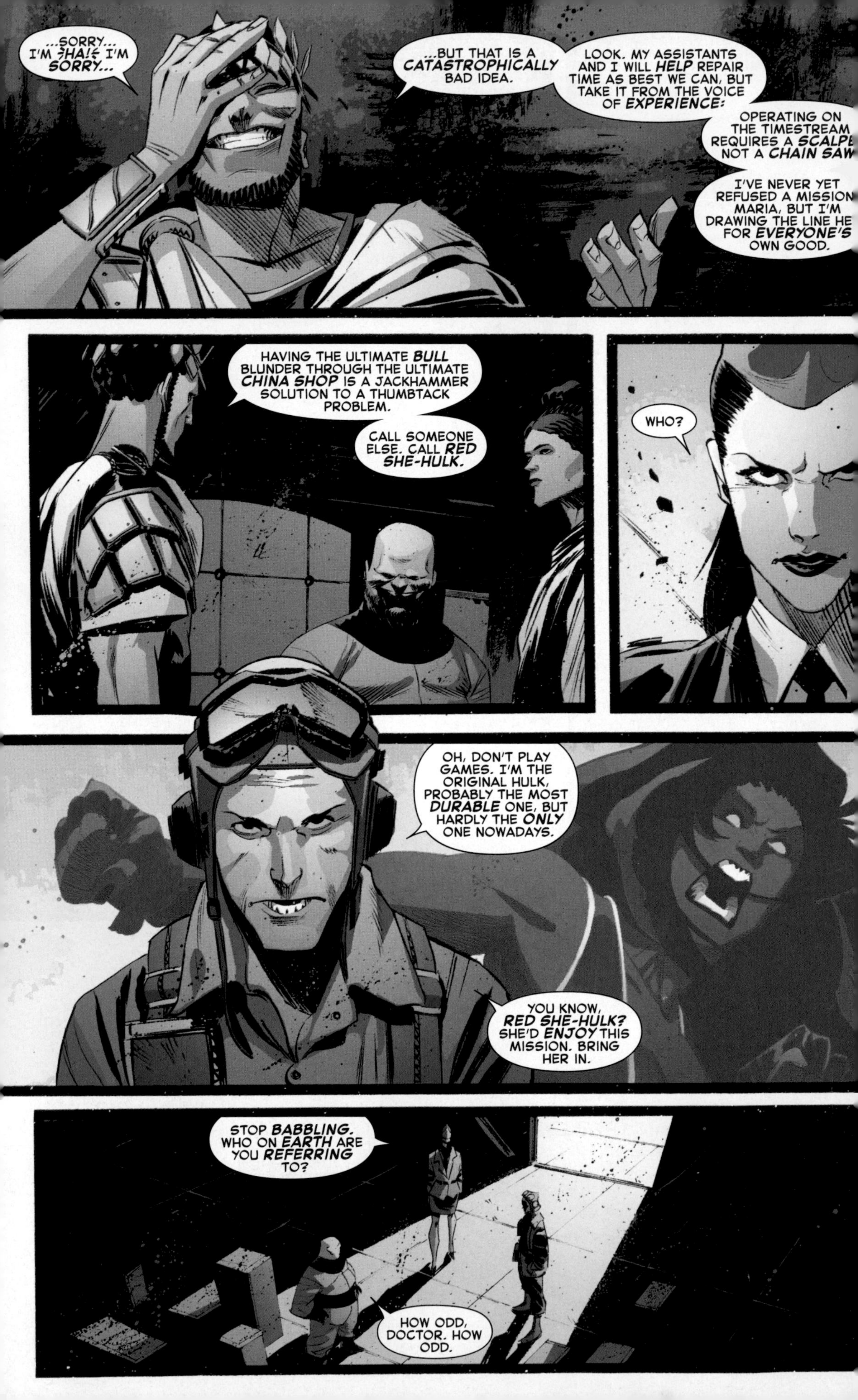
...SORRY... I'M ≠HA!≠ I'M SORRY...
...BUT THAT IS A CATASTROPHICALLY BAD IDEA.
LOOK. MY ASSISTANTS AND I WILL HELP REPAIR TIME AS BEST WE CAN, BUT TAKE IT FROM THE VOICE OF EXPERIENCE:
OPERATING ON THE TIMESTREAM REQUIRES A SCALPE NOT A CHAIN SAW
I'VE NEVER YET REFUSED A MISSION MARIA, BUT I'M DRAWING THE LINE HE FOR EVERYONE'S OWN GOOD.
HAVING THE ULTIMATE BULL BLUNDER THROUGH THE ULTIMATE CHINA SHOP IS A JACKHAMMER SOLUTION TO A THUMBTACK PROBLEM.
CALL SOMEONE ELSE. CALL RED SHE-HULK.
WHO?
OH, DON'T PLAY GAMES. I'M THE ORIGINAL HULK, PROBABLY THE MOST DURABLE ONE, BUT HARDLY THE ONLY ONE NOWADAYS.
YOU KNOW, RED SHE-HULK? SHE'D ENJOY THIS MISSION. BRING HER IN.
STOP BABBLING. WHO ON EARTH ARE YOU REFERRING TO?
HOW ODD, DOCTOR. HOW ODD.

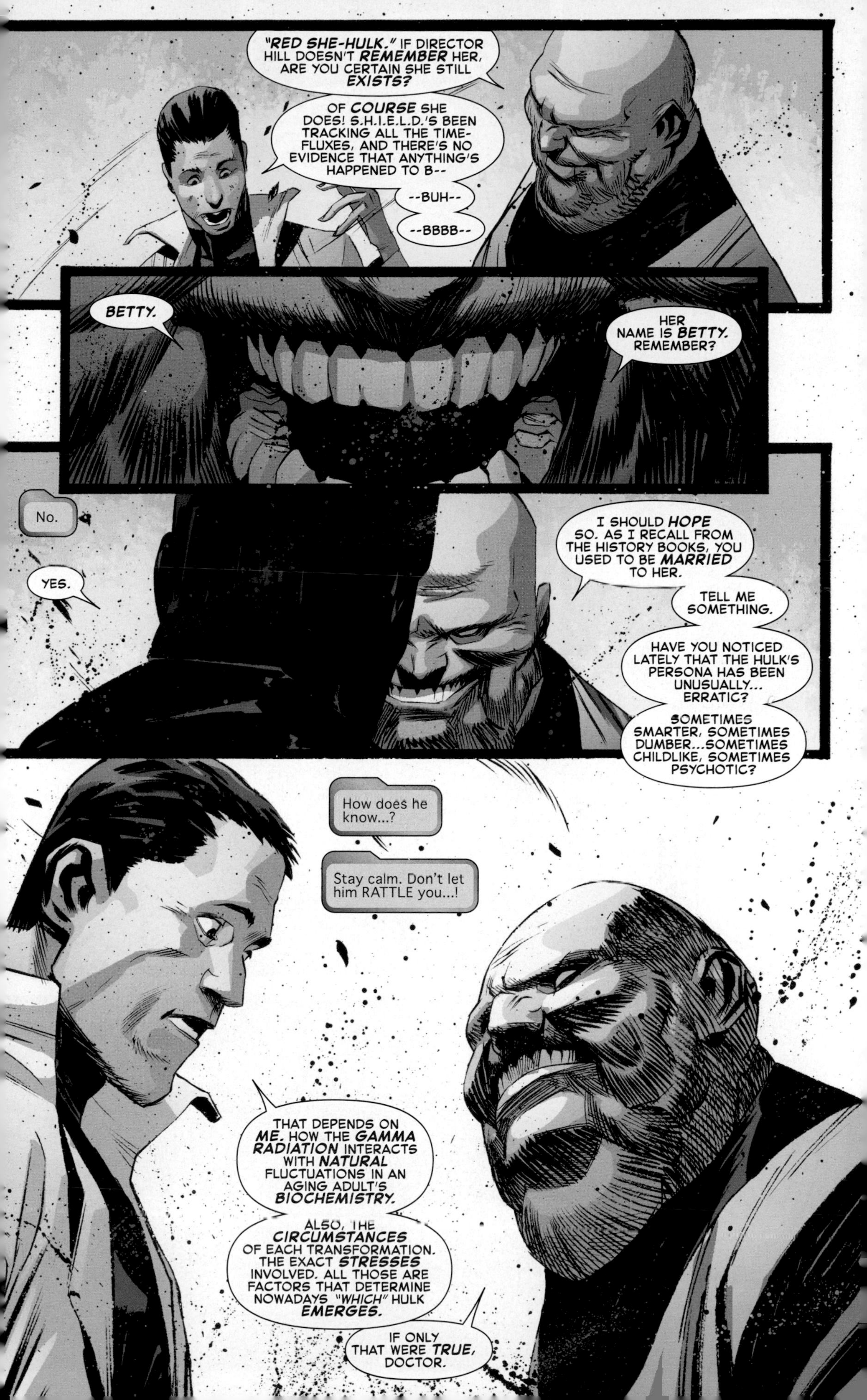
"RED SHE-HULK." IF DIRECTOR HILL DOESN'T REMEMBER HER, ARE YOU CERTAIN SHE STILL EXISTS?
OF COURSE SHE DOES! S.H.I.E.L.D.'S BEEN TRACKING ALL THE TIME-FLUXES, AND THERE'S NO EVIDENCE THAT ANYTHING'S HAPPENED TO B--
--BUH--
--BBBB--
BETTY.
HER NAME IS BETTY. REMEMBER?
No.
YES.
I SHOULD HOPE SO. AS I RECALL FROM THE HISTORY BOOKS, YOU USED TO BE MARRIED TO HER.
TELL ME SOMETHING.
HAVE YOU NOTICED LATELY THAT THE HULK'S PERSONA HAS BEEN UNUSUALLY... ERRATIC?
SOMETIMES SMARTER, SOMETIMES DUMBER...SOMETIMES CHILDLIKE, SOMETIMES PSYCHOTIC?
How does he know...?
Stay calm. Don't let him RATTLE you...!
THAT DEPENDS ON ME. HOW THE GAMMA RADIATION INTERACTS WITH NATURAL FLUCTUATIONS IN AN AGING ADULT'S BIOCHEMISTRY.
ALSO, THE CIRCUMSTANCES OF EACH TRANSFORMATION. THE EXACT STRESSES INVOLVED. ALL THOSE ARE FACTORS THAT DETERMINE NOWADAYS "WHICH" HULK EMERGES.
IF ONLY THAT WERE TRUE, DOCTOR.

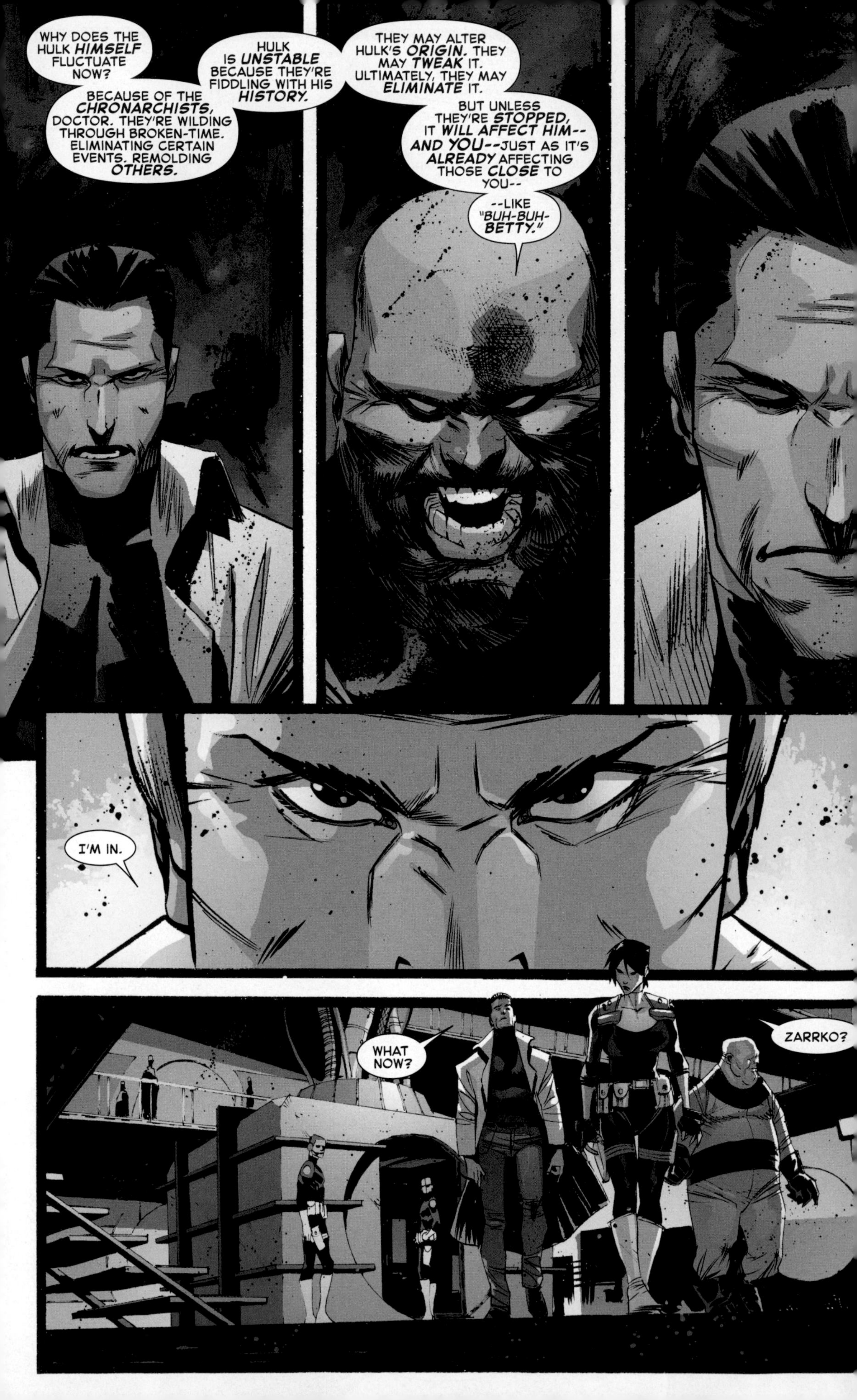
WHY DOES THE HULK HIMSELF FLUCTUATE NOW?
BECAUSE OF THE CHRONARCHISTS, DOCTOR. THEY'RE WILDING THROUGH BROKEN-TIME. ELIMINATING CERTAIN EVENTS. REMOLDING OTHERS.
HULK IS UNSTABLE BECAUSE THEY'RE FIDDLING WITH HIS HISTORY.
THEY MAY ALTER HULK'S ORIGIN. THEY MAY TWEAK IT. ULTIMATELY, THEY MAY ELIMINATE IT.
BUT UNLESS THEY'RE STOPPED, IT WILL AFFECT HIM-- AND YOU--JUST AS IT'S ALREADY AFFECTING THOSE CLOSE TO YOU--
--LIKE "BUH-BUH-BETTY."
I'M IN.
WHAT NOW?
ZARRKO?

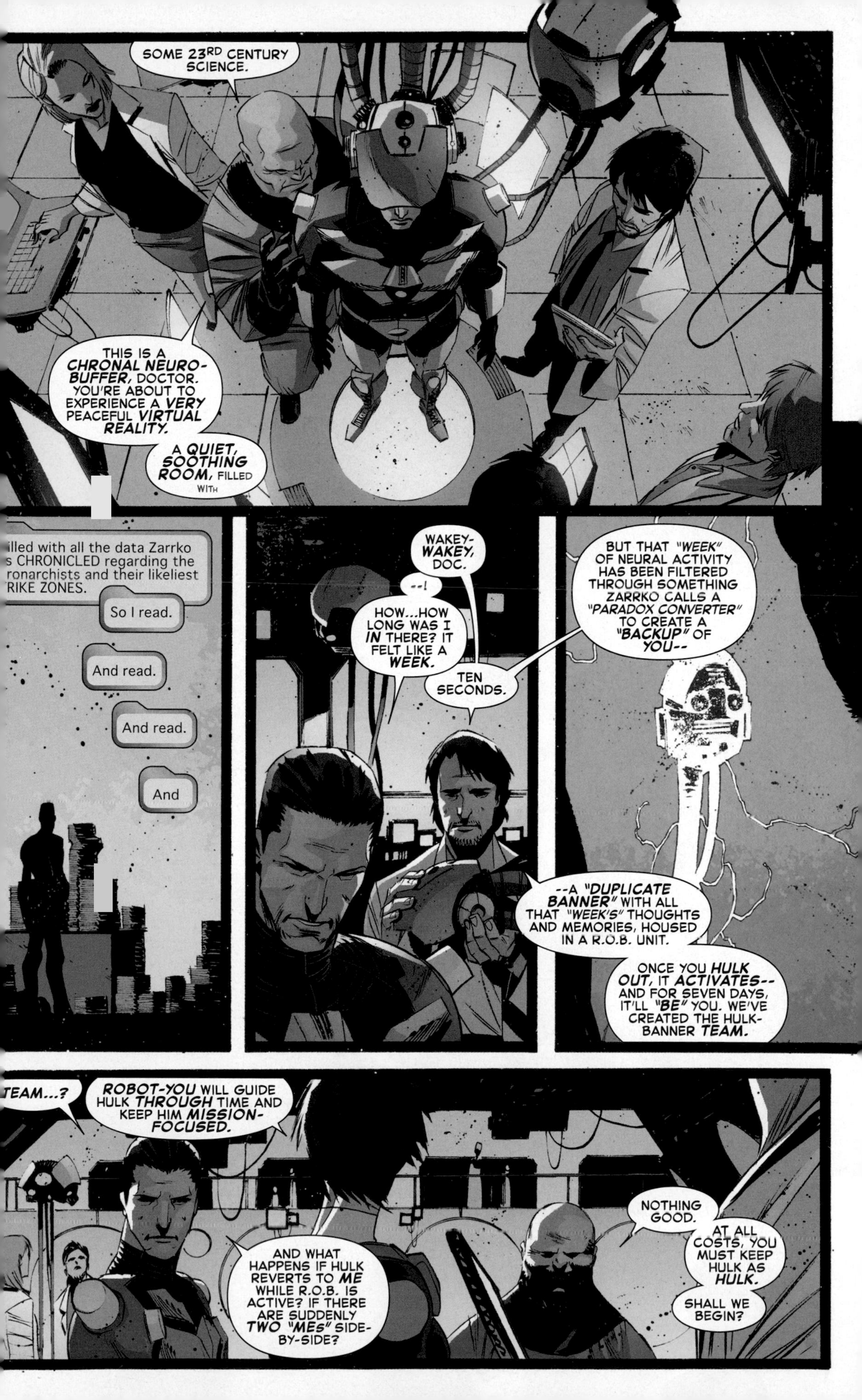
SOME 23RD CENTURY SCIENCE.
THIS IS A CHRONAL NEURO-BUFFER, DOCTOR. YOU'RE ABOUT TO EXPERIENCE A VERY PEACEFUL VIRTUAL REALITY.
A QUIET, SOOTHING ROOM, FILLED WITH
illed with all the data Zarrko s CHRONICLED regarding the ronarchists and their likeliest RIKE ZONES.
So I read.
And read.
And read.
And
WAKEY-WAKEY, DOC.
--!
HOW...HOW LONG WAS I IN THERE? IT FELT LIKE A WEEK.
TEN SECONDS.
BUT THAT "WEEK" OF NEURAL ACTIVITY HAS BEEN FILTERED THROUGH SOMETHING ZARRKO CALLS A "PARADOX CONVERTER" TO CREATE A "BACKUP" OF YOU--
--A "DUPLICATE BANNER" WITH ALL THAT "WEEK'S" THOUGHTS AND MEMORIES, HOUSED IN A R.O.B. UNIT.
ONCE YOU HULK OUT, IT ACTIVATES--AND FOR SEVEN DAYS, IT'LL "BE" YOU. WE'VE CREATED THE HULK-BANNER TEAM.
TEAM...?
ROBOT-YOU WILL GUIDE HULK THROUGH TIME AND KEEP HIM MISSION-FOCUSED.
AND WHAT HAPPENS IF HULK REVERTS TO ME WHILE R.O.B. IS ACTIVE? IF THERE ARE SUDDENLY TWO "MEs" SIDE-BY-SIDE?
NOTHING GOOD.
AT ALL COSTS, YOU MUST KEEP HULK AS HULK.
SHALL WE BEGIN?

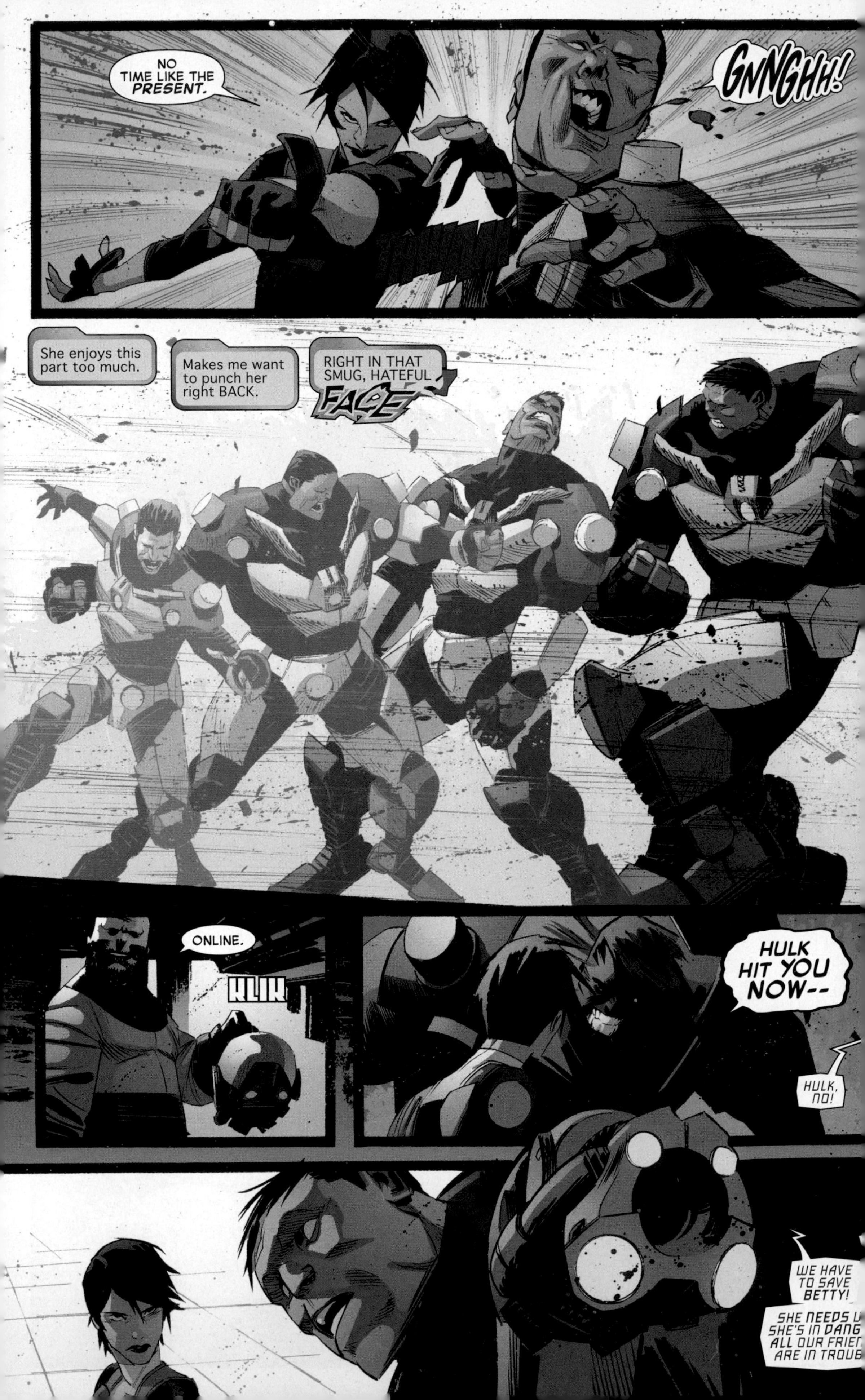
NO TIME LIKE THE PRESENT.
GNNGHH!
She enjoys this part too much.
Makes me want to punch her right BACK.
RIGHT IN THAT SMUG, HATEFUL FACE
ONLINE.
KLIK
HULK HIT YOU NOW--
HULK, NO!
WE HAVE TO SAVE BETTY!

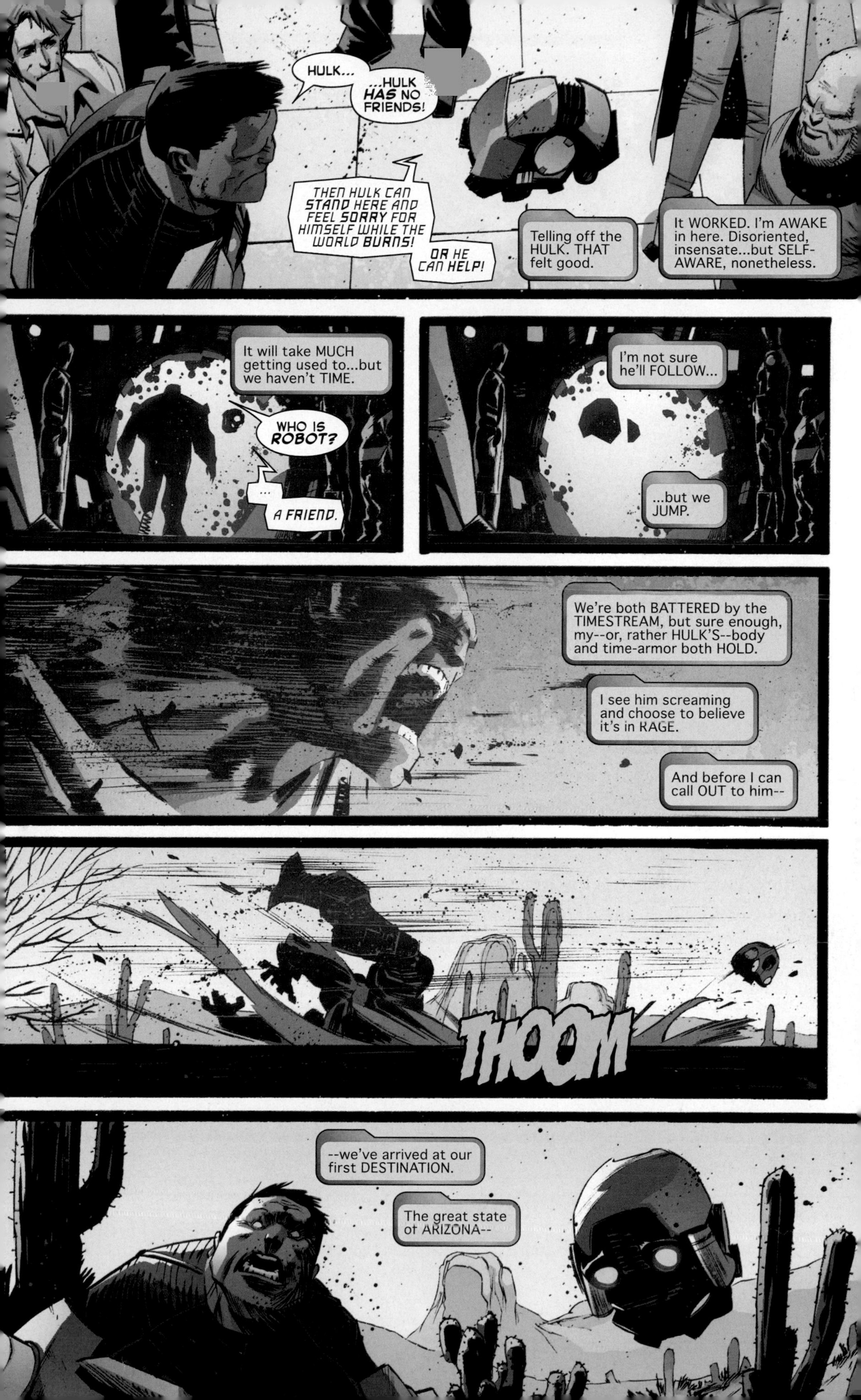
HULK...
...HULK HAS NO FRIENDS!
THEN HULK CAN STAND HERE AND FEEL SORRY FOR HIMSELF WHILE THE WORLD BURNS!
OR HE CAN HELP!
Telling off the HULK. THAT felt good.
It WORKED. I'm AWAKE in here. Disoriented, insensate...but SELF-AWARE, nonetheless.
It will take MUCH getting used to...but we haven't TIME.
WHO IS ROBOT?
... A FRIEND.
I'm not sure he'll FOLLOW...
...but we JUMP.
We're both BATTERED by the TIMESTREAM, but sure enough, my--or, rather HULK'S--body and time-armor both HOLD.
I see him screaming and choose to believe it's in RAGE.
And before I can call OUT to him--
THOOM
--we've arrived at our first DESTINATION.
The great state of ARIZONA--

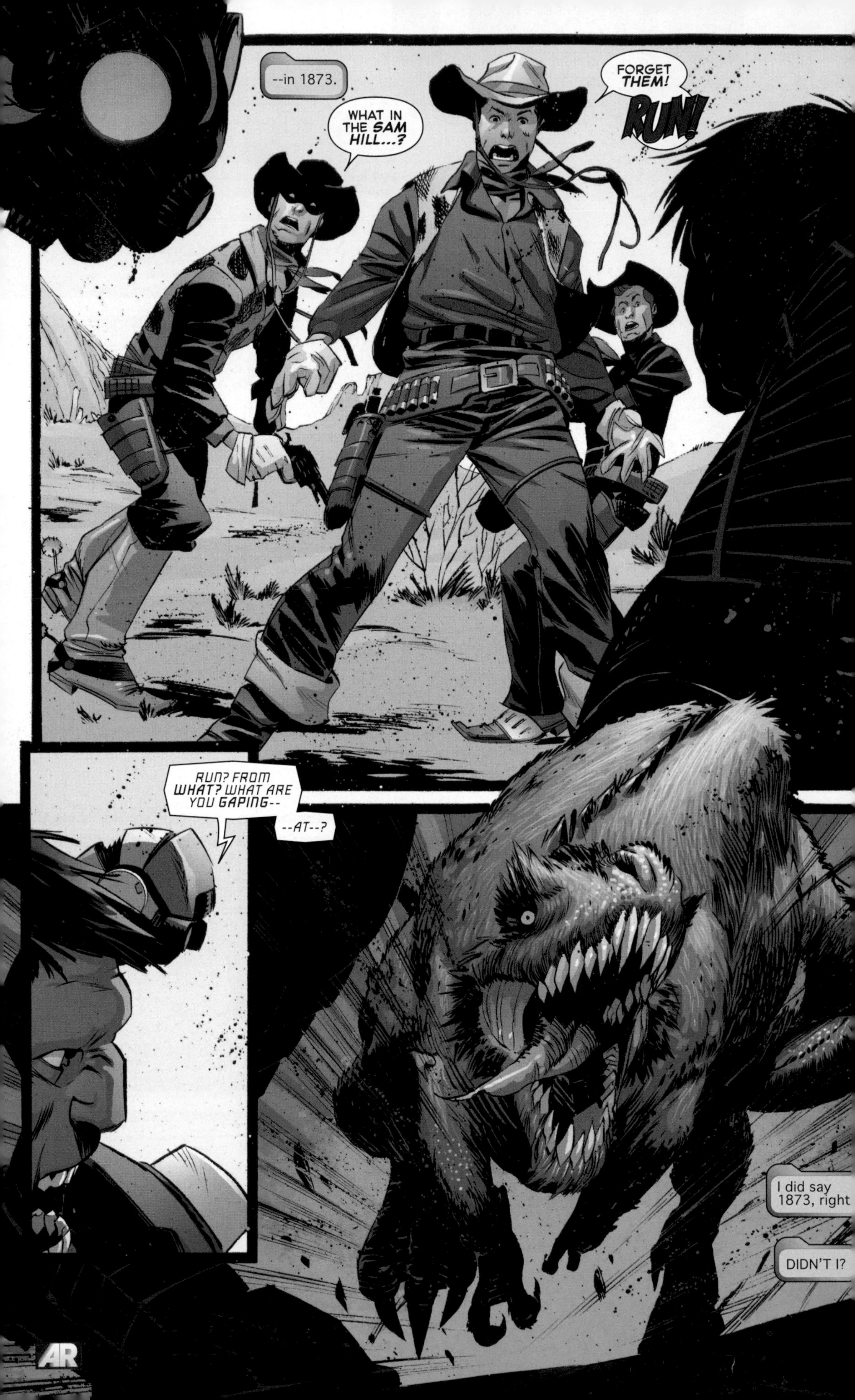
--in 1873.
WHAT IN THE SAM HILL...?
FORGET THEM! RUN!
RUN? FROM WHAT? WHAT ARE YOU GAPING--
--AT--?
I did say 1873, right
DIDN'T I?

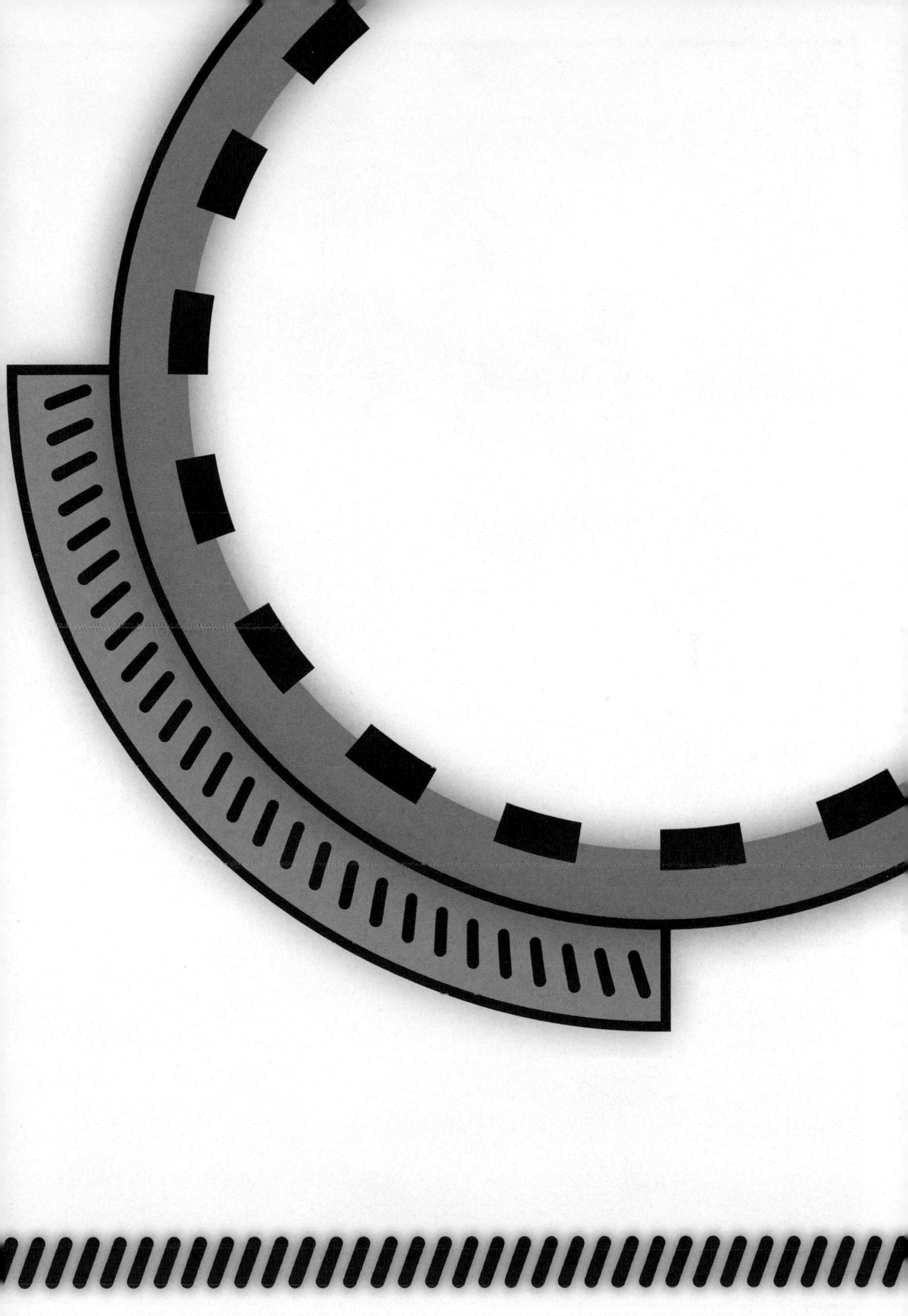

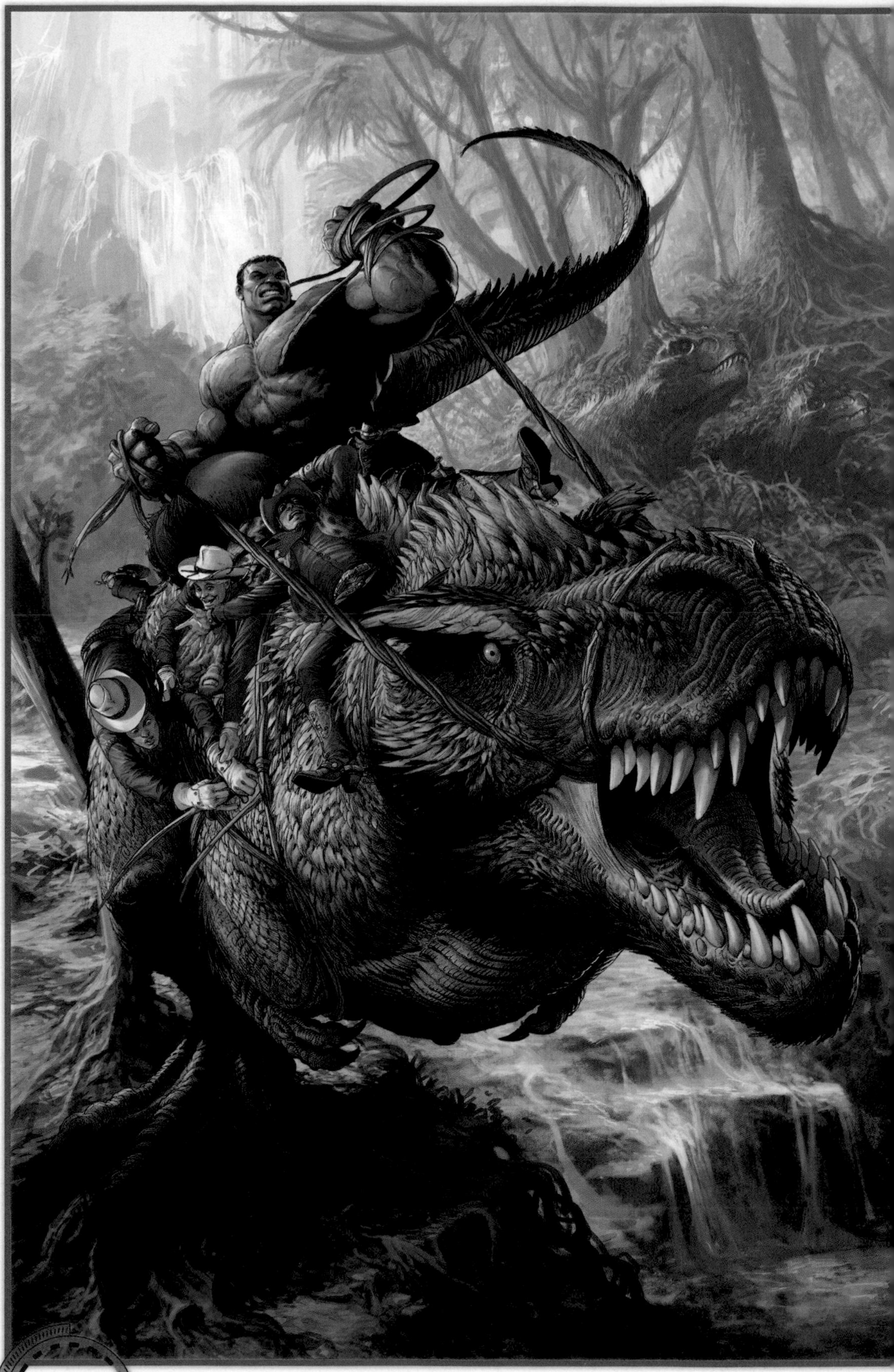

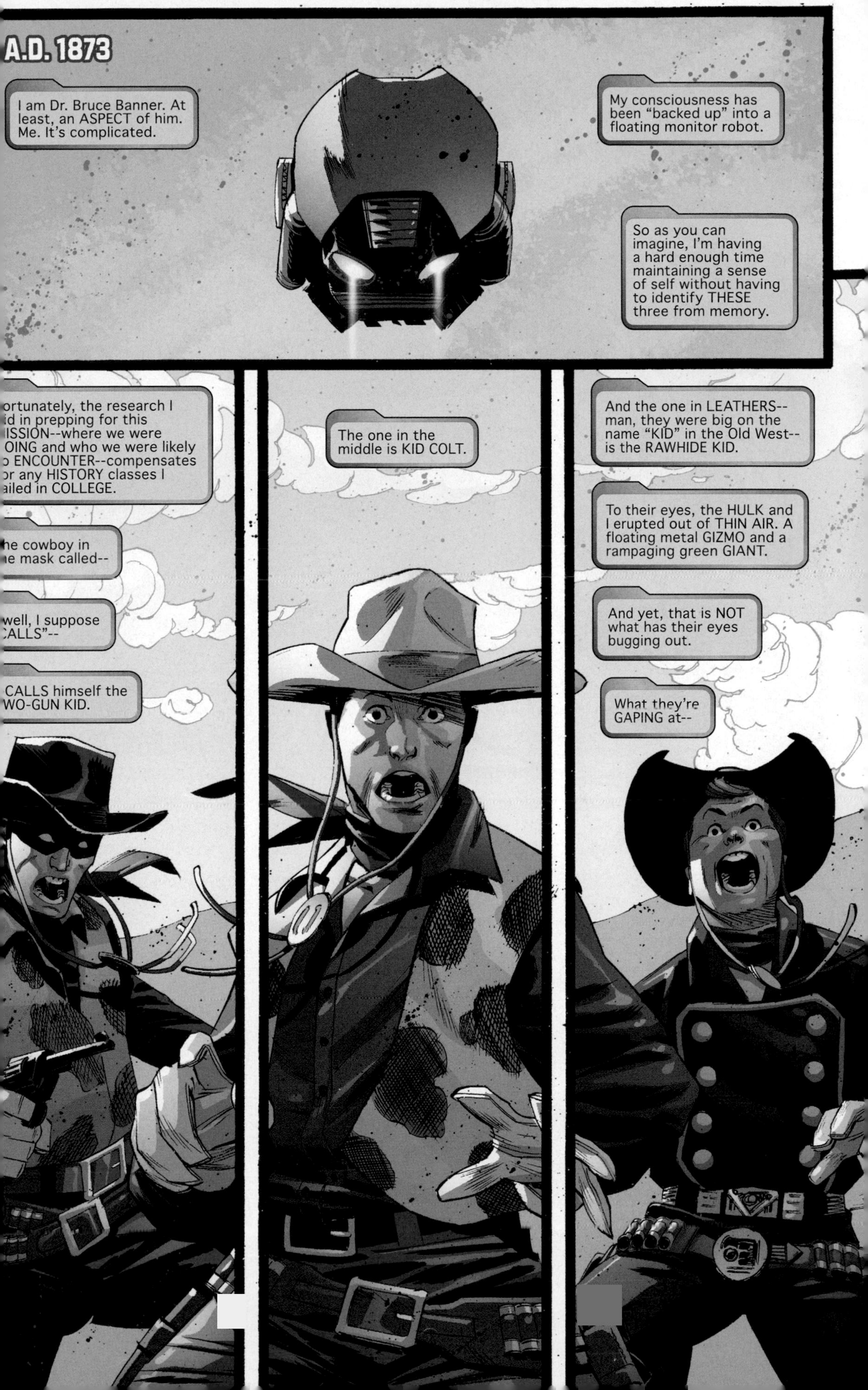
A.D. 1873
I am Dr. Bruce Banner. At least, an ASPECT of him. Me. It's complicated.
My consciousness has been "backed up" into a floating monitor robot.
So as you can imagine, I'm having a hard enough time maintaining a sense of self without having to identify THESE three from memory.
ortunately, the research I id in prepping for this ISSION--where we were OING and who we were likely o ENCOUNTER--compensates or any HISTORY classes I ailed in COLLEGE.
he cowboy in e mask called--
well, I suppose CALLS"--
CALLS himself the WO-GUN KID.
The one in the middle is KID COLT.
And the one in LEATHERS--man, they were big on the name "KID" in the Old West--is the RAWHIDE KID.
To their eyes, the HULK and I erupted out of THIN AIR. A floating metal GIZMO and a rampaging green GIANT.
And yet, that is NOT what has their eyes bugging out.
What they're GAPING at--

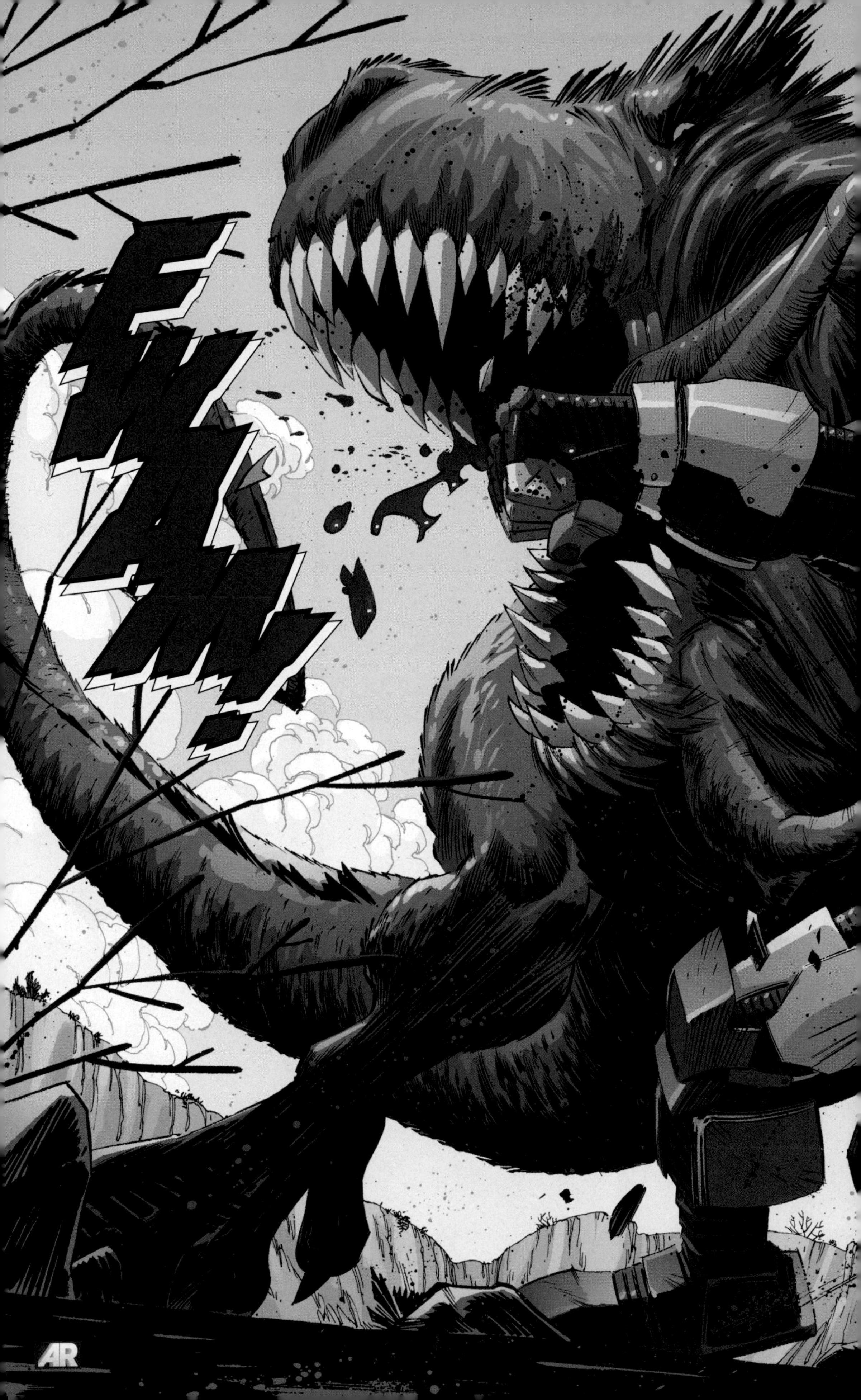

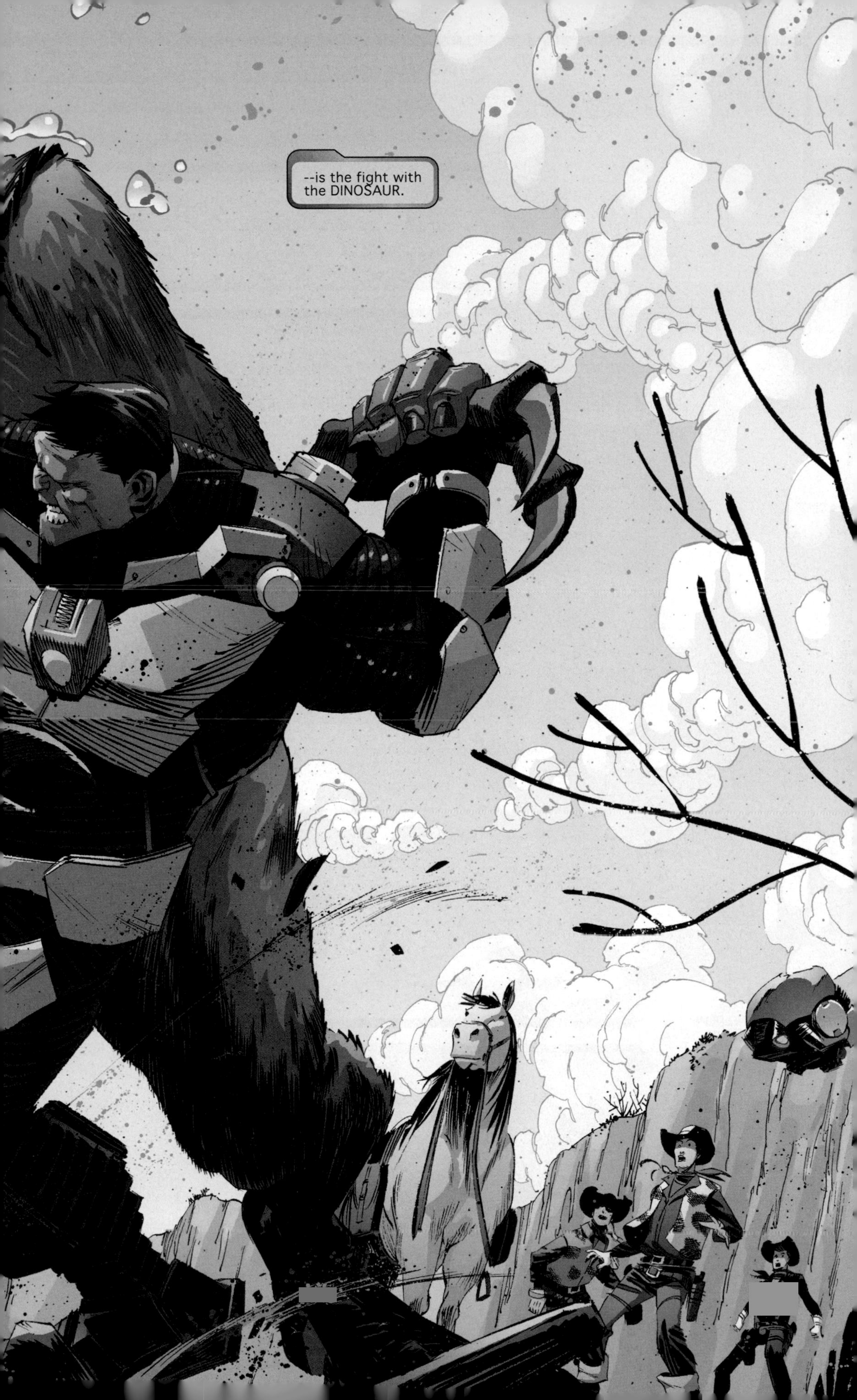
--is the fight with the DINOSAUR.

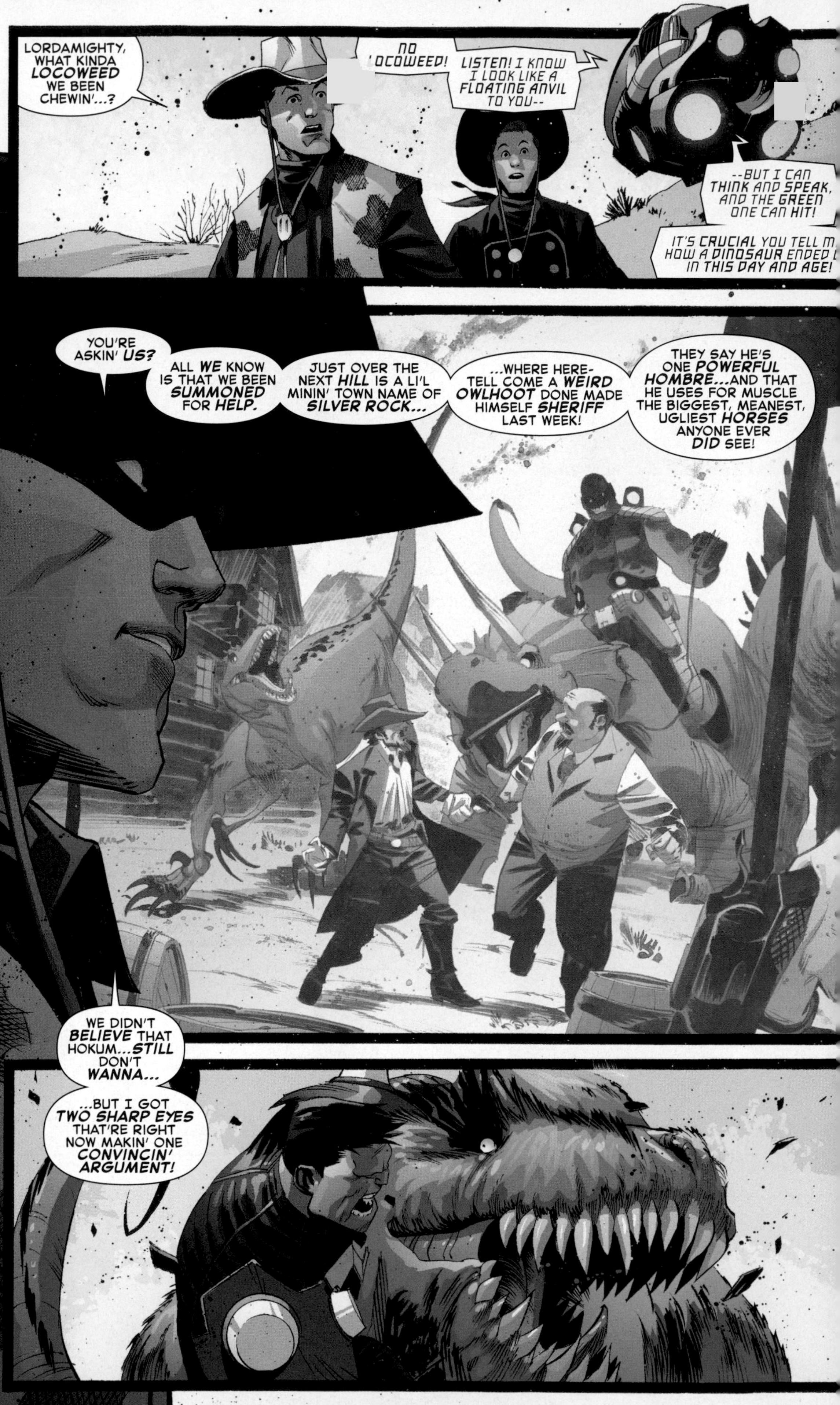
LORDAMIGHTY, WHAT KINDA LOCOWEED WE BEEN CHEWIN'...?
NO 'OCOWEED!
LISTEN! I KNOW I LOOK LIKE A FLOATING ANVIL TO YOU--
--BUT I CAN THINK AND SPEAK, AND THE GREEN ONE CAN HIT!
IT'S CRUCIAL YOU TELL M HOW A DINOSAUR ENDED IN THIS DAY AND AGE!
YOU'RE ASKIN' US?
ALL WE KNOW IS THAT WE BEEN SUMMONED FOR HELP.
JUST OVER THE NEXT HILL IS A LI'L MININ' TOWN NAME OF SILVER ROCK...
...WHERE HERE-TELL COME A WEIRD OWLHOOT DONE MADE HIMSELF SHERIFF LAST WEEK!
THEY SAY HE'S ONE POWERFUL HOMBRE...AND THAT HE USES FOR MUSCLE THE BIGGEST, MEANEST, UGLIEST HORSES ANYONE EVER DID SEE!
WE DIDN'T BELIEVE THAT HOKUM...STILL DON'T WANNA...
...BUT I GOT TWO SHARP EYES THAT'RE RIGHT NOW MAKIN' ONE CONVINCIN' ARGUMENT!

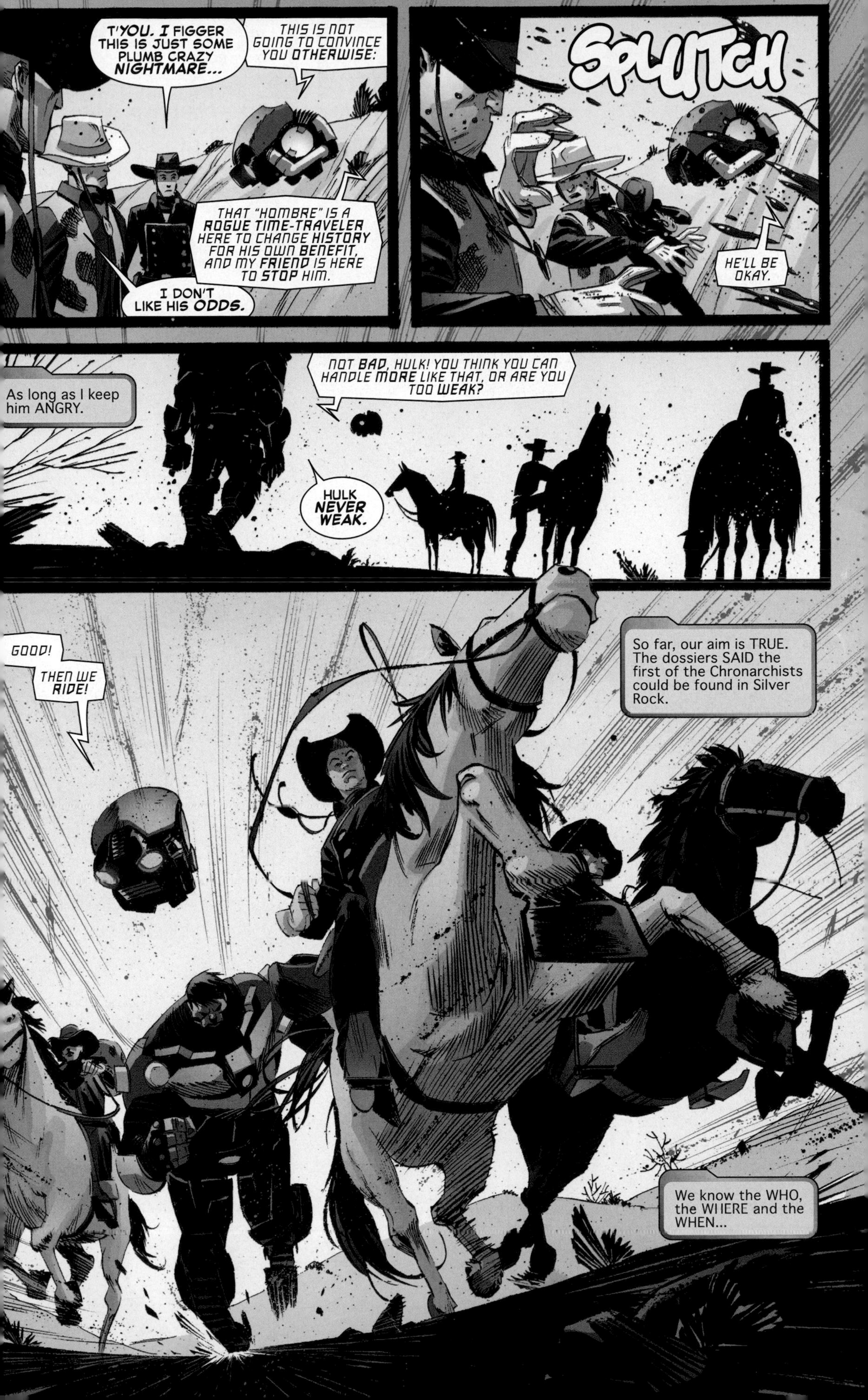
T'YOU. I FIGGER THIS IS JUST SOME PLUMB CRAZY NIGHTMARE...
THIS IS NOT GOING TO CONVINCE YOU OTHERWISE:
THAT "HOMBRE" IS A ROGUE TIME-TRAVELER HERE TO CHANGE HISTORY FOR HIS OWN BENEFIT, AND MY FRIEND IS HERE TO STOP HIM.
I DON'T LIKE HIS ODDS.
SPLUTCH
HE'LL BE OKAY.
As long as I keep him ANGRY.
NOT BAD, HULK! YOU THINK YOU CAN HANDLE MORE LIKE THAT, OR ARE YOU TOO WEAK?
HULK NEVER WEAK.
GOOD!
THEN WE RIDE!
So far, our aim is TRUE. The dossiers SAID the first of the Chronarchists could be found in Silver Rock.
We know the WHO, the WHERE and the WHEN...

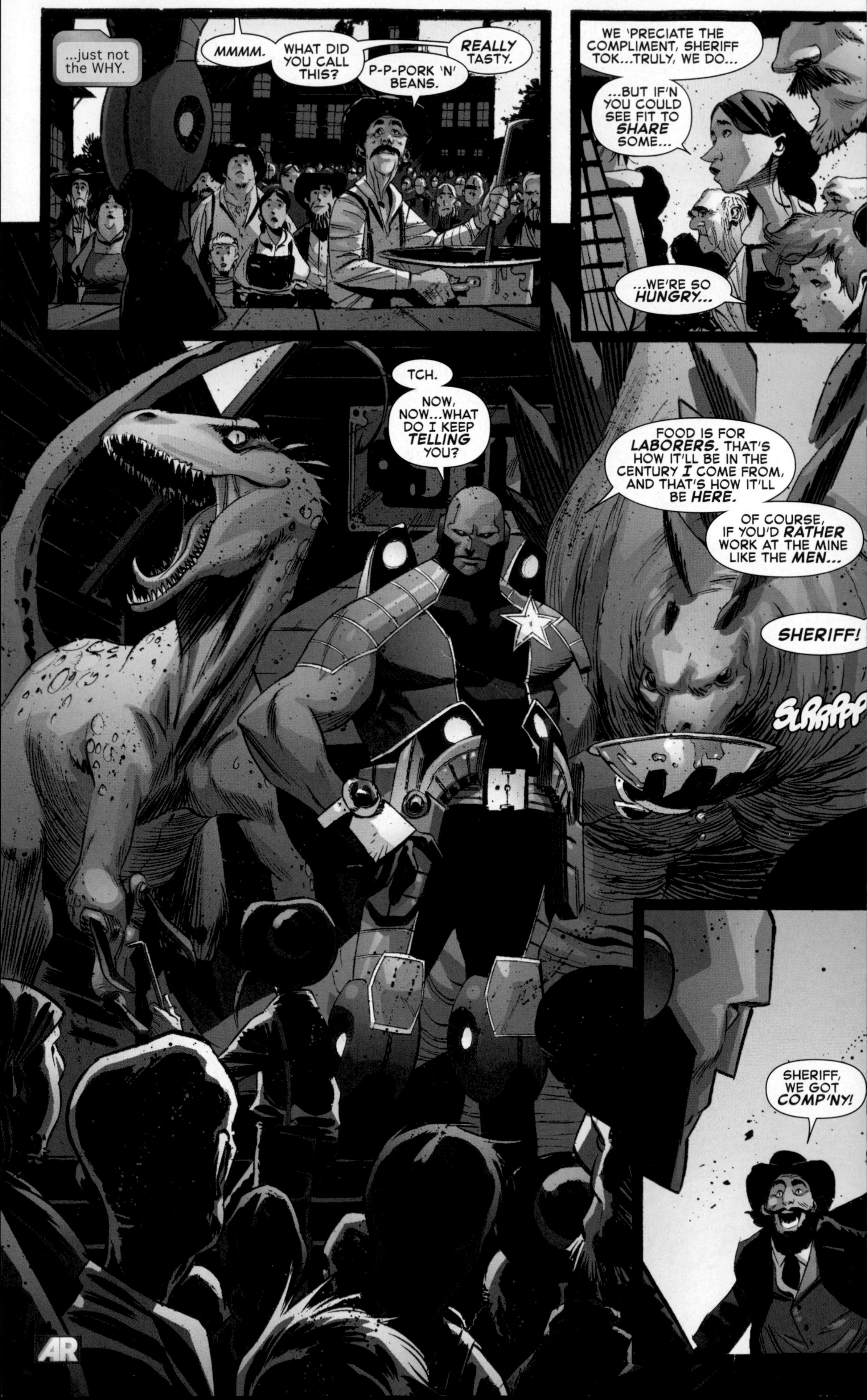

...just not the WHY.
MMMM.
WHAT DID YOU CALL THIS?
REALLY TASTY.
P-P-PORK 'N' BEANS.
WE 'PRECIATE THE COMPLIMENT, SHERIFF TOK...TRULY, WE DO...
...BUT IF'N YOU COULD SEE FIT TO SHARE SOME...
...WE'RE SO HUNGRY...
TCH.
NOW, NOW...WHAT DO I KEEP TELLING YOU?
FOOD IS FOR LABORERS. THAT'S HOW IT'LL BE IN THE CENTURY I COME FROM, AND THAT'S HOW IT'LL BE HERE.
OF COURSE, IF YOU'D RATHER WORK AT THE MINE LIKE THE MEN...
SHERIFF!
SLRRPP
SHERIFF, WE GOT COMP'NY!

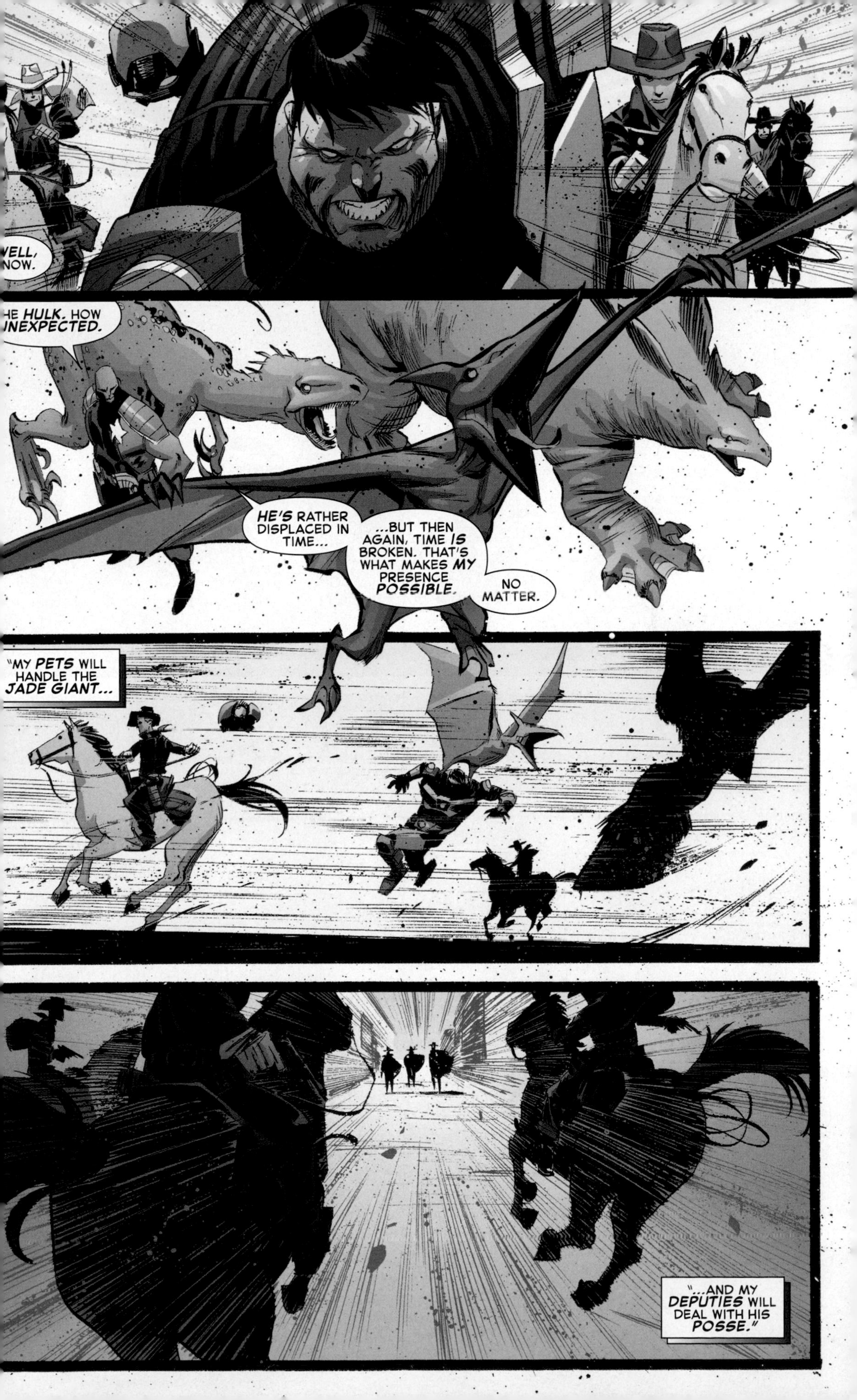
WELL, NOW.
THE HULK. HOW UNEXPECTED.
HE'S RATHER DISPLACED IN TIME...
...BUT THEN AGAIN, TIME IS BROKEN. THAT'S WHAT MAKES MY PRESENCE POSSIBLE.
NO MATTER.
"MY PETS WILL HANDLE THE JADE GIANT...
"...AND MY DEPUTIES WILL DEAL WITH HIS POSSE."

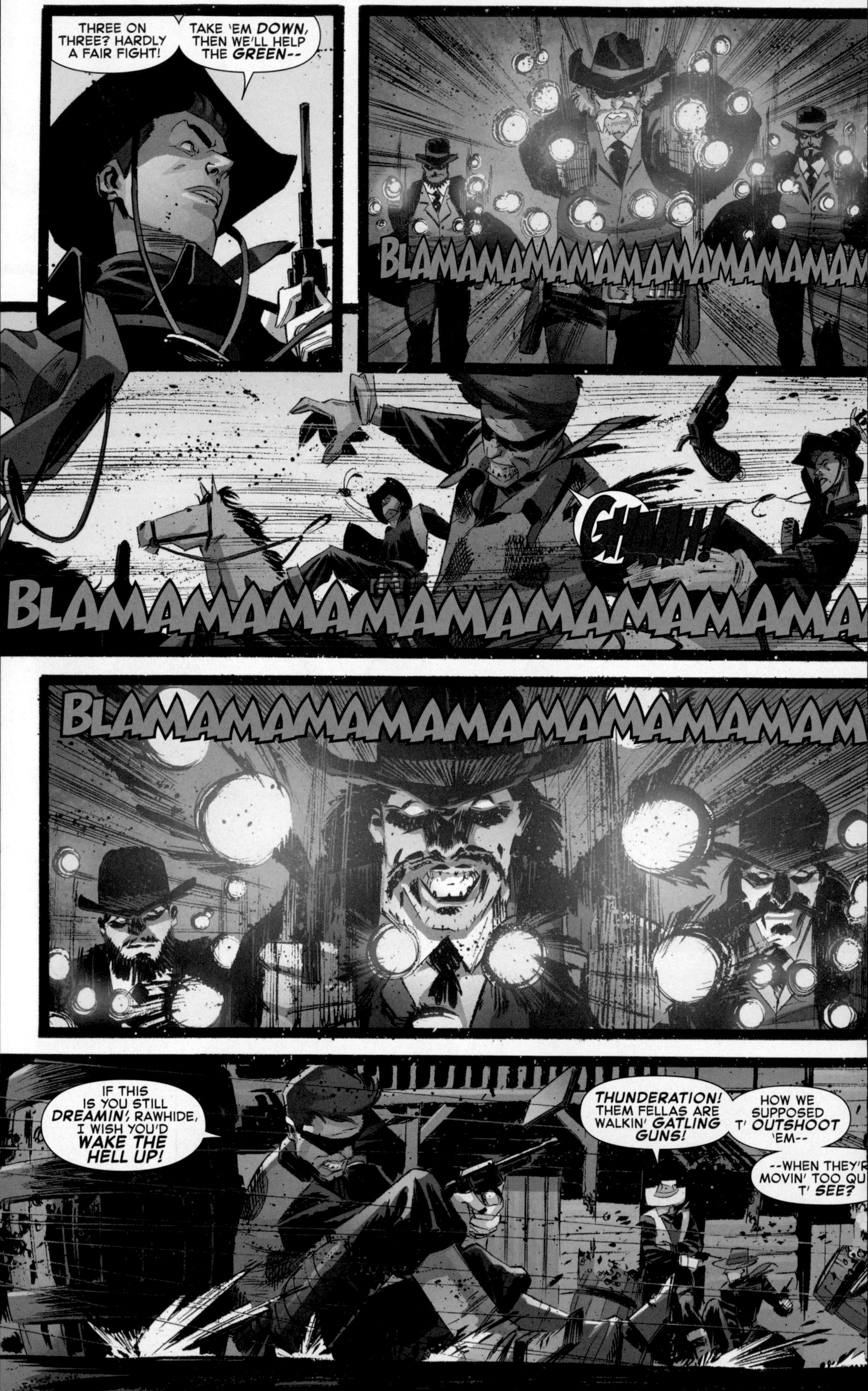

THREE ON THREE? HARDLY A FAIR FIGHT!
TAKE 'EM DOWN, THEN WE'LL HELP THE GREEN--
BLAMAMAMAMAMAMAMAMAMAMAM
GHHH!
BLAMAMAMAMAMAMAMAMAMAMAMA
BLAMAMAMAMAMAMAMAMAMAMAM
IF THIS IS YOU STILL DREAMIN', RAWHIDE, I WISH YOU'D WAKE THE HELL UP!
THUNDERATION! THEM FELLAS ARE WALKIN' GATLING GUNS!
HOW WE SUPPOSED T' OUTSHOOT 'EM--
--WHEN THEY'R MOVIN' TOO QU T' SEE?

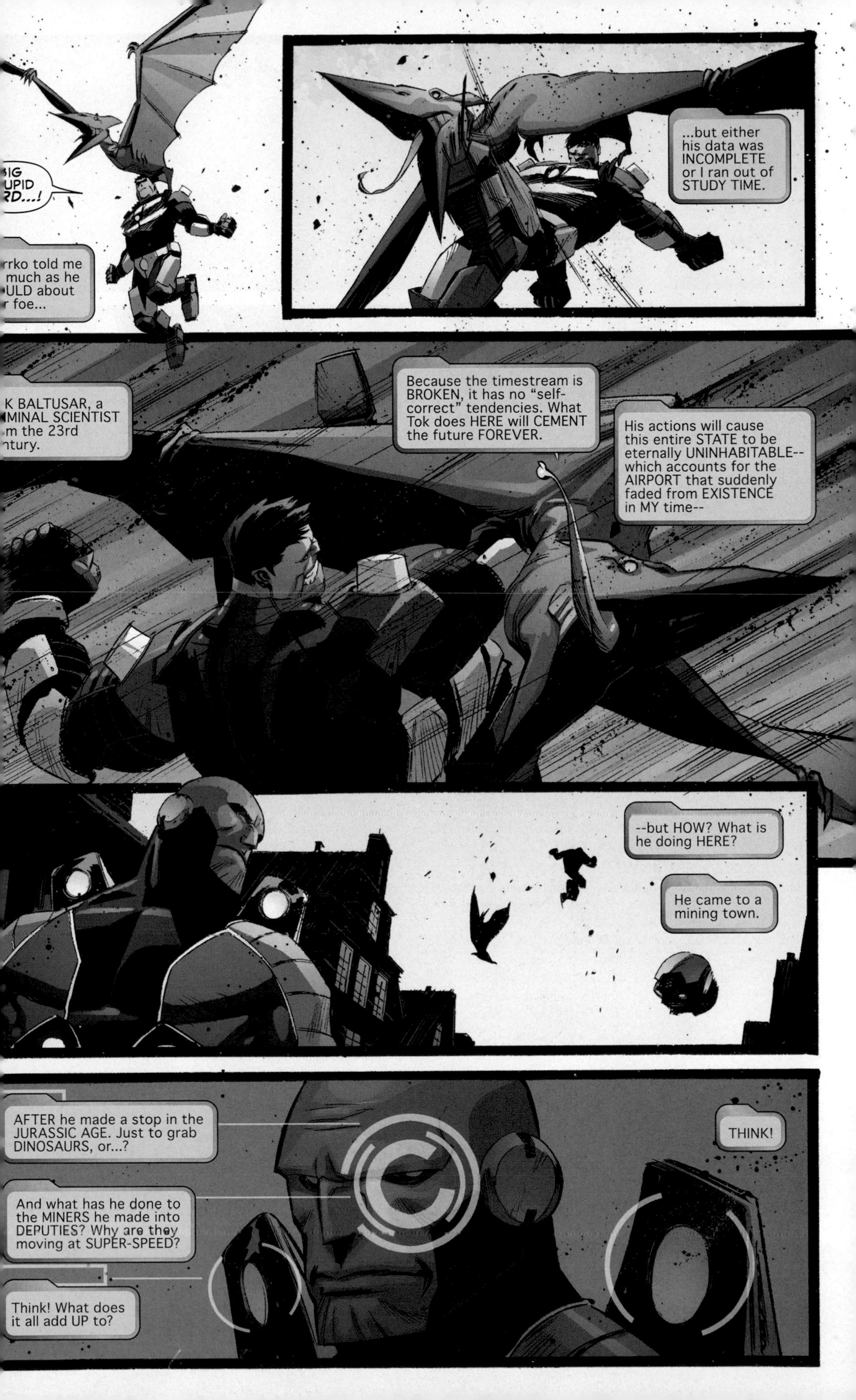

IG
UPID
RD...!
rrko told me
much as he
ULD about
r foe...
...but either
his data was
INCOMPLETE
or I ran out of
STUDY TIME.
K BALTUSAR, a
MINAL SCIENTIST
m the 23rd
ntury.
Because the timestream is
BROKEN, it has no "self-
correct" tendencies. What
Tok does HERE will CEMENT
the future FOREVER.
His actions will cause
this entire STATE to be
eternally UNINHABITABLE--
which accounts for the
AIRPORT that suddenly
faded from EXISTENCE
in MY time--
--but HOW? What is
he doing HERE?
He came to a
mining town.
AFTER he made a stop in the
JURASSIC AGE. Just to grab
DINOSAURS, or...?
And what has he done to
the MINERS he made into
DEPUTIES? Why are they
moving at SUPER-SPEED?
Think! What does
it all add UP to?
THINK!

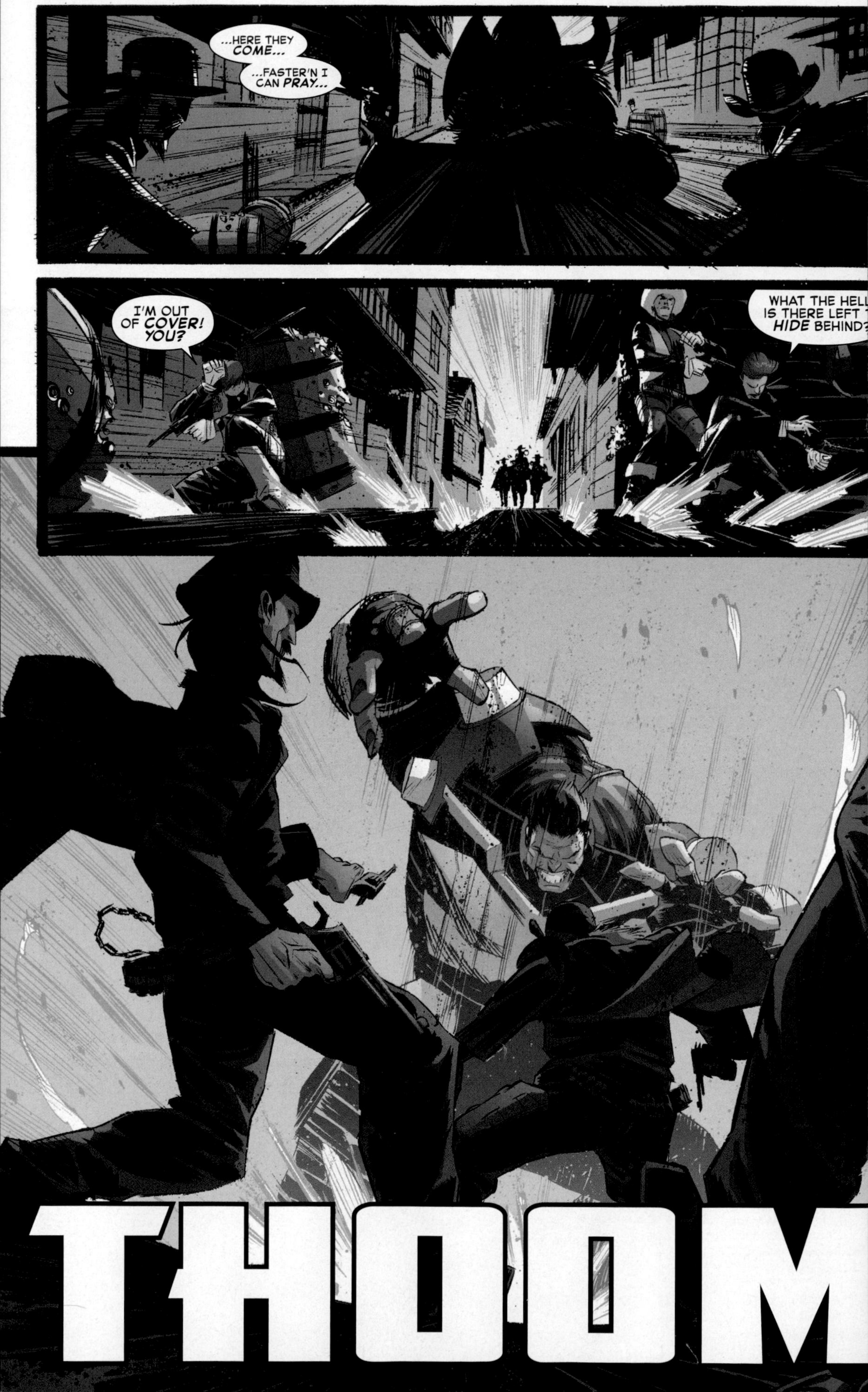
...HERE THEY COME...
...FASTER'N I CAN PRAY...
I'M OUT OF COVER! YOU?
WHAT THE HELL IS THERE LEFT T HIDE BEHIND?
THOOM

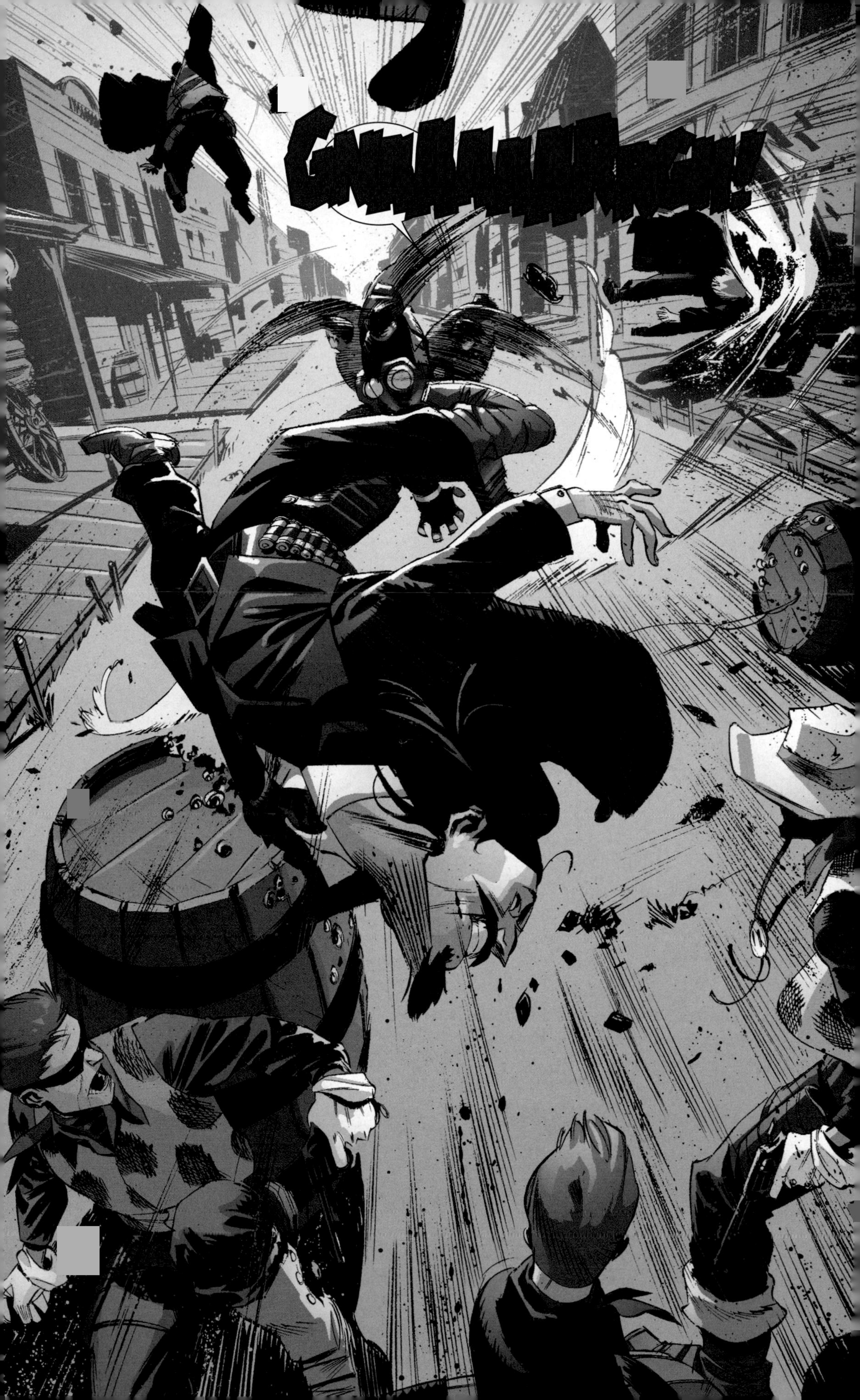

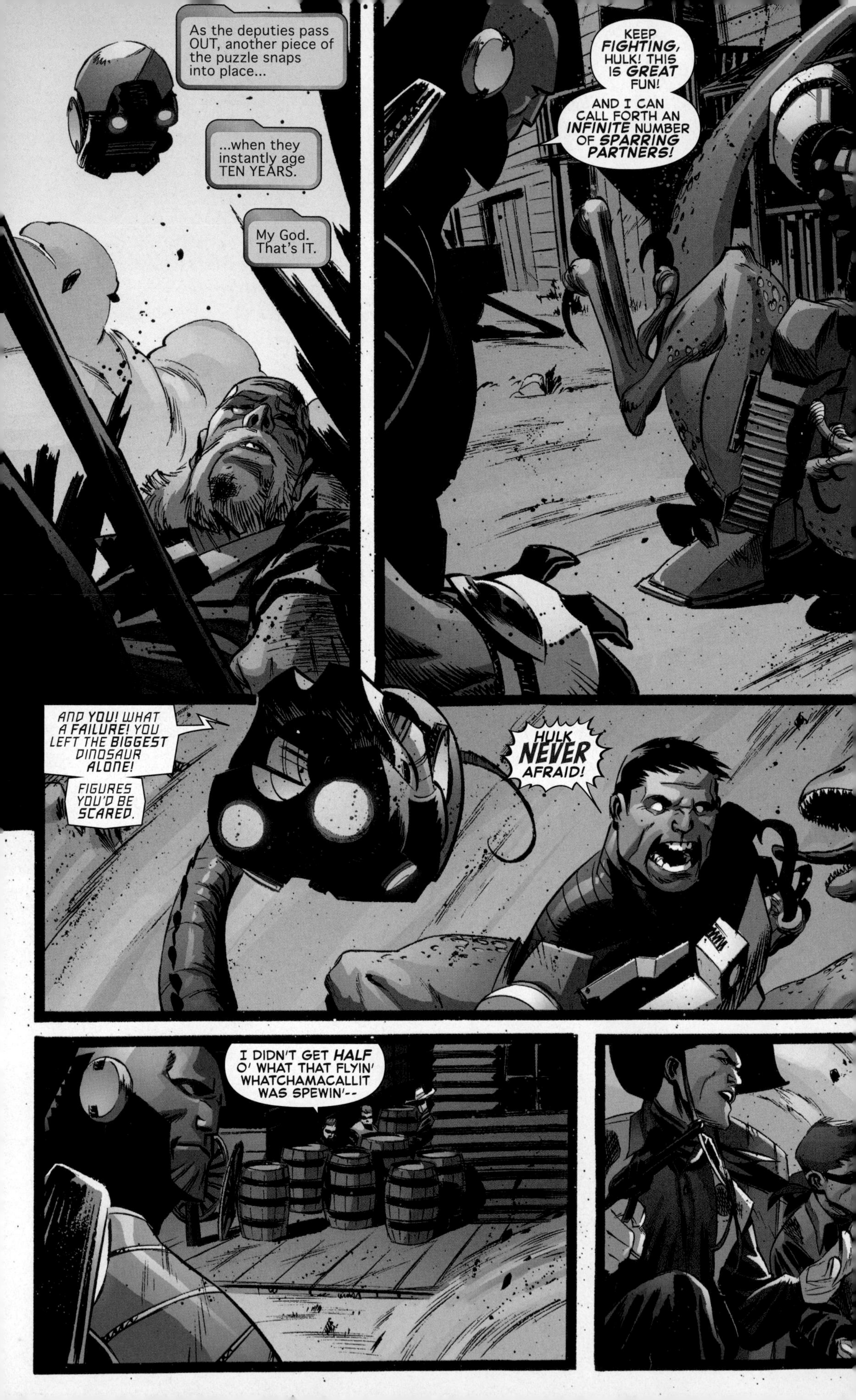

As the deputies pass OUT, another piece of the puzzle snaps into place...
...when they instantly age TEN YEARS.
My God. That's IT.
KEEP FIGHTING, HULK! THIS IS GREAT FUN!
AND I CAN CALL FORTH AN INFINITE NUMBER OF SPARRING PARTNERS!
AND YOU! WHAT A FAILURE! YOU LEFT THE BIGGEST DINOSAUR ALONE!
FIGURES YOU'D BE SCARED.
HULK NEVER AFRAID!
I DIDN'T GET HALF O' WHAT THAT FLYIN' WHATCHAMACALLIT WAS SPEWIN'--

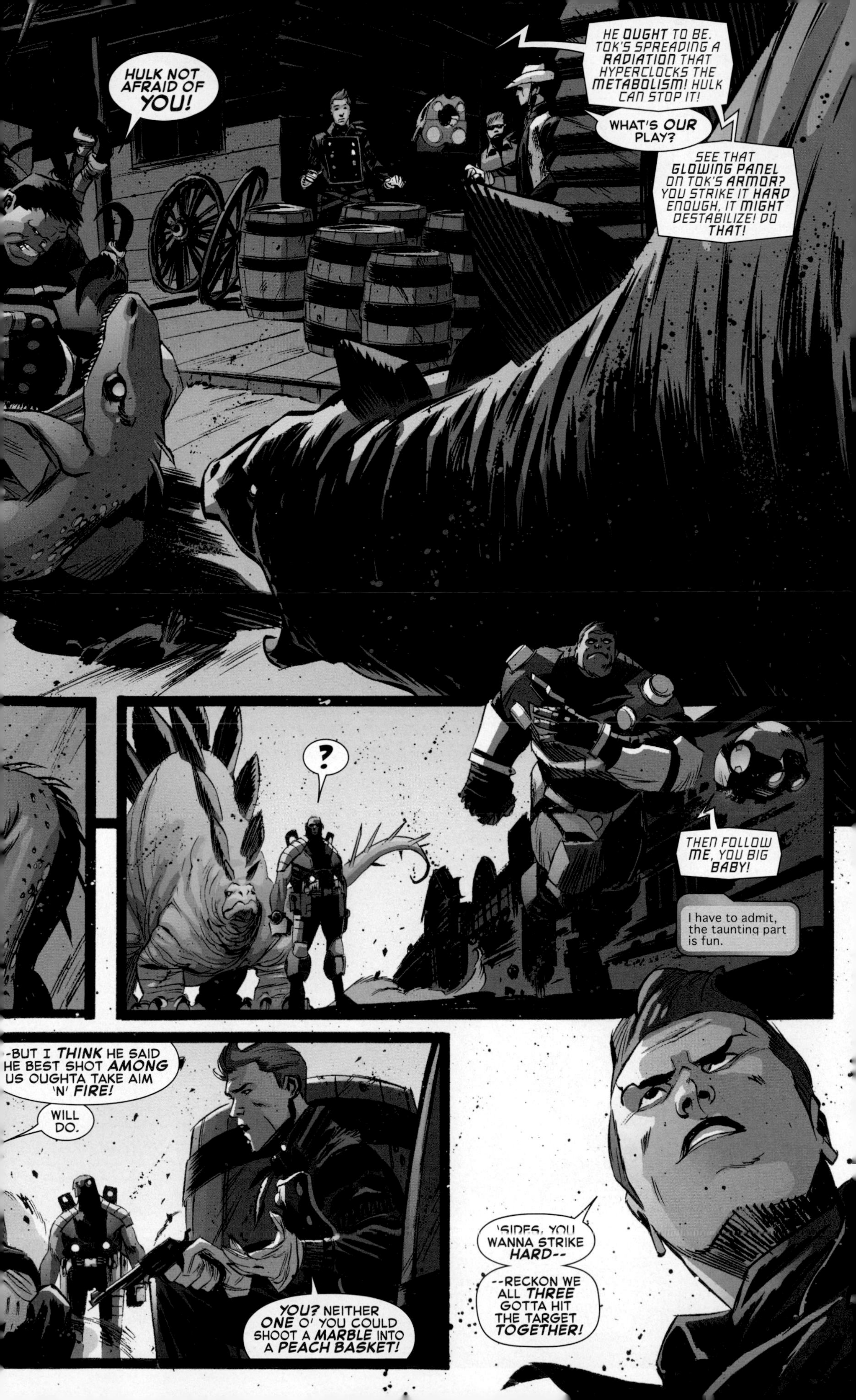
HULK NOT AFRAID OF YOU!
HE OUGHT TO BE. TOK'S SPREADING A RADIATION THAT HYPERCLOCKS THE METABOLISM! HULK CAN STOP IT!
WHAT'S OUR PLAY?
SEE THAT GLOWING PANEL ON TOK'S ARMOR? YOU STRIKE IT HARD ENOUGH, IT MIGHT DESTABILIZE! DO THAT!
?
THEN FOLLOW ME, YOU BIG BABY!
I have to admit, the taunting part is fun.
-BUT I THINK HE SAID HE BEST SHOT AMONG US OUGHTA TAKE AIM 'N' FIRE!
WILL DO.
YOU? NEITHER ONE O' YOU COULD SHOOT A MARBLE INTO A PEACH BASKET!
'SIDES, YOU WANNA STRIKE HARD--
--RECKON WE ALL THREE GOTTA HIT THE TARGET TOGETHER!

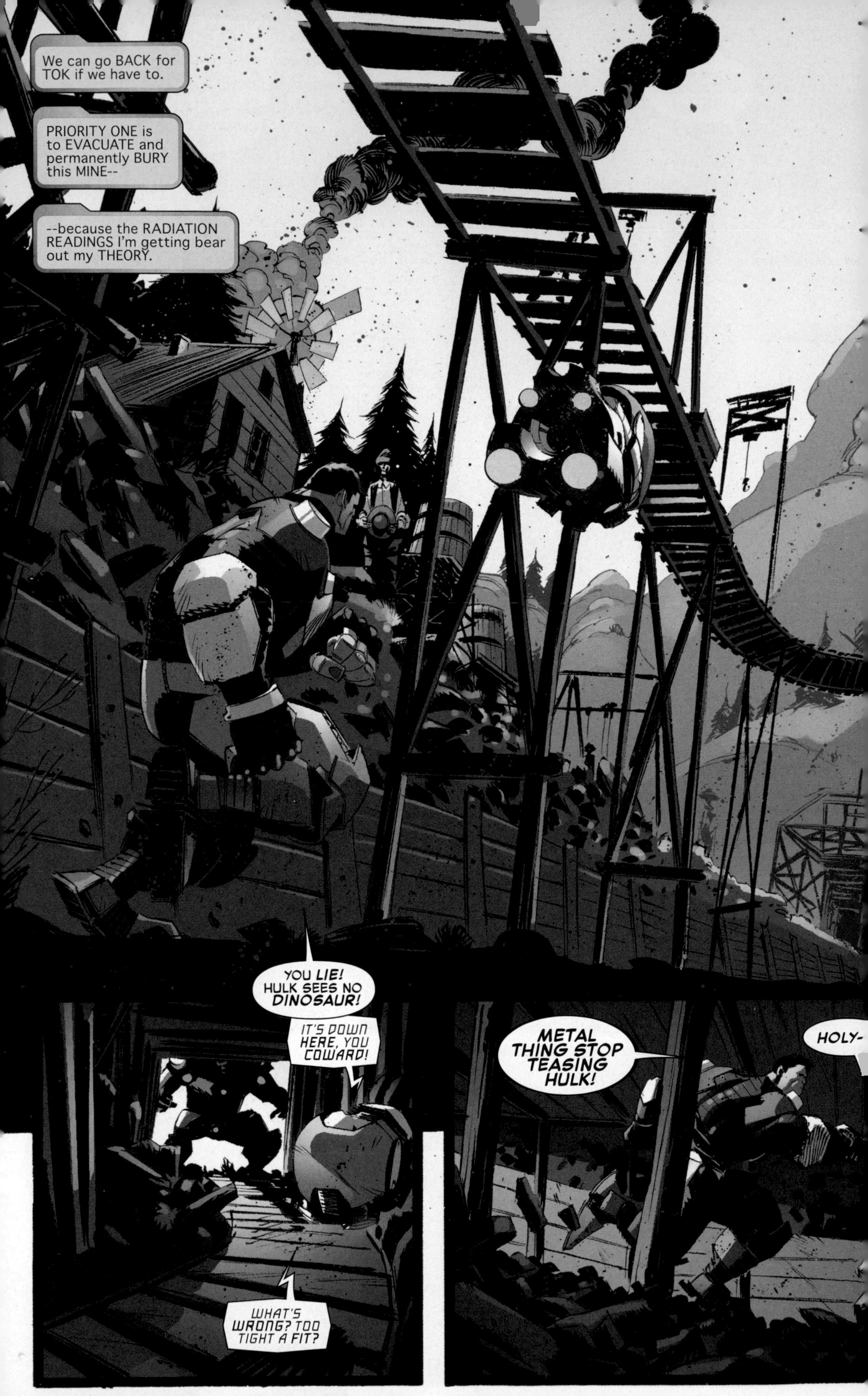
We can go BACK for TOK if we have to.
PRIORITY ONE is to EVACUATE and permanently BURY this MINE--
--because the RADIATION READINGS I'm getting bear out my THEORY.
YOU LIE! HULK SEES NO DINOSAUR!
IT'S DOWN HERE, YOU COWARD!
WHAT'S WRONG? TOO TIGHT A FIT?
METAL THING STOP TEASING HULK!
HOLY-

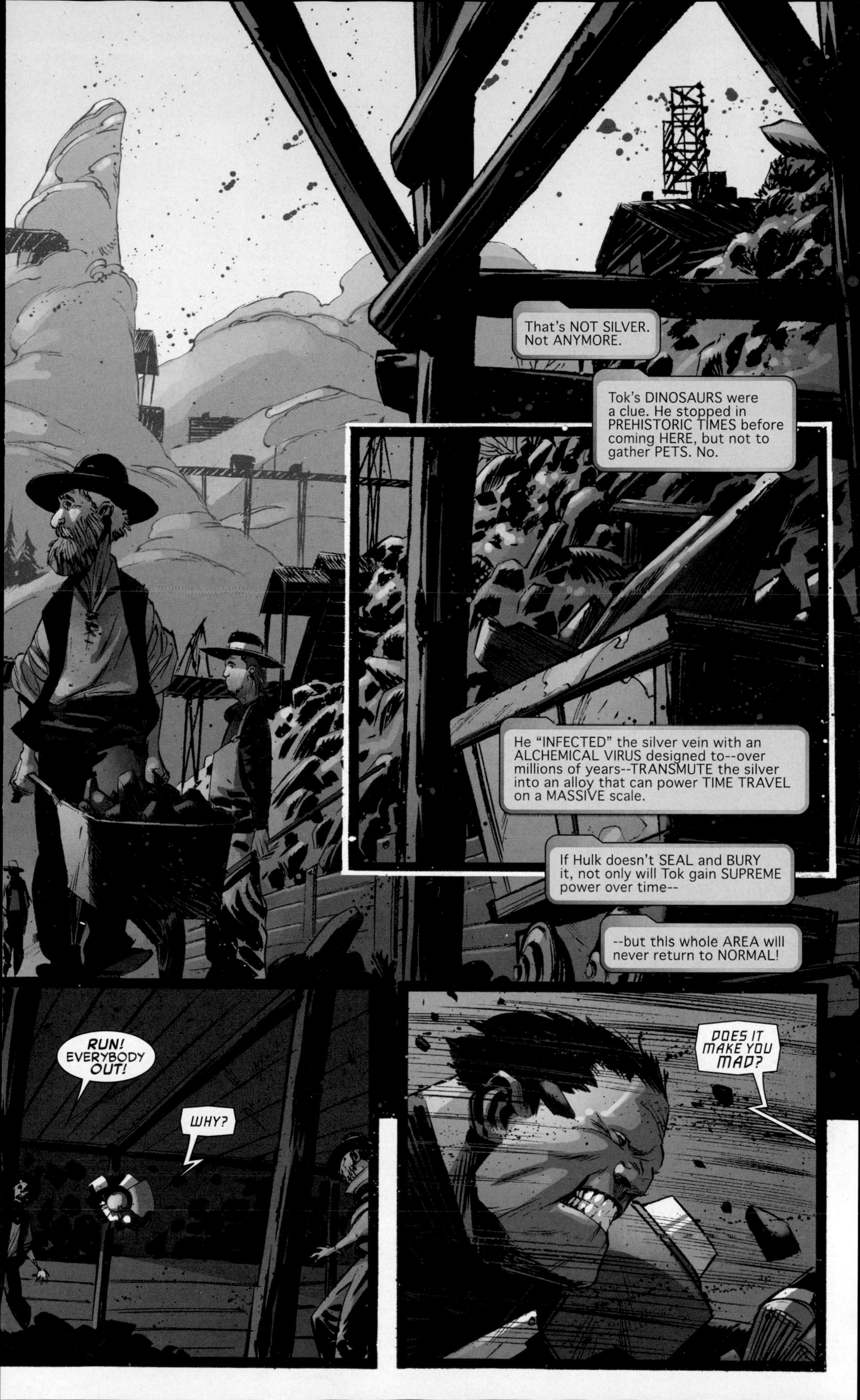

That's NOT SILVER. Not ANYMORE.
Tok's DINOSAURS were a clue. He stopped in PREHISTORIC TIMES before coming HERE, but not to gather PETS. No.
He "INFECTED" the silver vein with an ALCHEMICAL VIRUS designed to--over millions of years--TRANSMUTE the silver into an alloy that can power TIME TRAVEL on a MASSIVE scale.
If Hulk doesn't SEAL and BURY it, not only will Tok gain SUPREME power over time--
--but this whole AREA will never return to NORMAL!
RUN! EVERYBODY OUT!
WHY?
DOES IT MAKE YOU MAD?

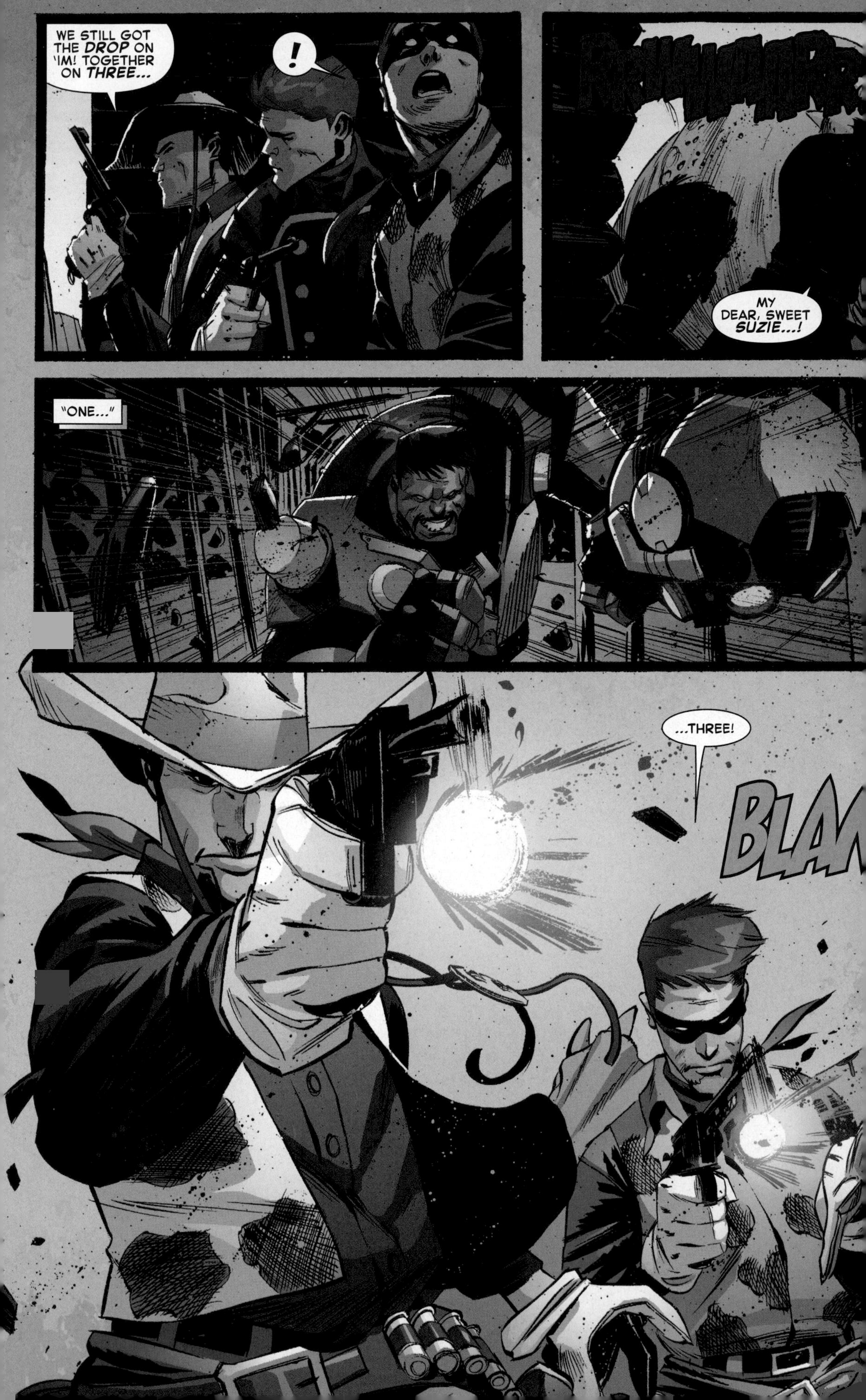
WE STILL GOT THE DROP ON 'IM! TOGETHER ON THREE...
!
MY DEAR, SWEET SUZIE...!
"ONE..."
...THREE!

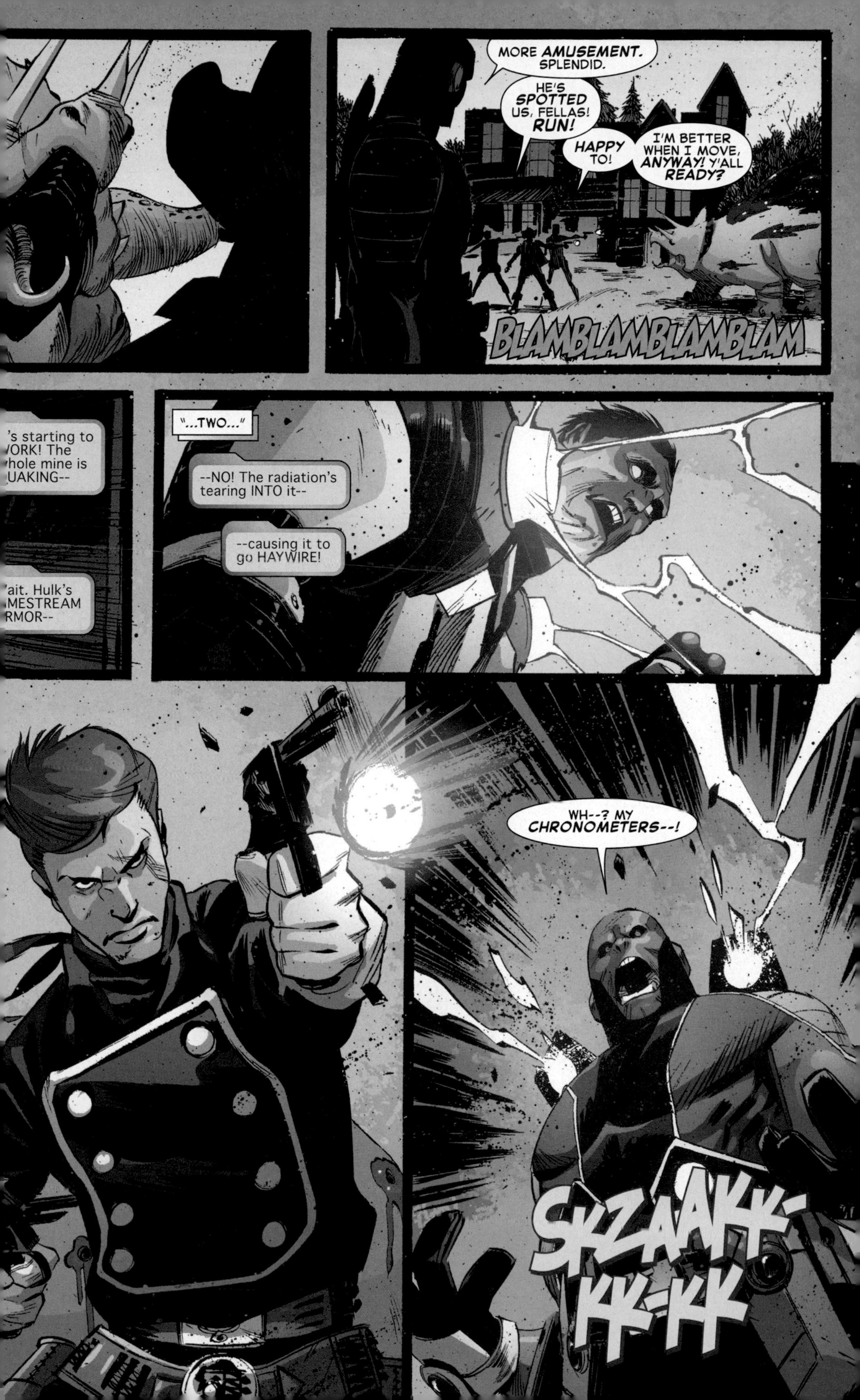

MORE AMUSEMENT. SPLENDID.
HE'S SPOTTED US, FELLAS! RUN!
HAPPY TO!
I'M BETTER WHEN I MOVE, ANYWAY! Y'ALL READY?
BLAMBLAMBLAMBLAM
'S starting to
/ORK! The
'hole mine is
UAKING--
'ait. Hulk's
MESTREAM
RMOR--
"...TWO..."
--NO! The radiation's tearing INTO it--
--causing it to go HAYWIRE!
WH--? MY CHRONOMETERS--!
SKZAAKK-KK-KK

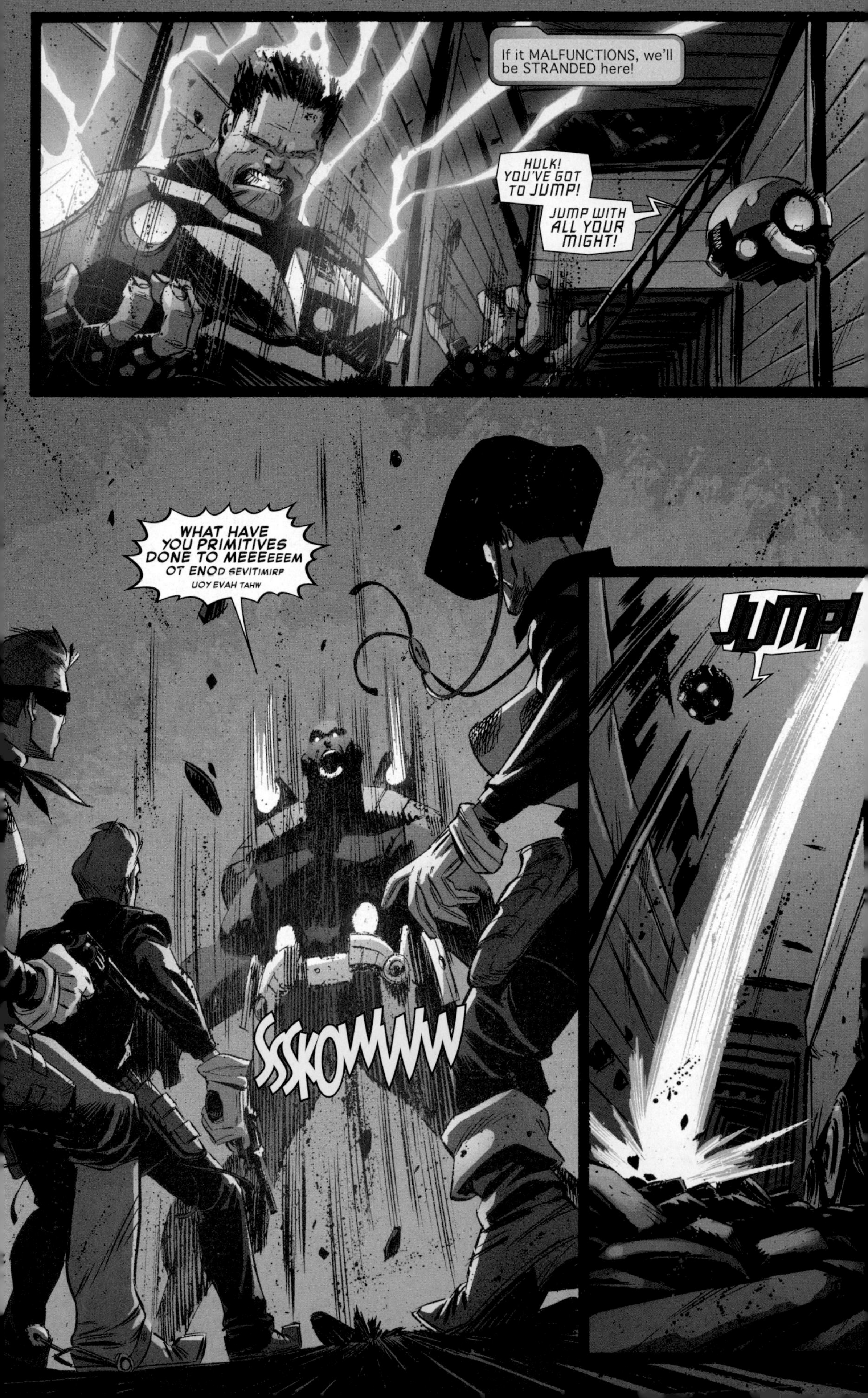
If it MALFUNCTIONS, we'll be STRANDED here!
HULK! YOU'VE GOT TO JUMP!
JUMP WITH ALL YOUR MIGHT!
WHAT HAVE YOU PRIMITIVES DONE TO MEEEeeem
OT ENOd SEVITIMIRP
UOY EVAH TAHW
JUMP!
SSSKOMMM

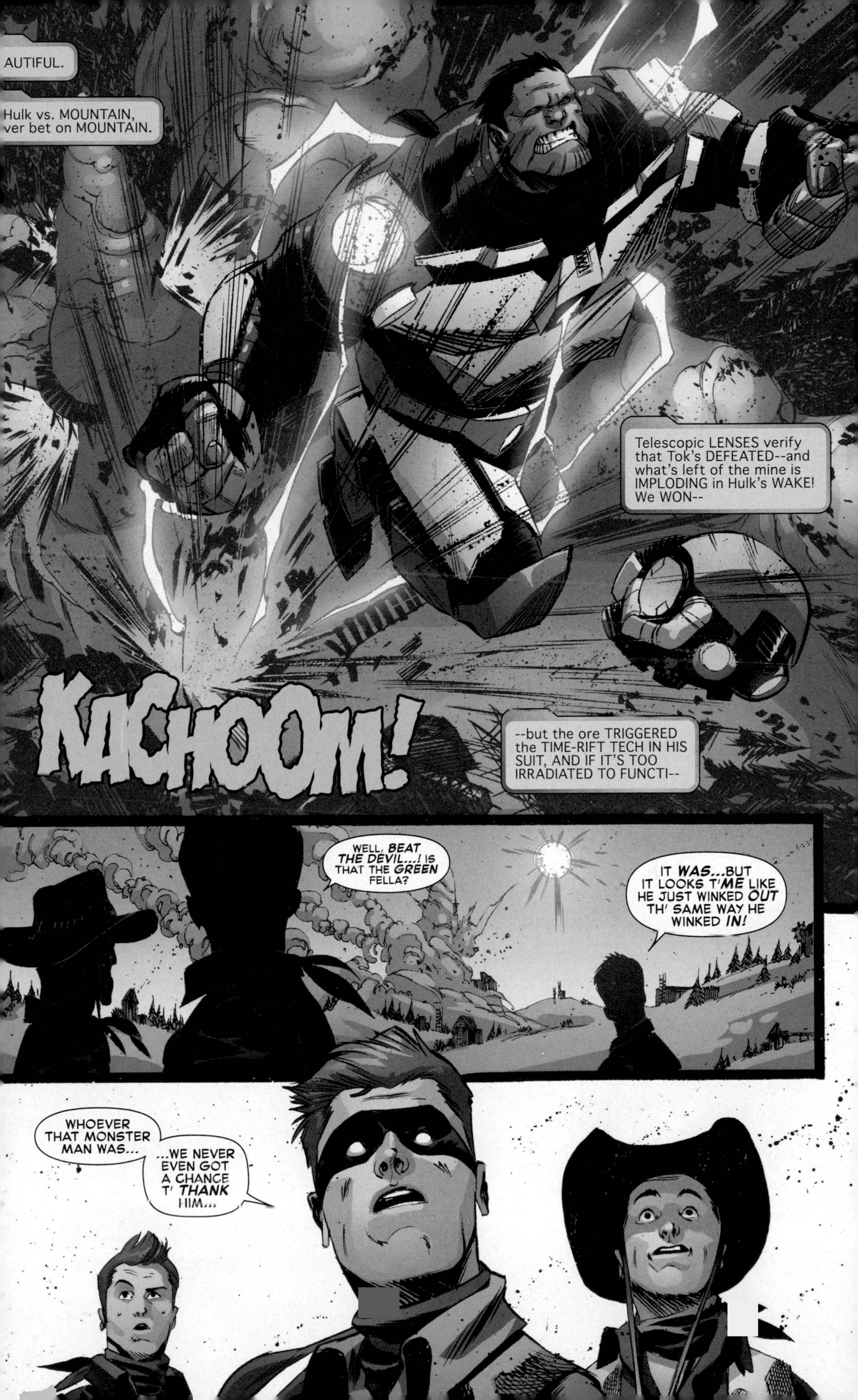
AUTIFUL.
Hulk vs. MOUNTAIN, ver bet on MOUNTAIN.
Telescopic LENSES verify that Tok's DEFEATED--and what's left of the mine is IMPLODING in Hulk's WAKE! We WON--
KACHOOM!
--but the ore TRIGGERED the TIME-RIFT TECH IN HIS SUIT, AND IF IT'S TOO IRRADIATED TO FUNCTI--
WELL, BEAT THE DEVIL...! IS THAT THE GREEN FELLA?
IT WAS...BUT IT LOOKS T'ME LIKE HE JUST WINKED OUT TH' SAME WAY HE WINKED IN!
WHOEVER THAT MONSTER MAN WAS...
...WE NEVER EVEN GOT A CHANCE T' THANK HIM...

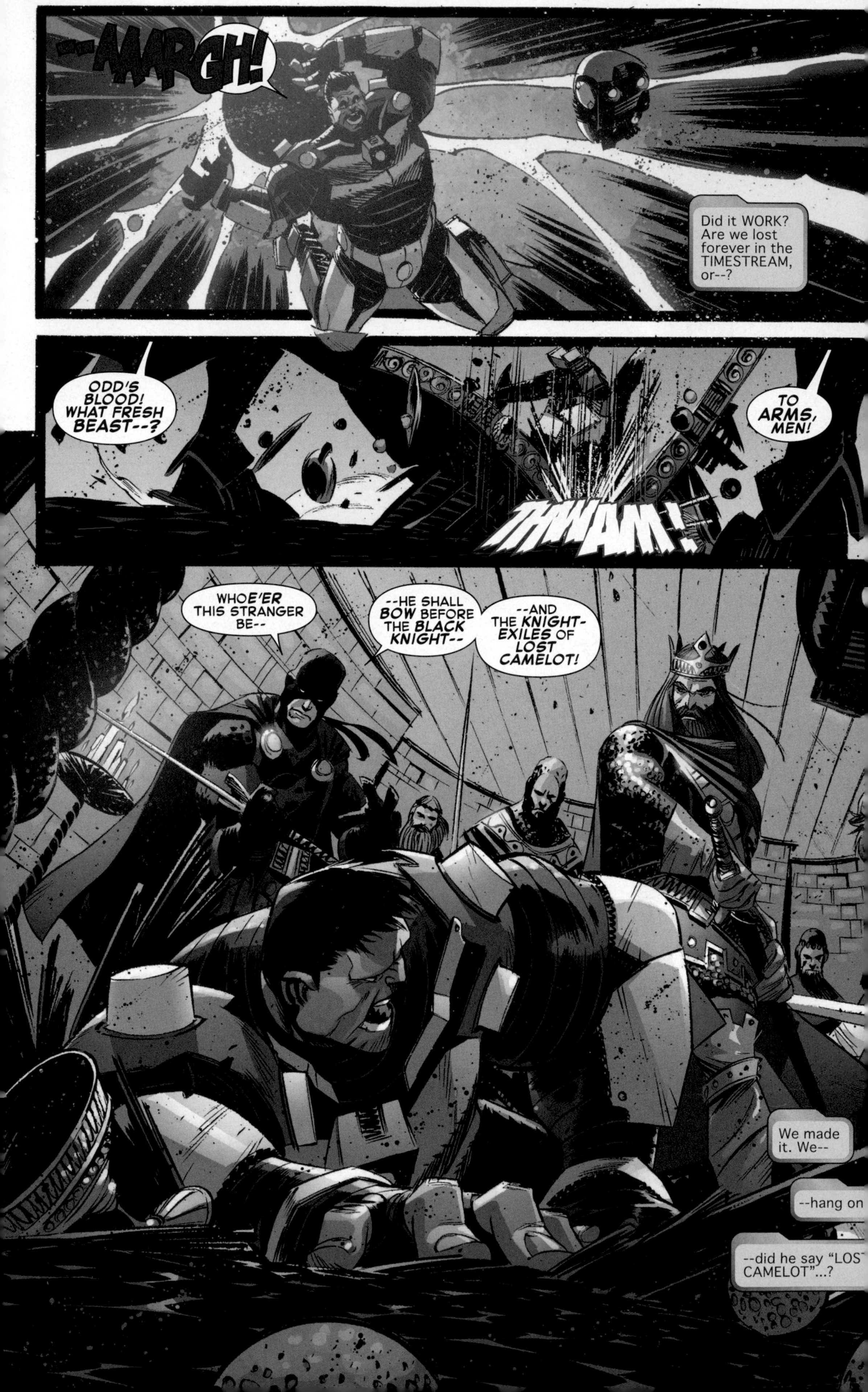
--AAARGH!
Did it WORK? Are we lost forever in the TIMESTREAM, or--?
ODD'S BLOOD! WHAT FRESH BEAST--?
TO ARMS, MEN!
THWAM!
WHOE'ER THIS STRANGER BE--
--HE SHALL BOW BEFORE THE BLACK KNIGHT--
--AND THE KNIGHT-EXILES OF LOST CAMELOT!
We made it. We--
--hang on
--did he say "LOST CAMELOT"...?

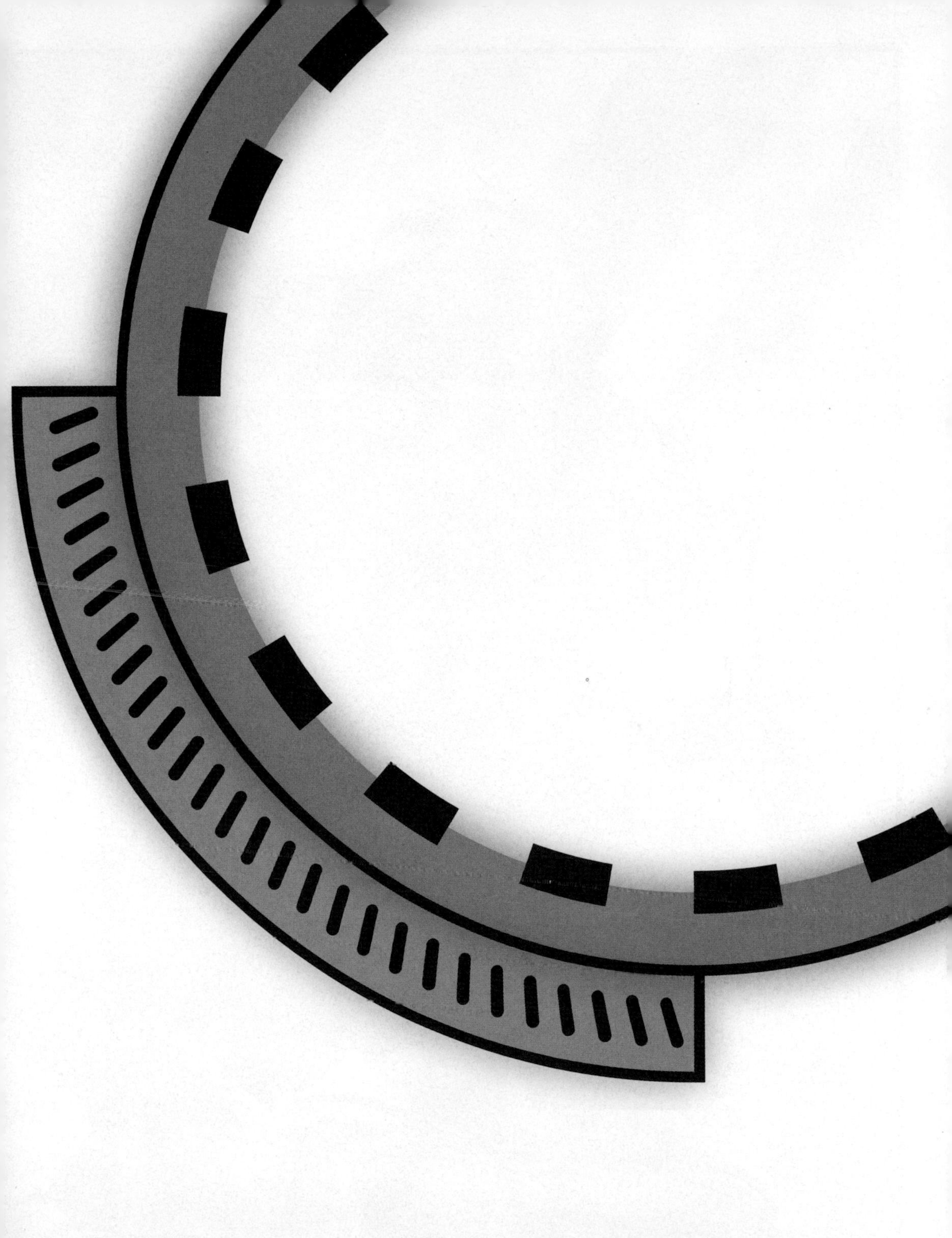

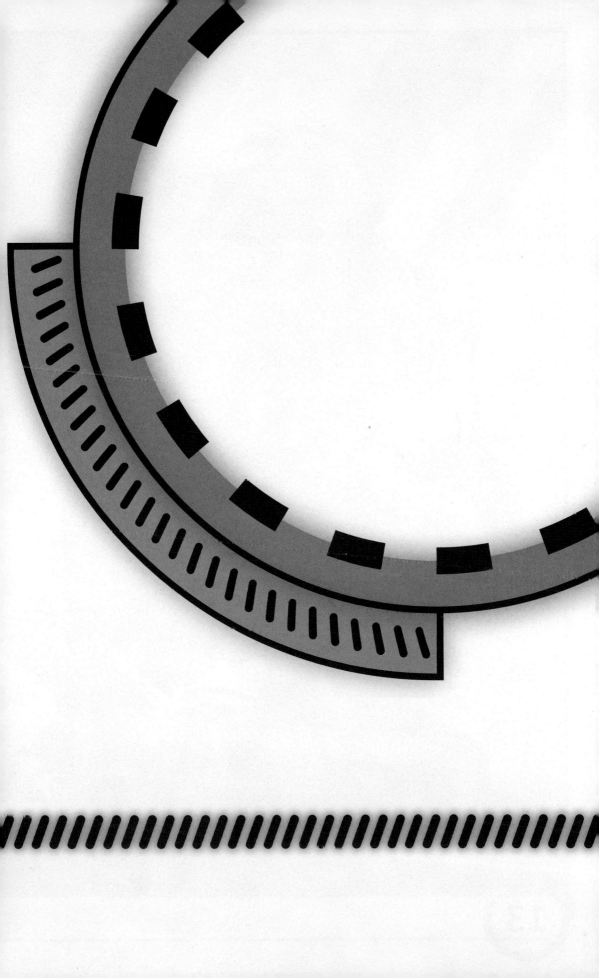

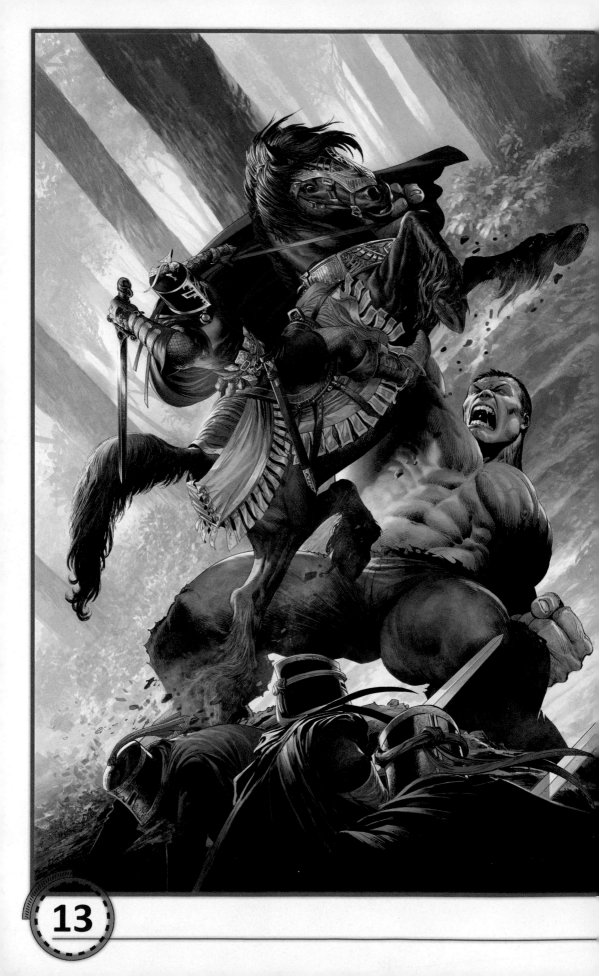

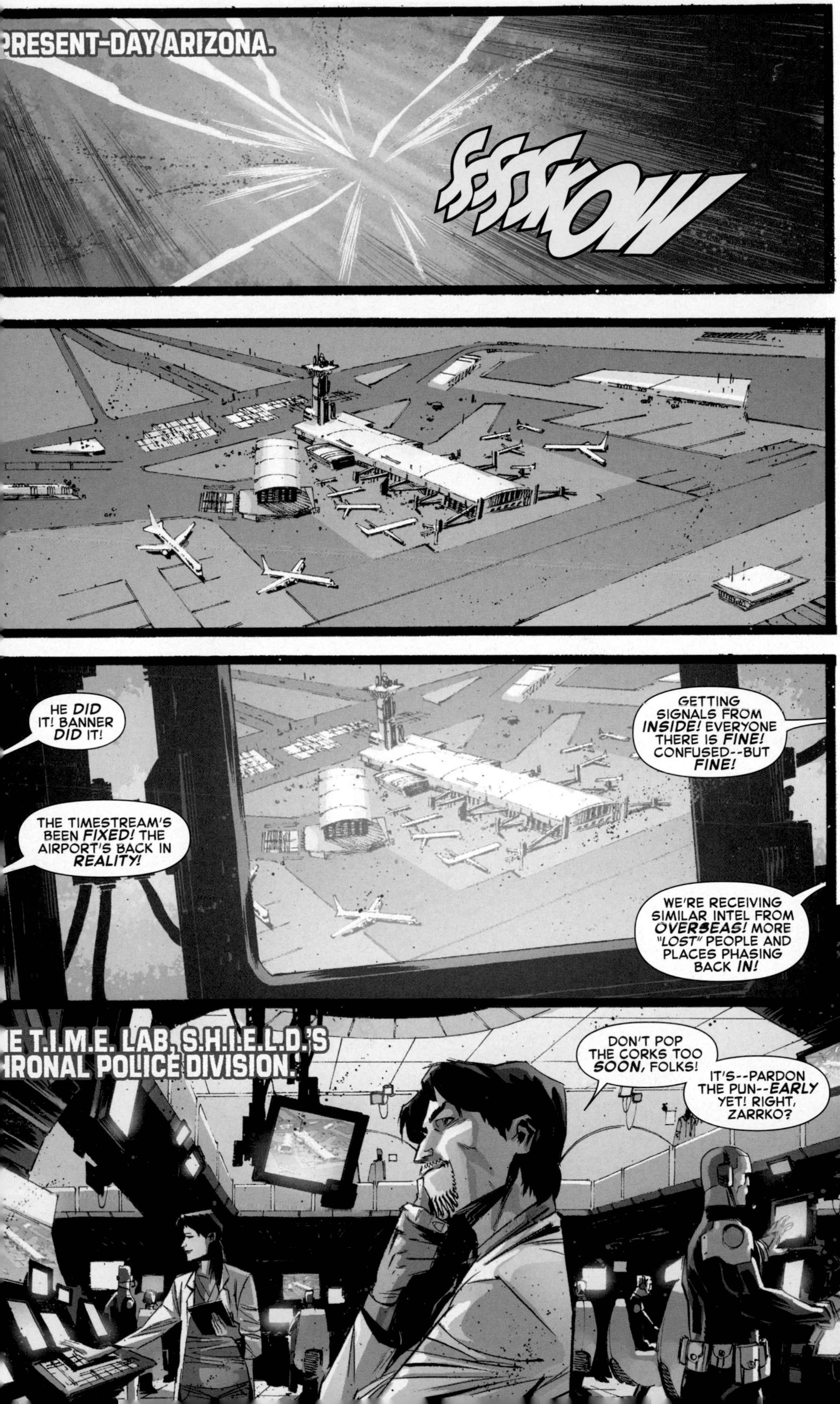
PRESENT-DAY ARIZONA.
SSSKOW
HE DID IT! BANNER DID IT!
THE TIMESTREAM'S BEEN FIXED! THE AIRPORT'S BACK IN REALITY!
GETTING SIGNALS FROM INSIDE! EVERYONE THERE IS FINE! CONFUSED--BUT FINE!
WE'RE RECEIVING SIMILAR INTEL FROM OVERSEAS! MORE "LOST" PEOPLE AND PLACES PHASING BACK IN!
E T.I.M.E. LAB, S.H.I.E.L.D.'S
IRONAL POLICE DIVISION.
DON'T POP THE CORKS TOO SOON, FOLKS!
IT'S--PARDON THE PUN--EARLY YET! RIGHT, ZARRKO?

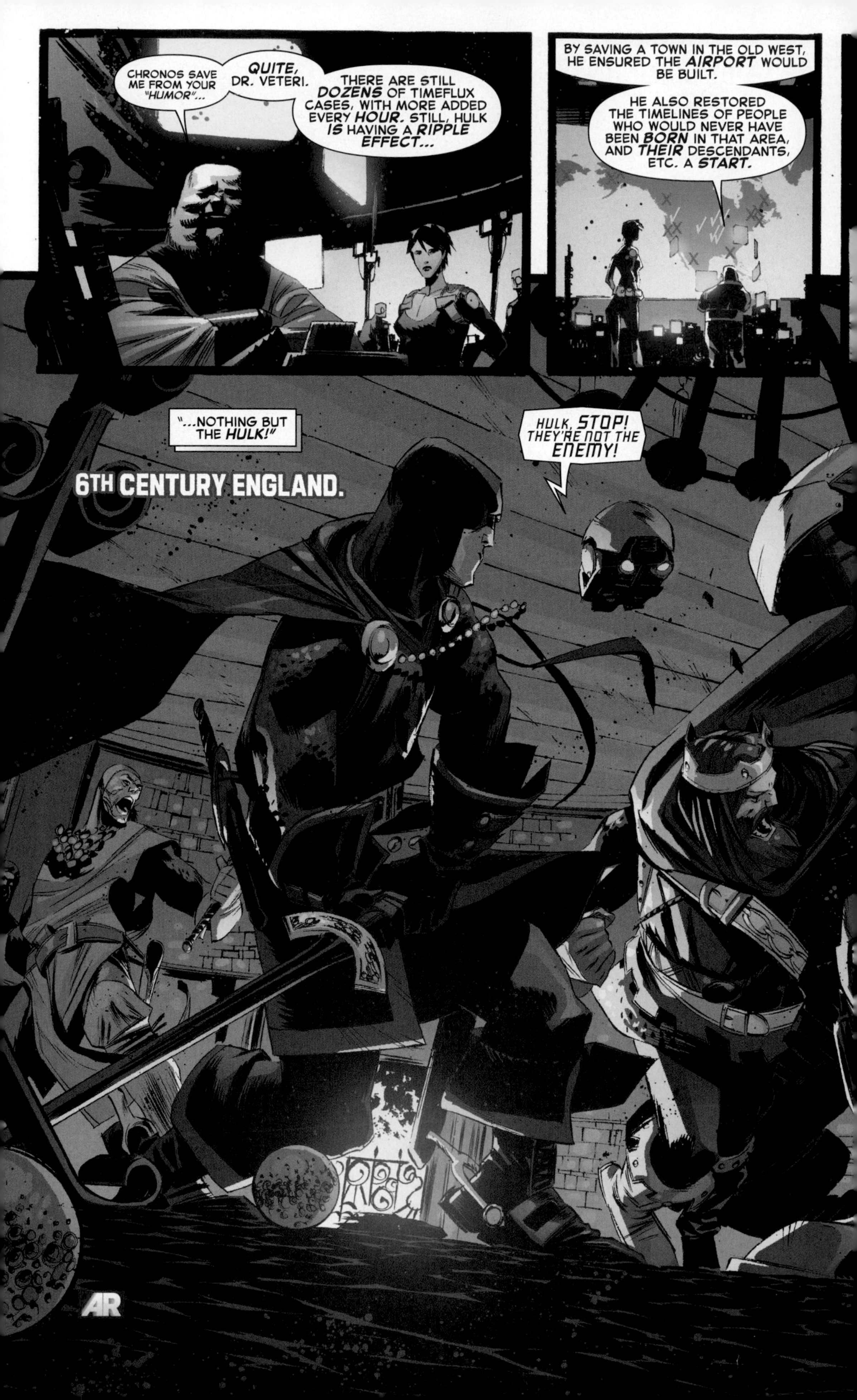
CHRONOS SAVE ME FROM YOUR "HUMOR"...
QUITE, DR. VETERI.
THERE ARE STILL DOZENS OF TIMEFLUX CASES, WITH MORE ADDED EVERY HOUR. STILL, HULK IS HAVING A RIPPLE EFFECT...
BY SAVING A TOWN IN THE OLD WEST, HE ENSURED THE AIRPORT WOULD BE BUILT.
HE ALSO RESTORED THE TIMELINES OF PEOPLE WHO WOULD NEVER HAVE BEEN BORN IN THAT AREA, AND THEIR DESCENDANTS, ETC. A START.
"...NOTHING BUT THE HULK!"
6TH CENTURY ENGLAND.
HULK, STOP! THEY'RE NOT THE ENEMY!
AR

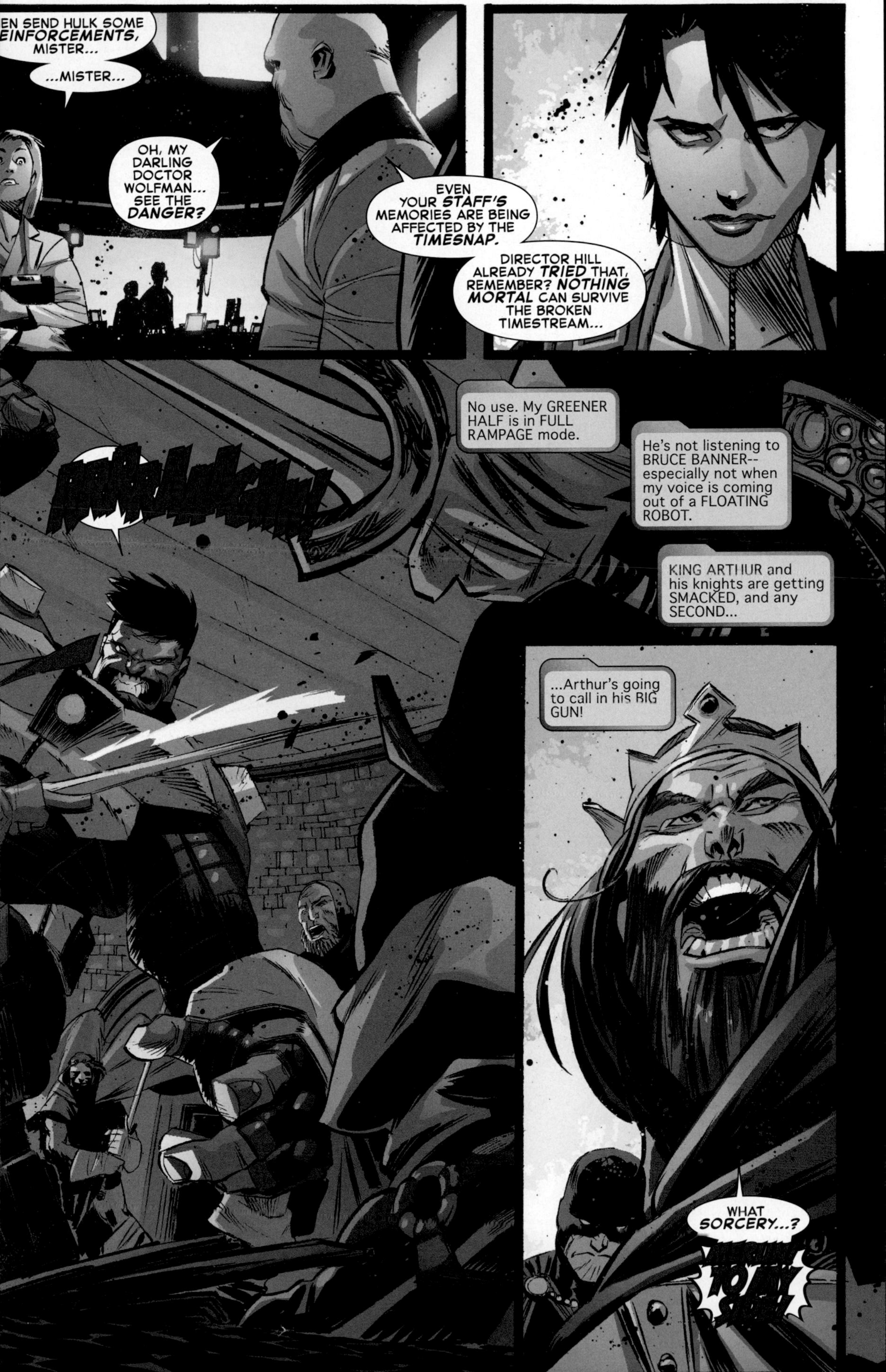

EN SEND HULK SOME EINFORCEMENTS, MISTER...
...MISTER...
OH, MY DARLING DOCTOR WOLFMAN... SEE THE DANGER?
EVEN YOUR STAFF'S MEMORIES ARE BEING AFFECTED BY THE TIMESNAP.
DIRECTOR HILL ALREADY TRIED THAT, REMEMBER? NOTHING MORTAL CAN SURVIVE THE BROKEN TIMESTREAM...
No use. My GREENER HALF is in FULL RAMPAGE mode.
He's not listening to BRUCE BANNER--especially not when my voice is coming out of a FLOATING ROBOT.
KING ARTHUR and his knights are getting SMACKED, and any SECOND...
...Arthur's going to call in his BIG GUN!
WHAT SORCERY...?

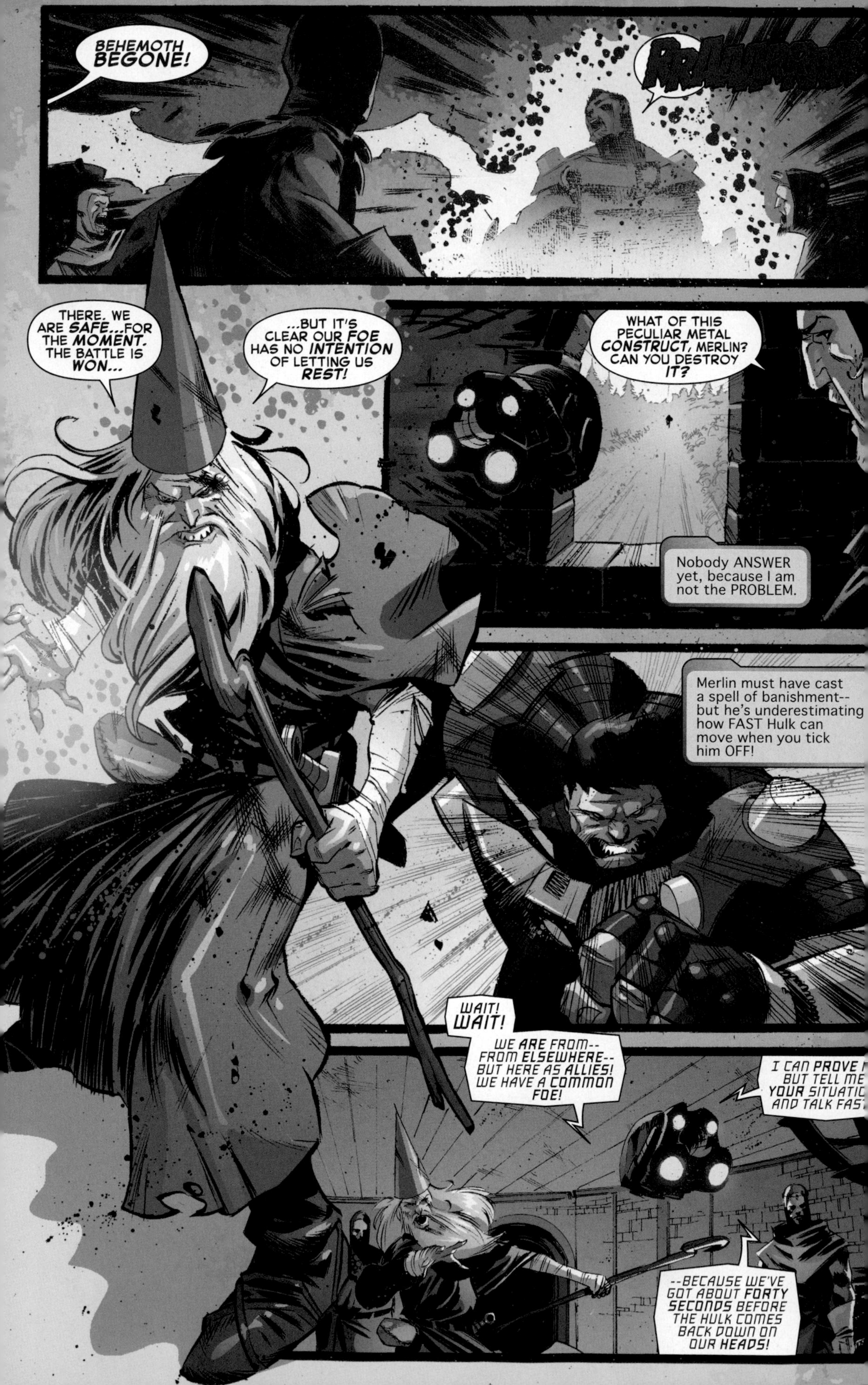
BEHEMOTH BEGONE!
THERE. WE ARE SAFE...FOR THE MOMENT. THE BATTLE IS WON...
...BUT IT'S CLEAR OUR FOE HAS NO INTENTION OF LETTING US REST!
WHAT OF THIS PECULIAR METAL CONSTRUCT, MERLIN? CAN YOU DESTROY IT?
Nobody ANSWER yet, because I am not the PROBLEM.
Merlin must have cast a spell of banishment-- but he's underestimating how FAST Hulk can move when you tick him OFF!
WAIT! WAIT!
WE ARE FROM-- FROM ELSEWHERE-- BUT HERE AS ALLIES! WE HAVE A COMMON FOE!
I CAN PROVE
BUT TELL ME
YOUR
AND TALK
--BECAUSE WE'VE GOT ABOUT FORTY SECONDS BEFORE THE HULK COMES BACK DOWN ON OUR HEADS!

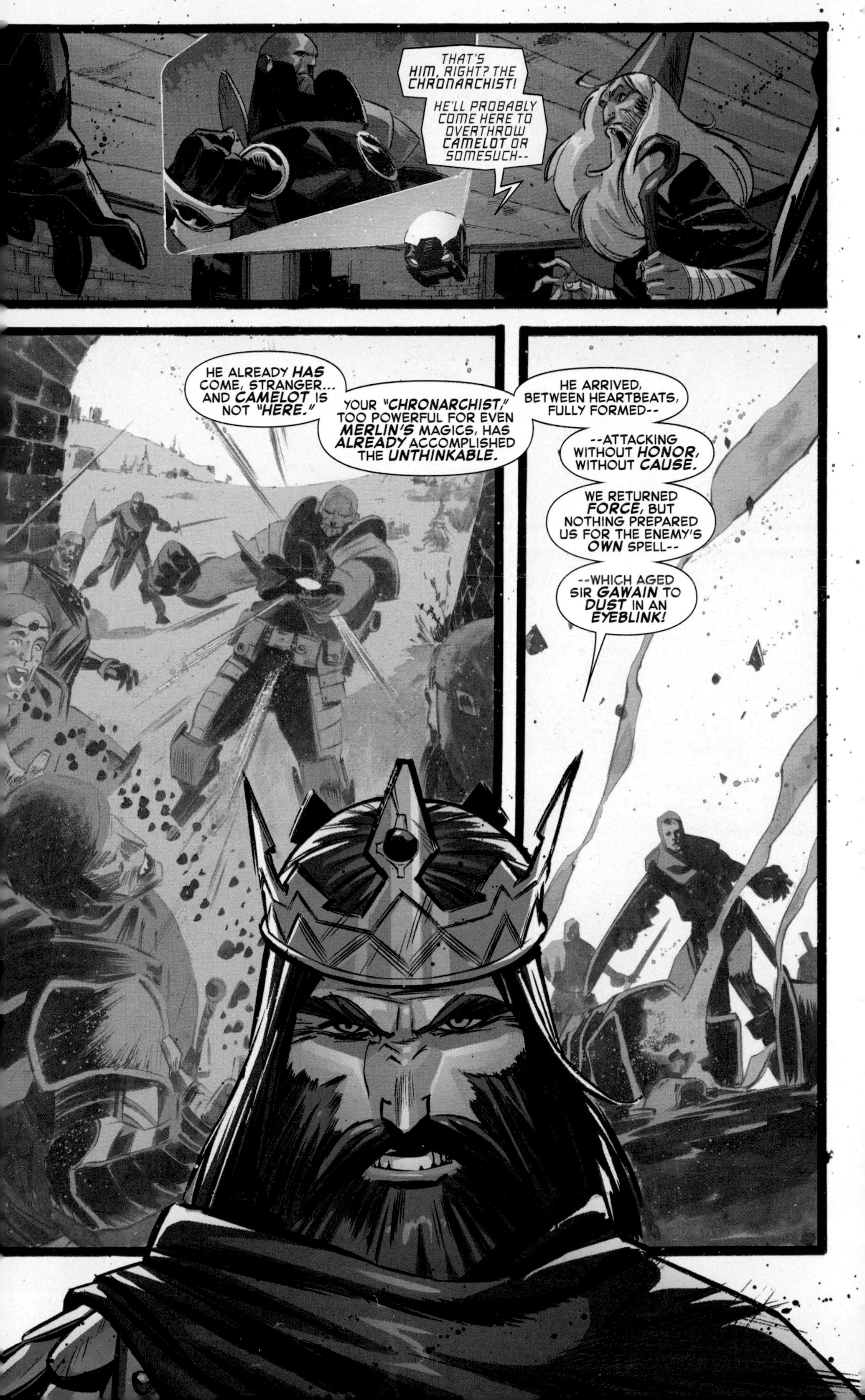
THAT'S HIM, RIGHT? THE CHRONARCHIST!
HE'LL PROBABLY COME HERE TO OVERTHROW CAMELOT OR SOMESUCH--
HE ALREADY HAS COME, STRANGER... AND CAMELOT IS NOT "HERE."
YOUR "CHRONARCHIST," TOO POWERFUL FOR EVEN MERLIN'S MAGICS, HAS ALREADY ACCOMPLISHED THE UNTHINKABLE.
HE ARRIVED, BETWEEN HEARTBEATS, FULLY FORMED--
--ATTACKING WITHOUT HONOR, WITHOUT CAUSE.
WE RETURNED FORCE, BUT NOTHING PREPARED US FOR THE ENEMY'S OWN SPELL--
--WHICH AGED SIR GAWAIN TO DUST IN AN EYEBLINK!

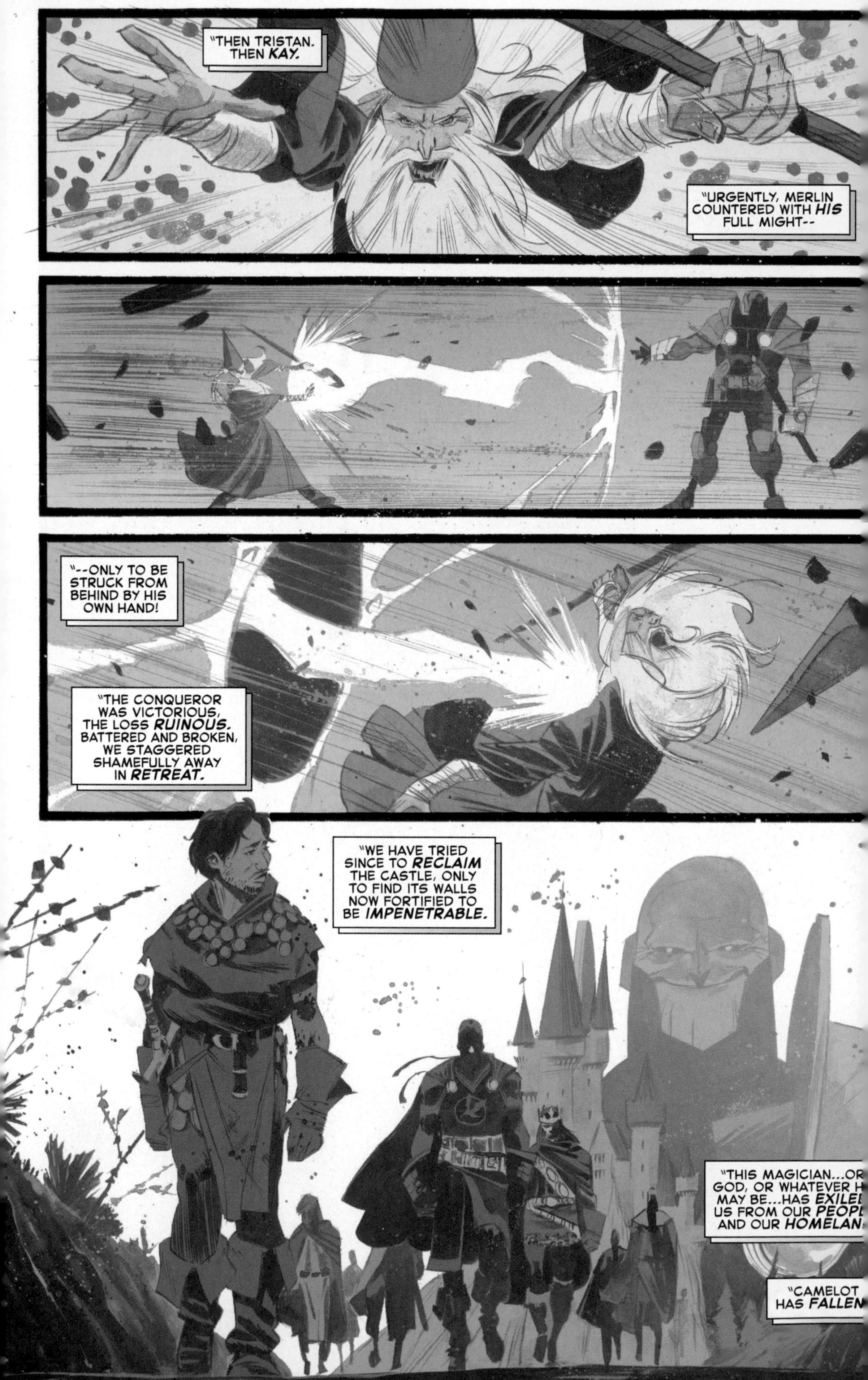
"THEN TRISTAN. THEN KAY.
"URGENTLY, MERLIN COUNTERED WITH HIS FULL MIGHT--
"--ONLY TO BE STRUCK FROM BEHIND BY HIS OWN HAND!
"THE CONQUEROR WAS VICTORIOUS, THE LOSS RUINOUS. BATTERED AND BROKEN, WE STAGGERED SHAMEFULLY AWAY IN RETREAT.
"WE HAVE TRIED SINCE TO RECLAIM THE CASTLE, ONLY TO FIND ITS WALLS NOW FORTIFIED TO BE IMPENETRABLE.
"THIS MAGICIAN...OR GOD, OR WHATEVER H MAY BE...HAS EXILE US FROM OUR PEOPL AND OUR HOMELAN
"CAMELOT HAS FALLEN

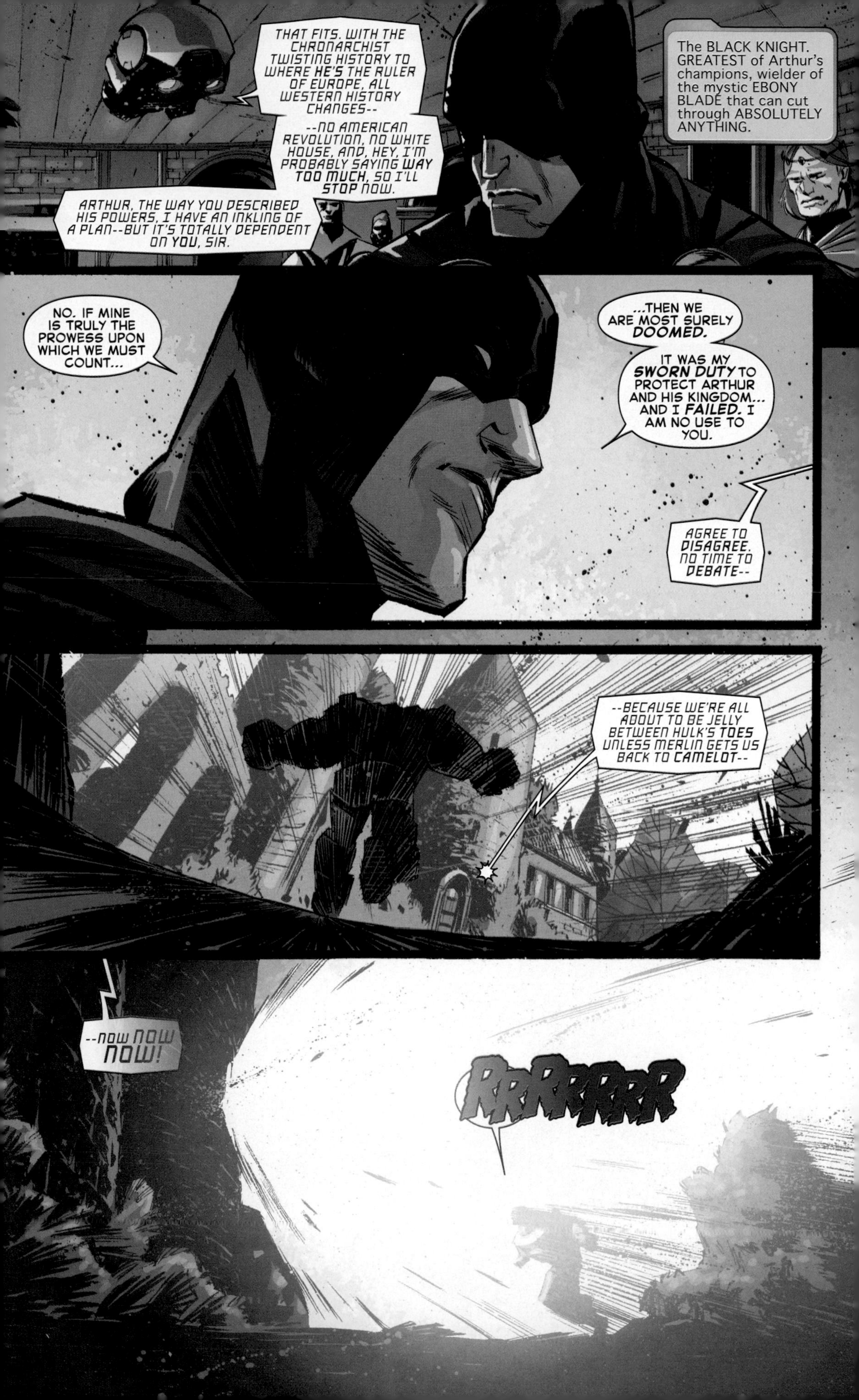
THAT FITS. WITH THE CHRONARCHIST TWISTING HISTORY TO WHERE HE'S THE RULER OF EUROPE, ALL WESTERN HISTORY CHANGES--
--NO AMERICAN REVOLUTION, NO WHITE HOUSE, AND, HEY, I'M PROBABLY SAYING WAY TOO MUCH, SO I'LL STOP NOW.
The BLACK KNIGHT. GREATEST of Arthur's champions, wielder of the mystic EBONY BLADE that can cut through ABSOLUTELY ANYTHING.
ARTHUR, THE WAY YOU DESCRIBED HIS POWERS, I HAVE AN INKLING OF A PLAN--BUT IT'S TOTALLY DEPENDENT ON YOU, SIR.
NO. IF MINE IS TRULY THE PROWESS UPON WHICH WE MUST COUNT...
...THEN WE ARE MOST SURELY DOOMED.
IT WAS MY SWORN DUTY TO PROTECT ARTHUR AND HIS KINGDOM... AND I FAILED. I AM NO USE TO YOU.
AGREE TO DISAGREE. NO TIME TO DEBATE--
--BECAUSE WE'RE ALL ABOUT TO BE JELLY BETWEEN HULK'S TOES UNLESS MERLIN GETS US BACK TO CAMELOT--
--NOW NOW NOW!
RRRRRRRR

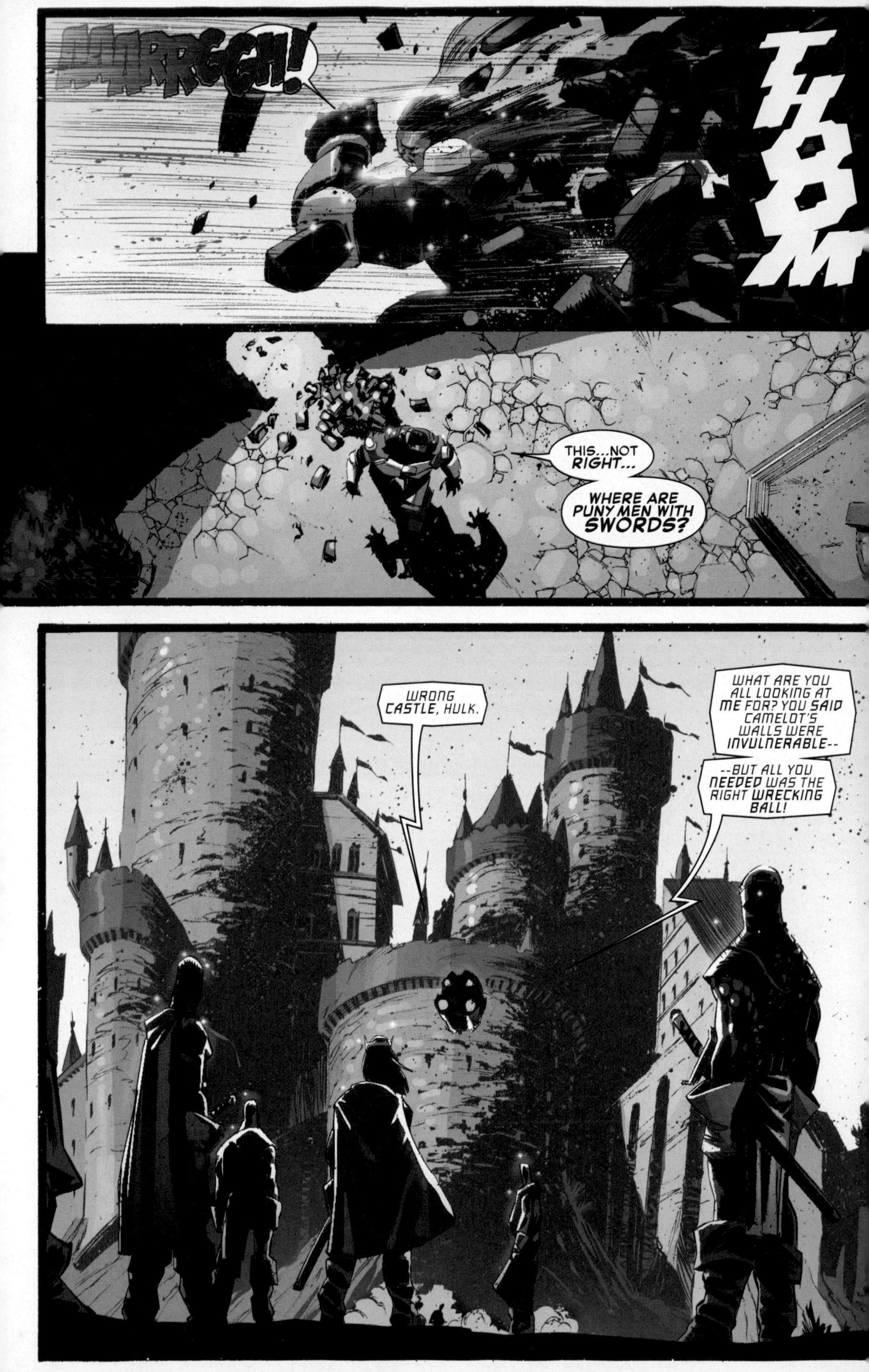
AAARRGH!
TOOM
THIS...NOT RIGHT...
WHERE ARE PUNY MEN WITH SWORDS?
WRONG CASTLE, HULK.
WHAT ARE YOU ALL LOOKING AT ME FOR? YOU SAID CAMELOT'S WALLS WERE INVULNERABLE--
--BUT ALL YOU NEEDED WAS THE RIGHT WRECKING BALL!

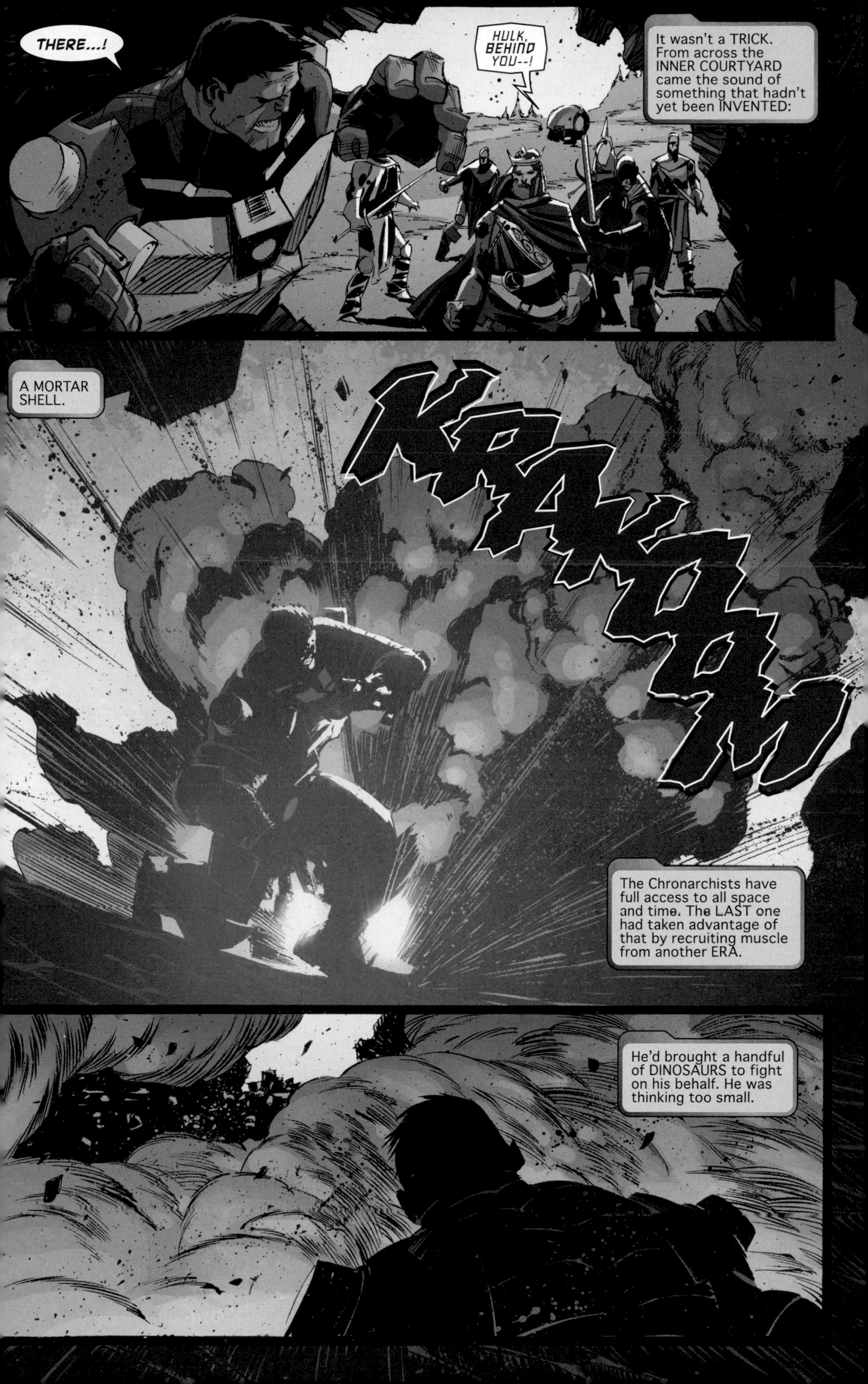

THERE...!
HULK, BEHIND YOU--!
It wasn't a TRICK. From across the INNER COURTYARD came the sound of something that hadn't yet been INVENTED:
A MORTAR SHELL.
KRAKOOM
The Chronarchists have full access to all space and time. The LAST one had taken advantage of that by recruiting muscle from another ERA.
He'd brought a handful of DINOSAURS to fight on his behalf. He was thinking too small.

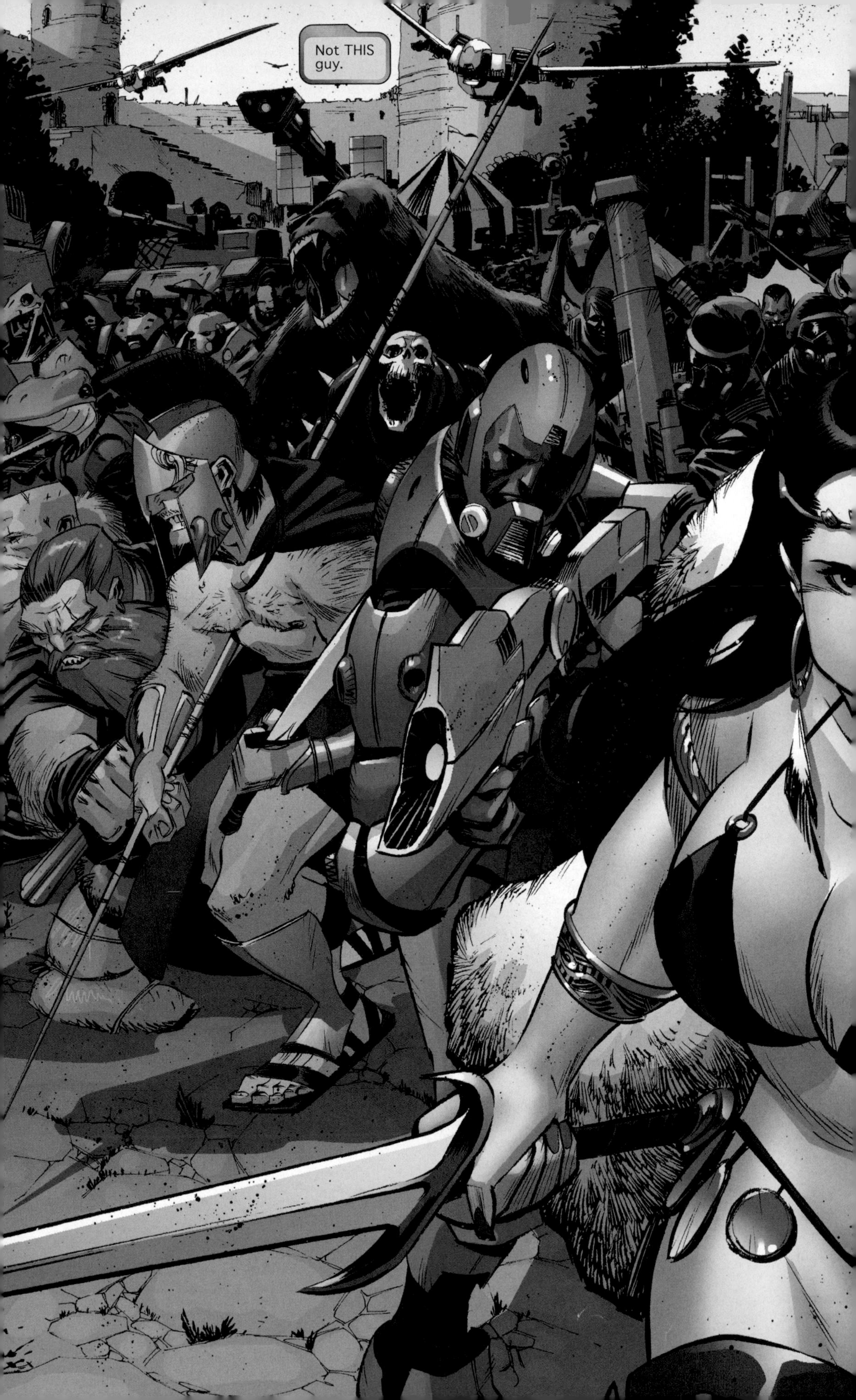
Not THIS guy.

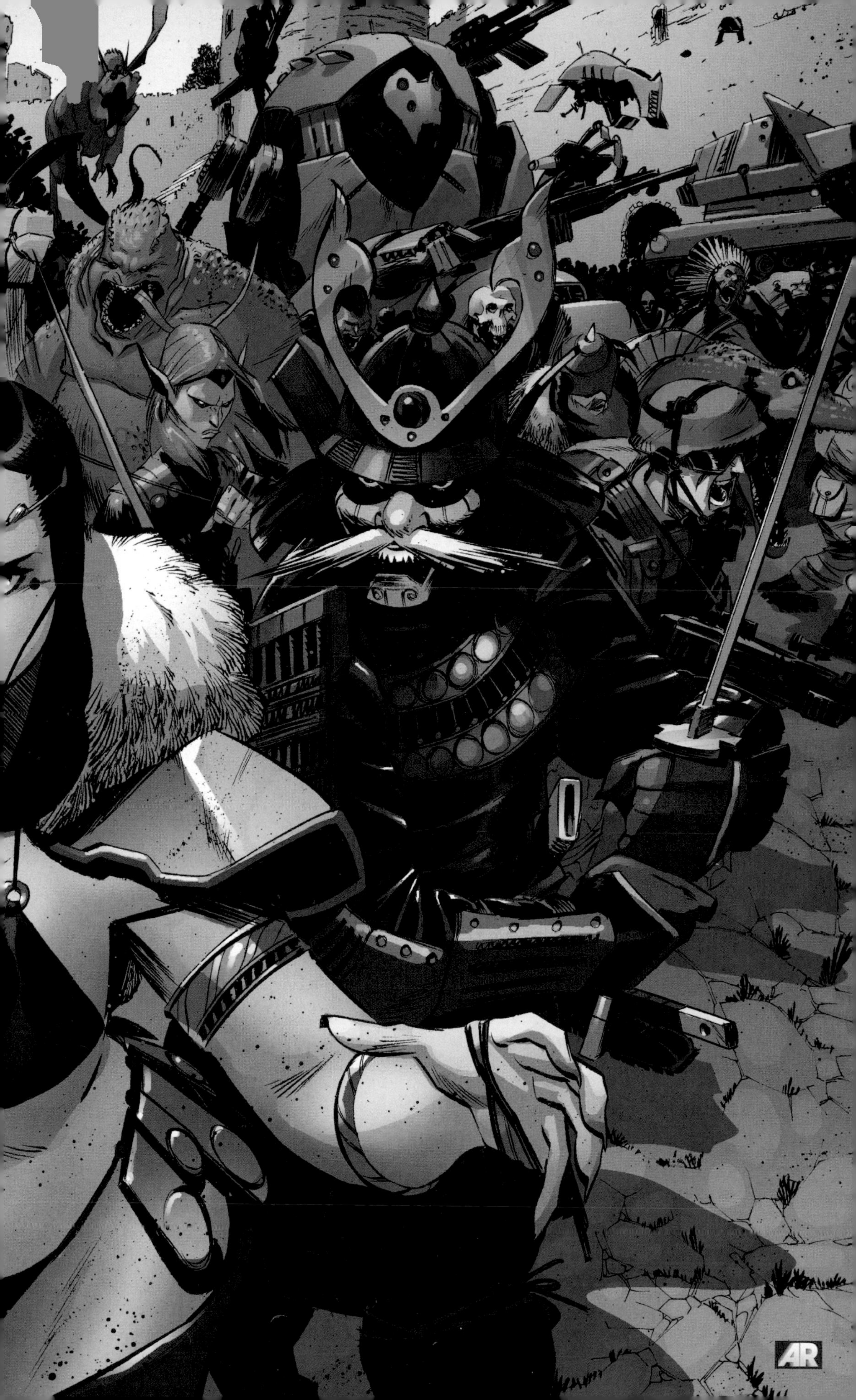

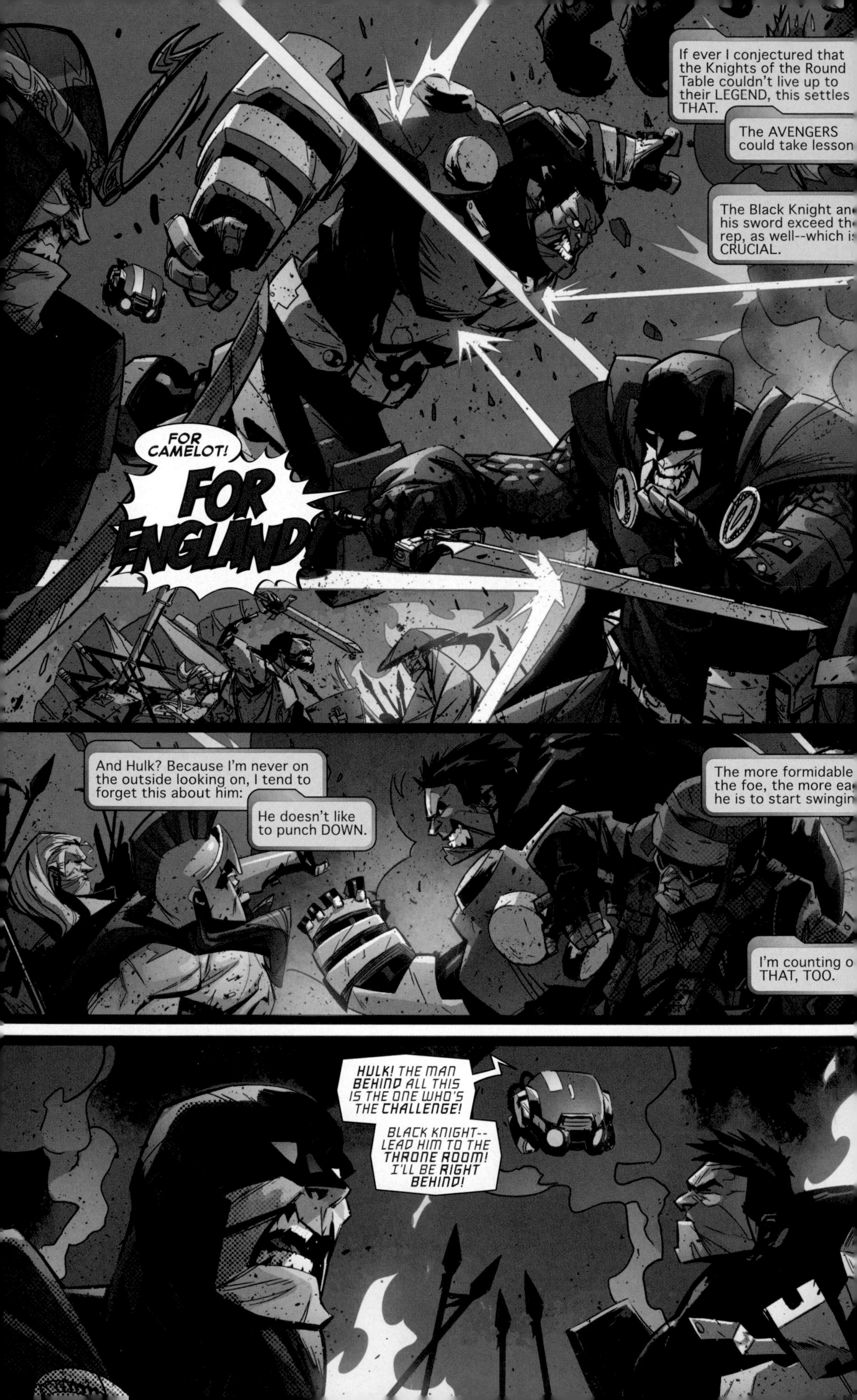

If ever I conjectured that the Knights of the Round Table couldn't live up to their LEGEND, this settles THAT.
The AVENGERS could take lesson
The Black Knight an his sword exceed th rep, as well--which i CRUCIAL.
FOR CAMELOT!
FOR ENGLAND!
And Hulk? Because I'm never on the outside looking on, I tend to forget this about him:
He doesn't like to punch DOWN.
The more formidable the foe, the more ea he is to start swingin
I'm counting o THAT, TOO.
HULK! THE MAN BEHIND ALL THIS IS THE ONE WHO'S THE CHALLENGE!
BLACK KNIGHT-- LEAD HIM TO THE THRONE ROOM! I'LL BE RIGHT BEHIND!

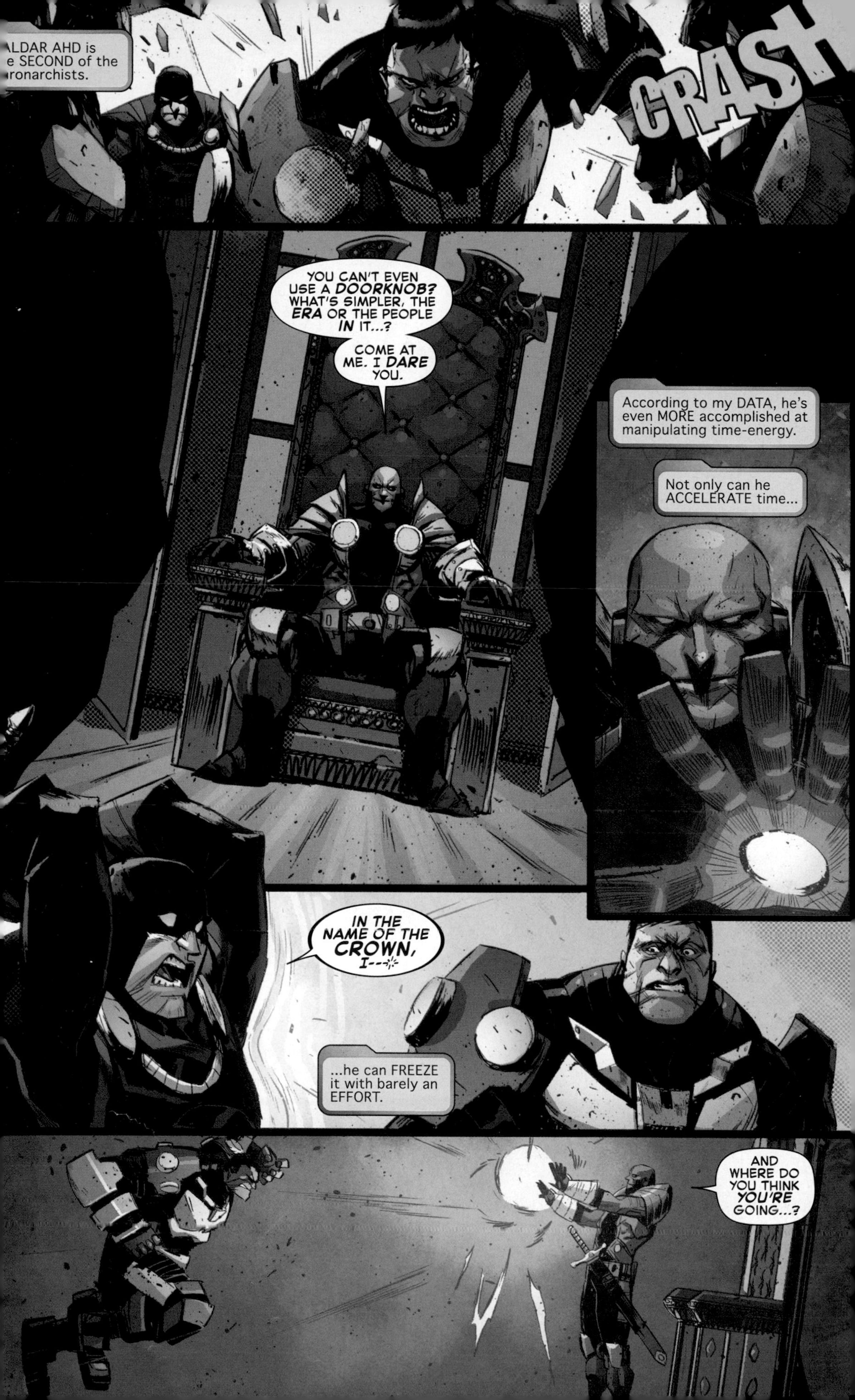
ALDAR AHD is
e SECOND of the
ronarchists.
CRASH
YOU CAN'T EVEN USE A DOORKNOB? WHAT'S SIMPLER, THE ERA OR THE PEOPLE IN IT...?
COME AT ME. I DARE YOU.
According to my DATA, he's even MORE accomplished at manipulating time-energy.
Not only can he ACCELERATE time...
IN THE NAME OF THE CROWN, I--
...he can FREEZE it with barely an EFFORT.
AND WHERE DO YOU THINK YOU'RE GOING...?

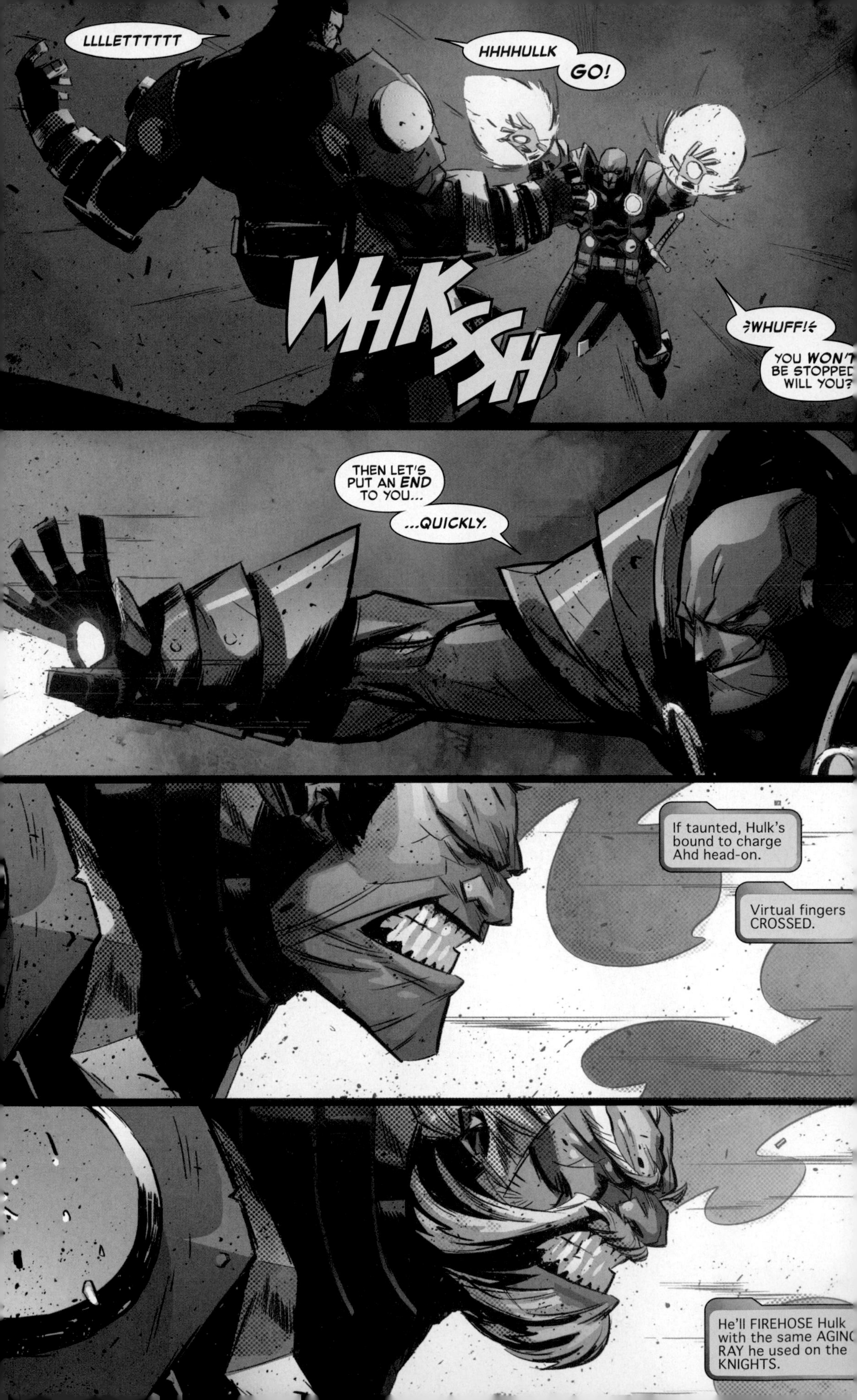

LLLLETTTTTT
HHHHULLK GO!
WHKSH
WHUFF!
YOU WON'T BE STOPPED WILL YOU?
THEN LET'S PUT AN END TO YOU...
...QUICKLY.
If taunted, Hulk's bound to charge Ahd head-on.
Virtual fingers CROSSED.
He'll FIREHOSE Hulk with the same AGING RAY he used on the KNIGHTS.

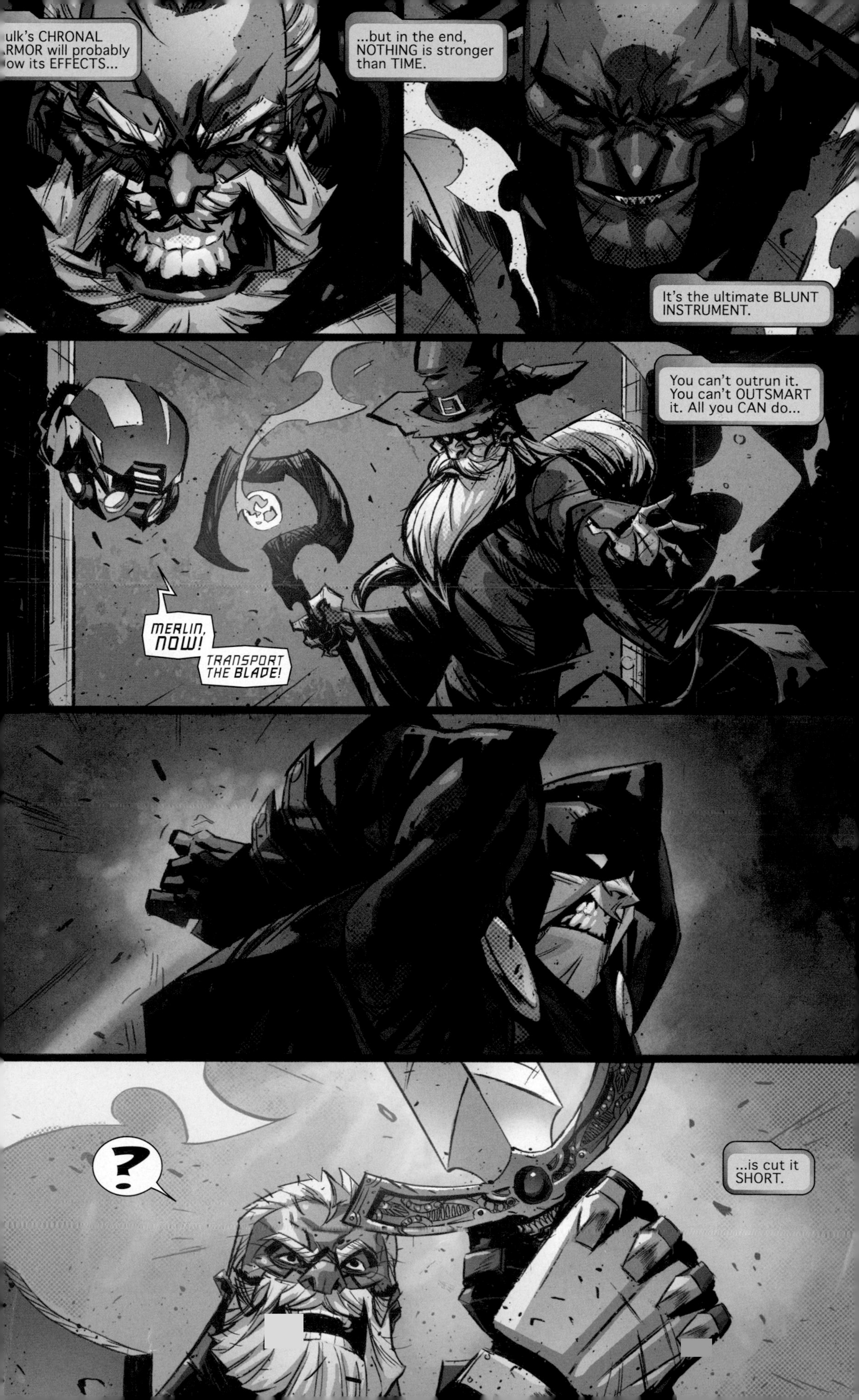
ulk's CHRONAL
RMOR will probably
ow its EFFECTS...
...but in the end, NOTHING is stronger than TIME.
It's the ultimate BLUNT INSTRUMENT.
You can't outrun it. You can't OUTSMART it. All you CAN do...
MERLIN, NOW!
TRANSPORT THE BLADE!
?
...is cut it SHORT.

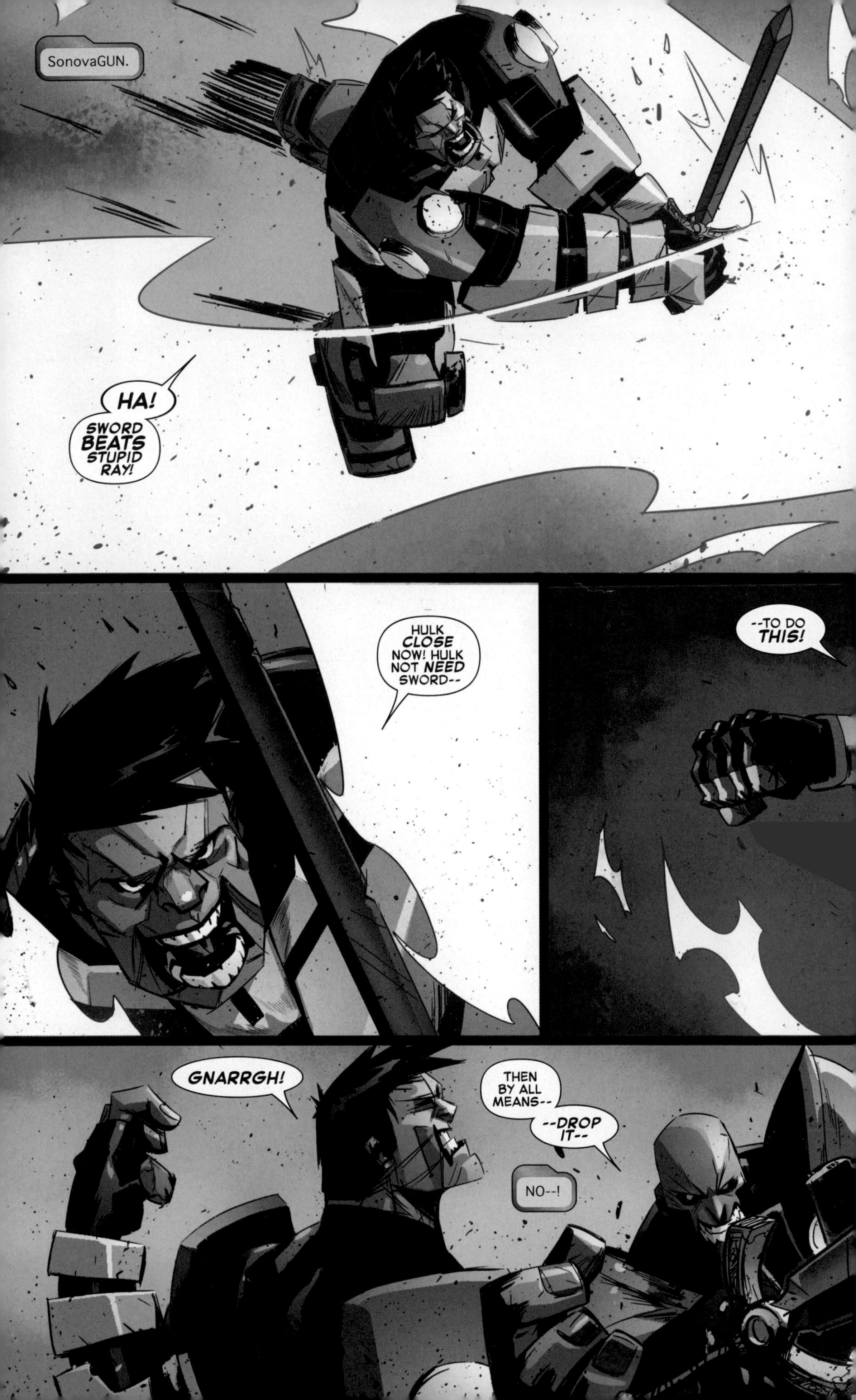

SonovaGUN.
HA! SWORD BEATS STUPID RAY!
HULK CLOSE NOW! HULK NOT NEED SWORD--
--TO DO THIS!
GNARRGH!
THEN BY ALL MEANS--
--DROP IT--
NO--!

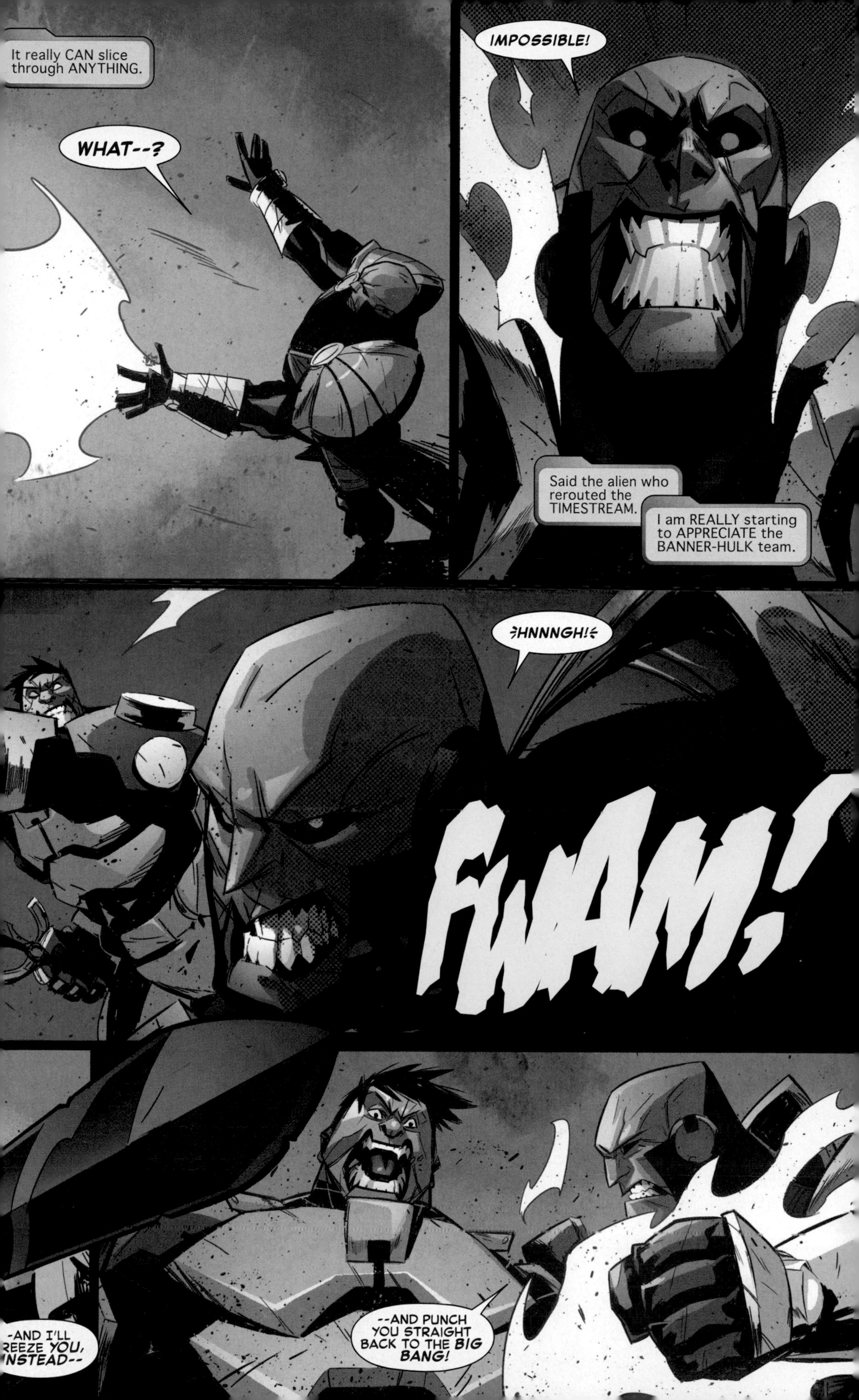
It really CAN slice through ANYTHING.
WHAT--?
IMPOSSIBLE!
Said the alien who rerouted the TIMESTREAM.
I am REALLY starting to APPRECIATE the BANNER-HULK team.
HNNNGH!
FWAM!
-AND I'LL REEZE YOU, NSTEAD--
--AND PUNCH YOU STRAIGHT BACK TO THE BIG BANG!

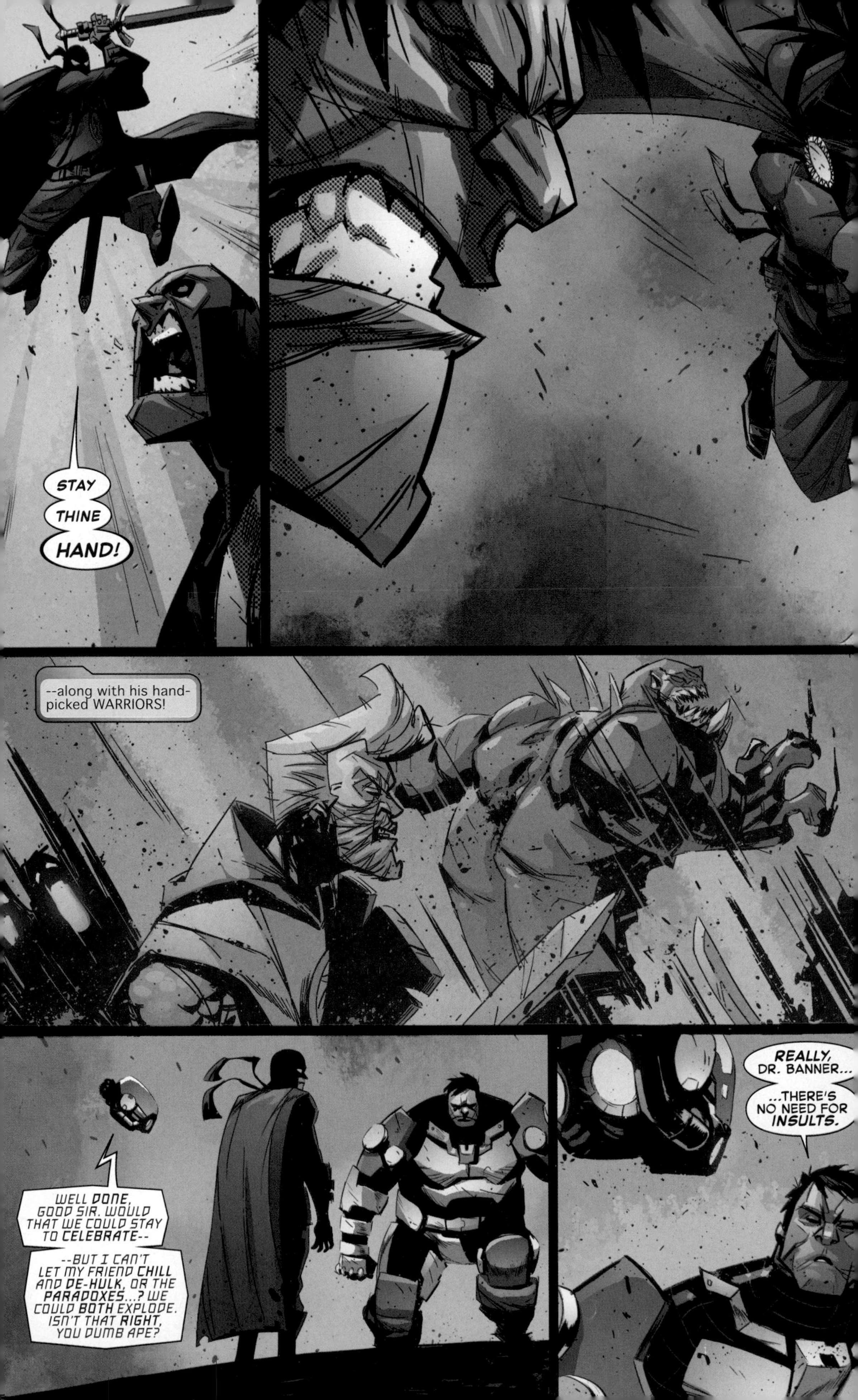
STAY THINE HAND!
--along with his hand-picked WARRIORS!
WELL DONE, GOOD SIR. WOULD THAT WE COULD STAY TO CELEBRATE--
--BUT I CAN'T LET MY FRIEND CHILL AND DE-HULK, OR THE PARADOXES...? WE COULD BOTH EXPLODE. ISN'T THAT RIGHT, YOU DUMB APE?
REALLY, DR. BANNER...
...THERE'S NO NEED FOR INSULTS.

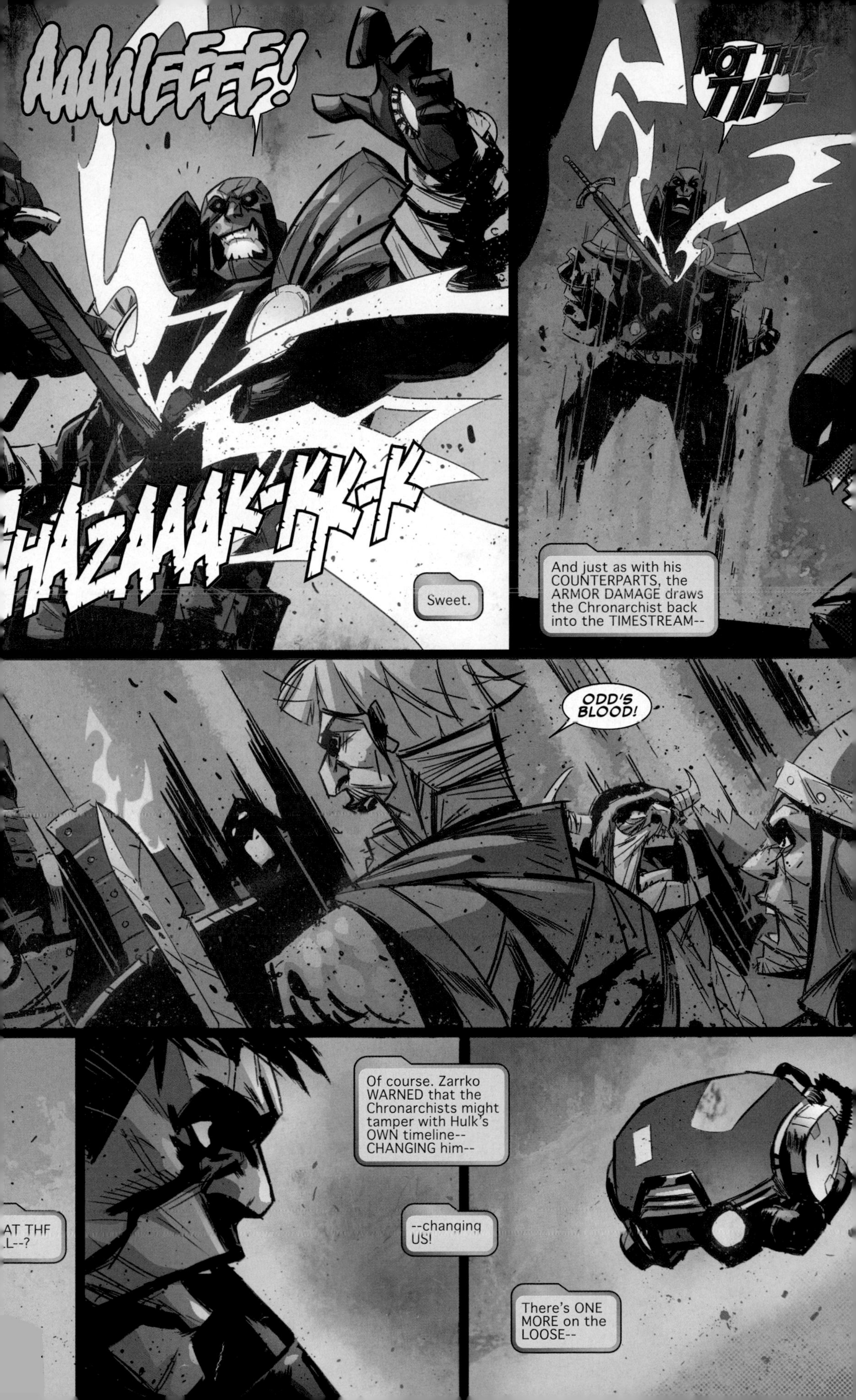
AAAAIEEEE!
CHAZAAAK-KK-K
Sweet.
NOT THIS TII--
And just as with his COUNTERPARTS, the ARMOR DAMAGE draws the Chronarchist back into the TIMESTREAM--
ODD'S BLOOD!
AT THE
L--?
Of course. Zarrko WARNED that the Chronarchists might tamper with Hulk's OWN timeline-- CHANGING him--
--changing US!
There's ONE MORE on the LOOSE--

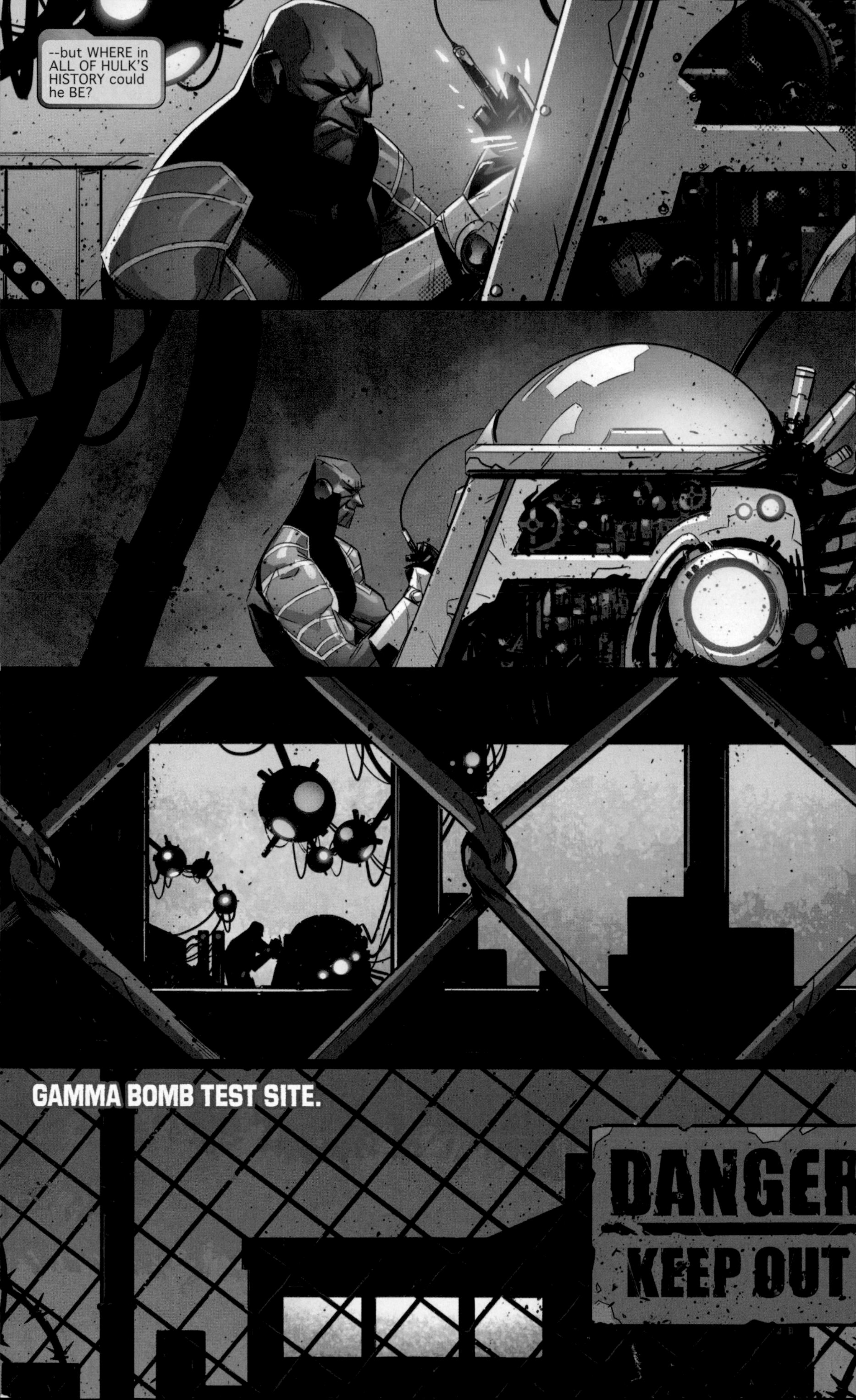
--but WHERE in ALL OF HULK'S HISTORY could he BE?
GAMMA BOMB TEST SITE.
DANGER
KEEP OUT

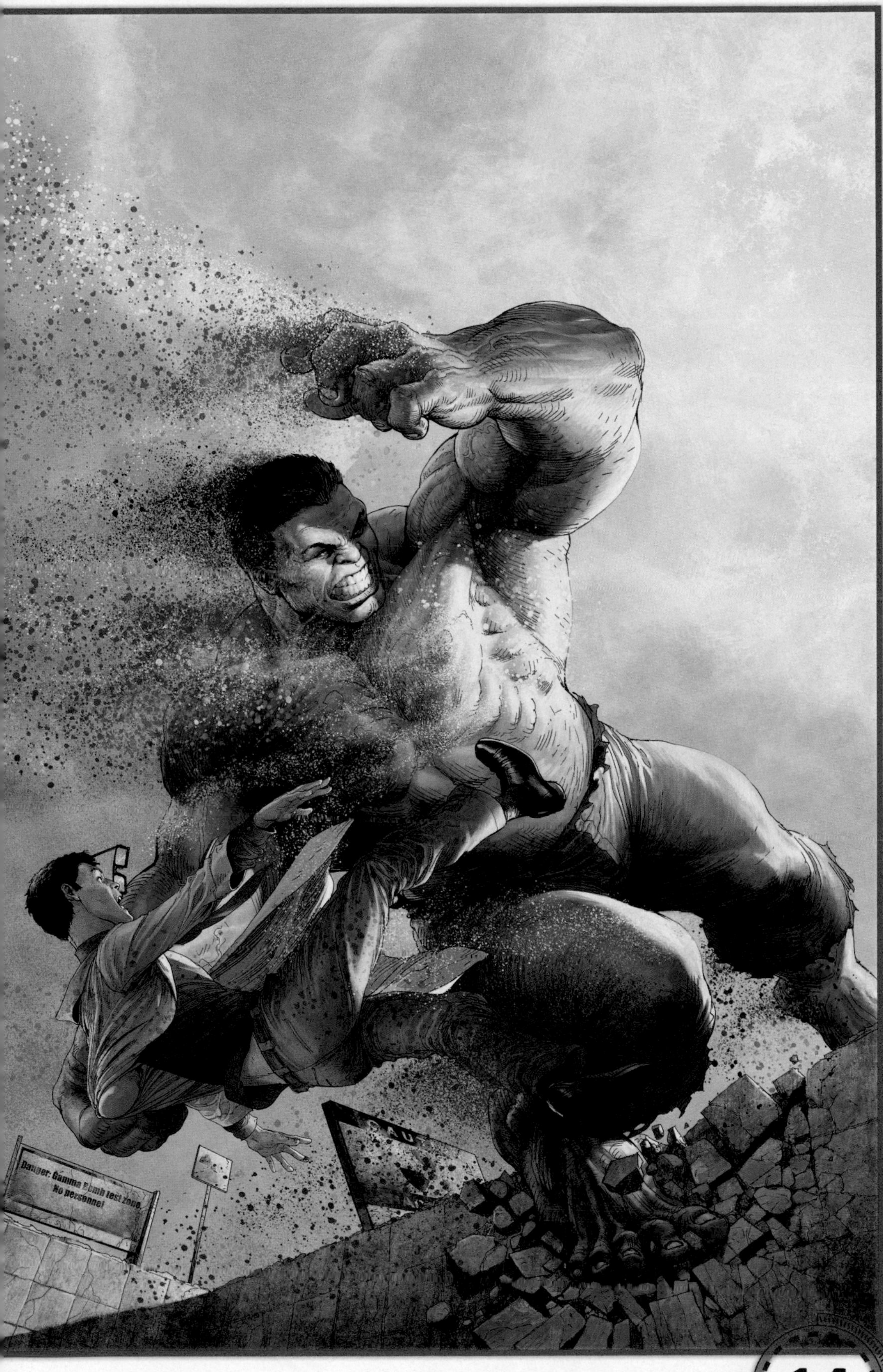
Danger: Gamma Bomb test zone.
No personnel

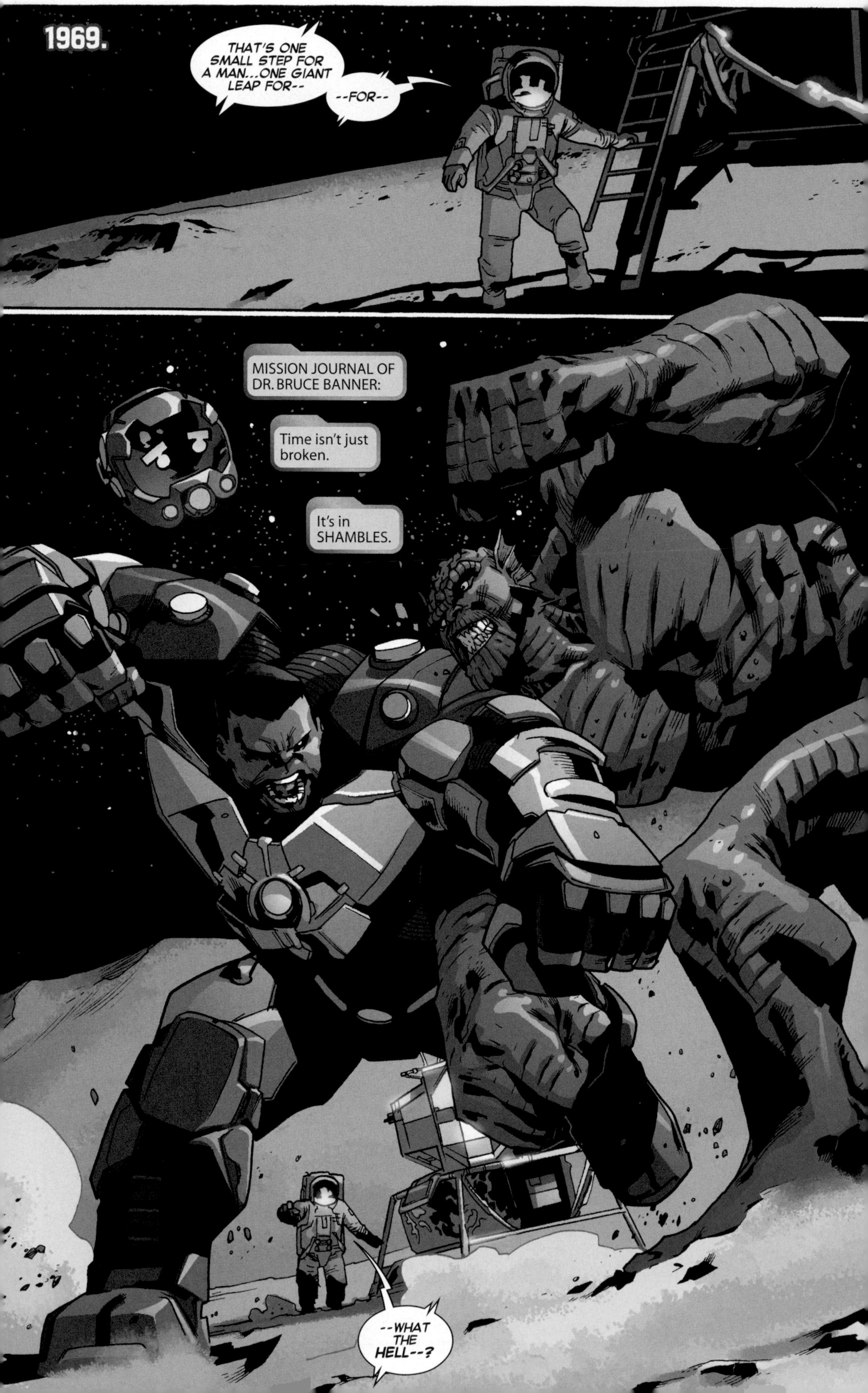
1969.
THAT'S ONE SMALL STEP FOR A MAN...ONE GIANT LEAP FOR--
--FOR--
MISSION JOURNAL OF DR. BRUCE BANNER:
Time isn't just broken.
It's in SHAMBLES.
--WHAT THE HELL--?

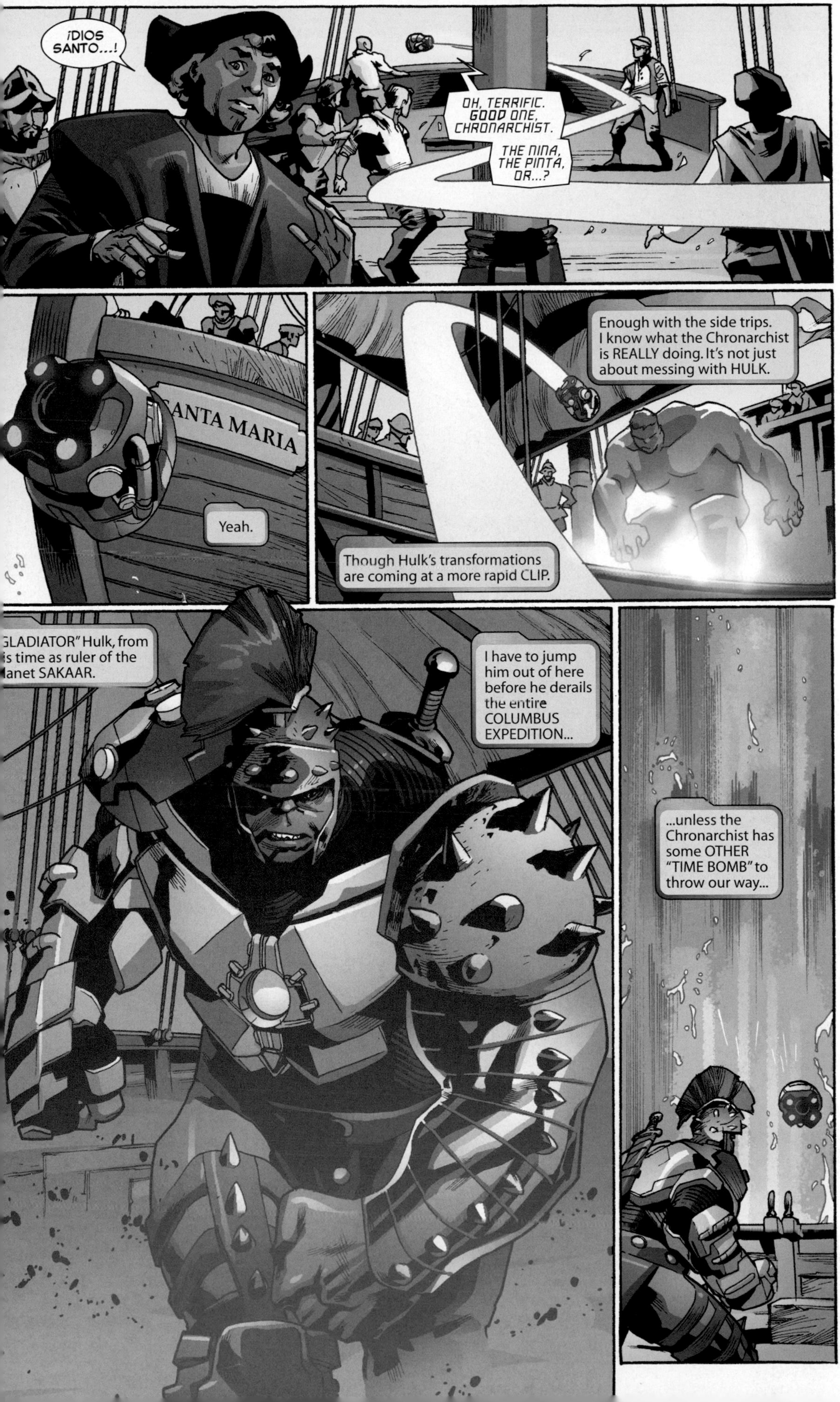

¡DIOS SANTO...!
OH, TERRIFIC. GOOD ONE, CHRONARCHIST.
THE NINA, THE PINTA, OR...?
ANTA MARIA
Yeah.
Enough with the side trips. I know what the Chronarchist is REALLY doing. It's not just about messing with HULK.
Though Hulk's transformations are coming at a more rapid CLIP.
GLADIATOR" Hulk, from is time as ruler of the lanet SAKAAR.
I have to jump him out of here before he derails the entire COLUMBUS EXPEDITION...
...unless the Chronarchist has some OTHER "TIME BOMB" to throw our way...

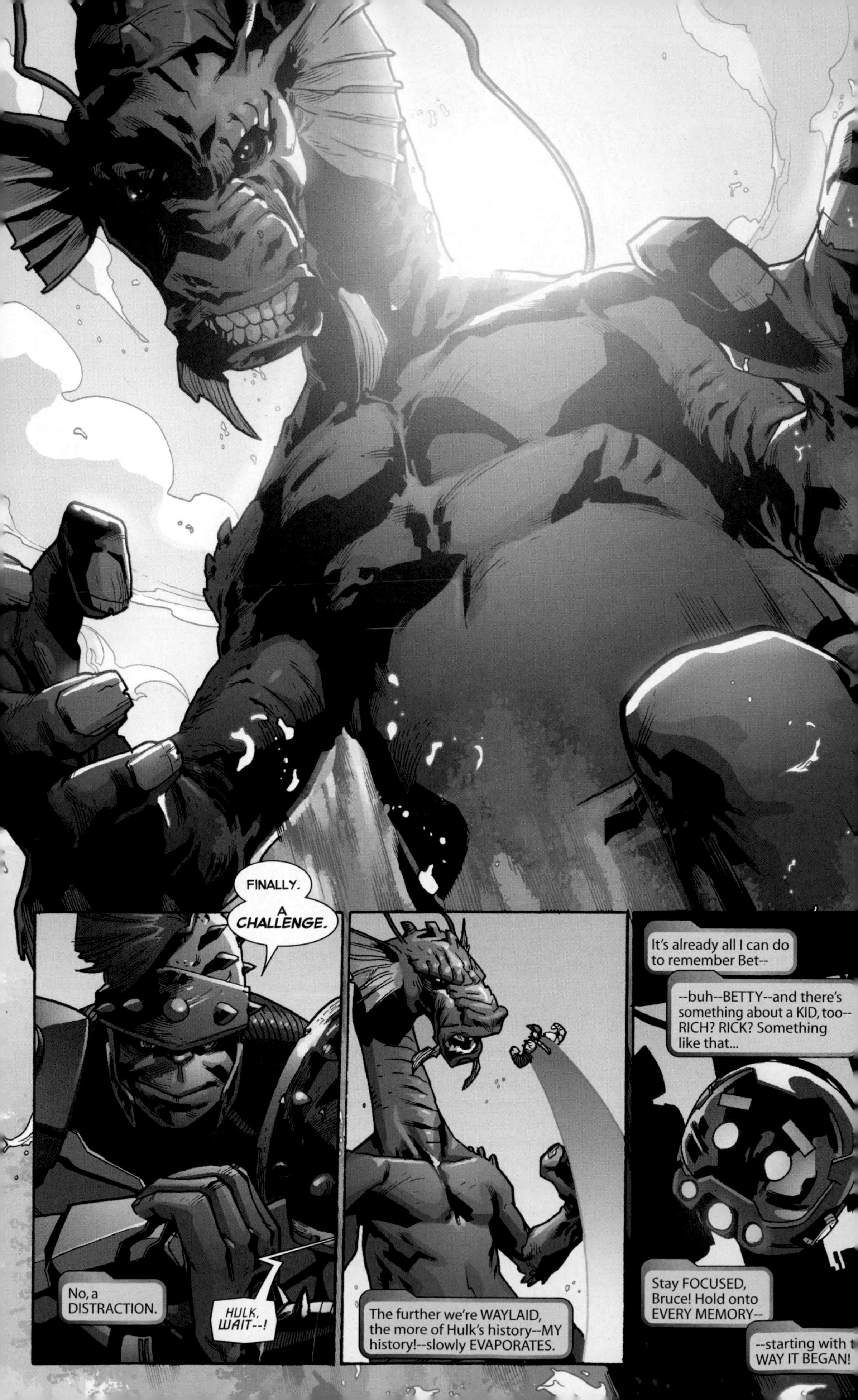
FINALLY.
A CHALLENGE.
No, a DISTRACTION.
HULK, WAIT--!
The further we're WAYLAID, the more of Hulk's history--MY history!--slowly EVAPORATES.
It's already all I can do to remember Bet--
--buh--BETTY--and there's something about a KID, too--RICH? RICK? Something like that...
Stay FOCUSED, Bruce! Hold onto EVERY MEMORY--
--starting with t
WAY IT BEGAN!

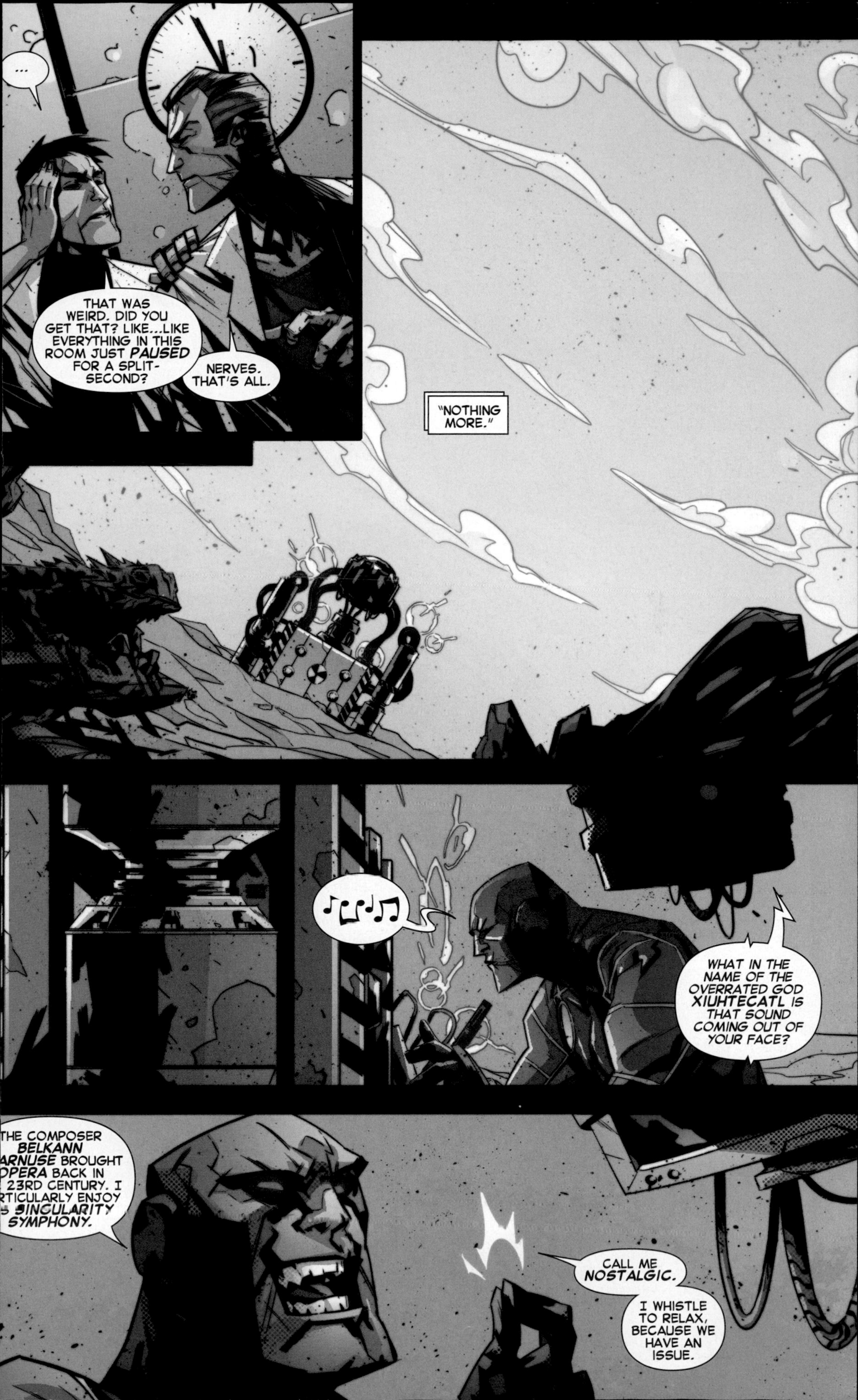
...
THAT WAS WEIRD. DID YOU GET THAT? LIKE...LIKE EVERYTHING IN THIS ROOM JUST PAUSED FOR A SPLIT-SECOND?
NERVES. THAT'S ALL.
"NOTHING MORE."
WHAT IN THE NAME OF THE OVERRATED GOD XIUHTECATL IS THAT SOUND COMING OUT OF YOUR FACE?
THE COMPOSER BELKANN
ARNUSE BROUGHT
OPERA BACK IN
23RD CENTURY. I
RTICULARLY ENJOY
SINGULARITY SYMPHONY.
CALL ME NOSTALGIC.
I WHISTLE TO RELAX, BECAUSE WE HAVE AN ISSUE.

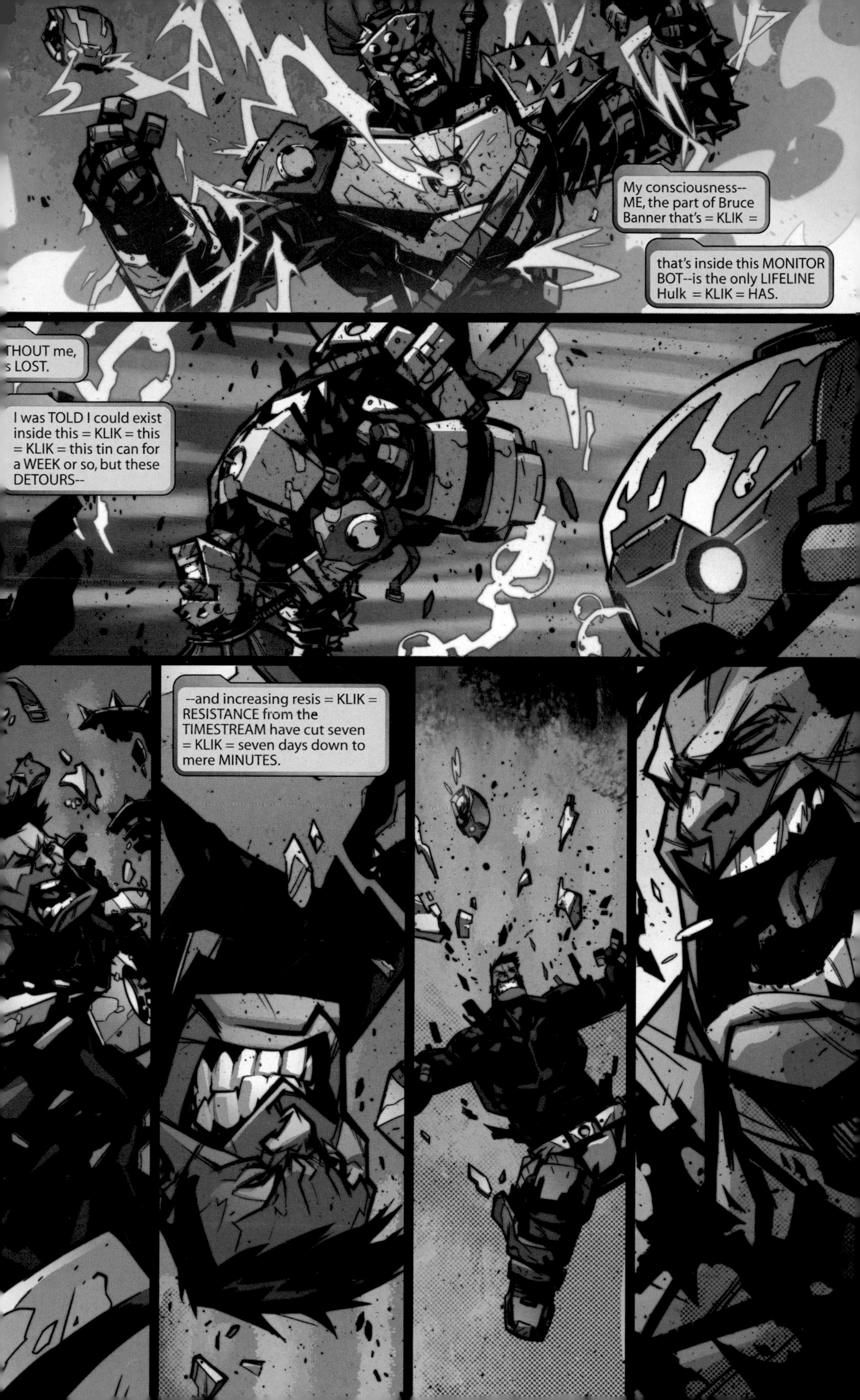
My consciousness-- ME, the part of Bruce Banner that's = KLIK =
that's inside this MONITOR BOT--is the only LIFELINE Hulk = KLIK = HAS.
THOUT me, s LOST.
I was TOLD I could exist inside this = KLIK = this = KLIK = this tin can for a WEEK or so, but these DETOURS--
--and increasing resis = KLIK = RESISTANCE from the TIMESTREAM have cut seven = KLIK = seven days down to mere MINUTES.

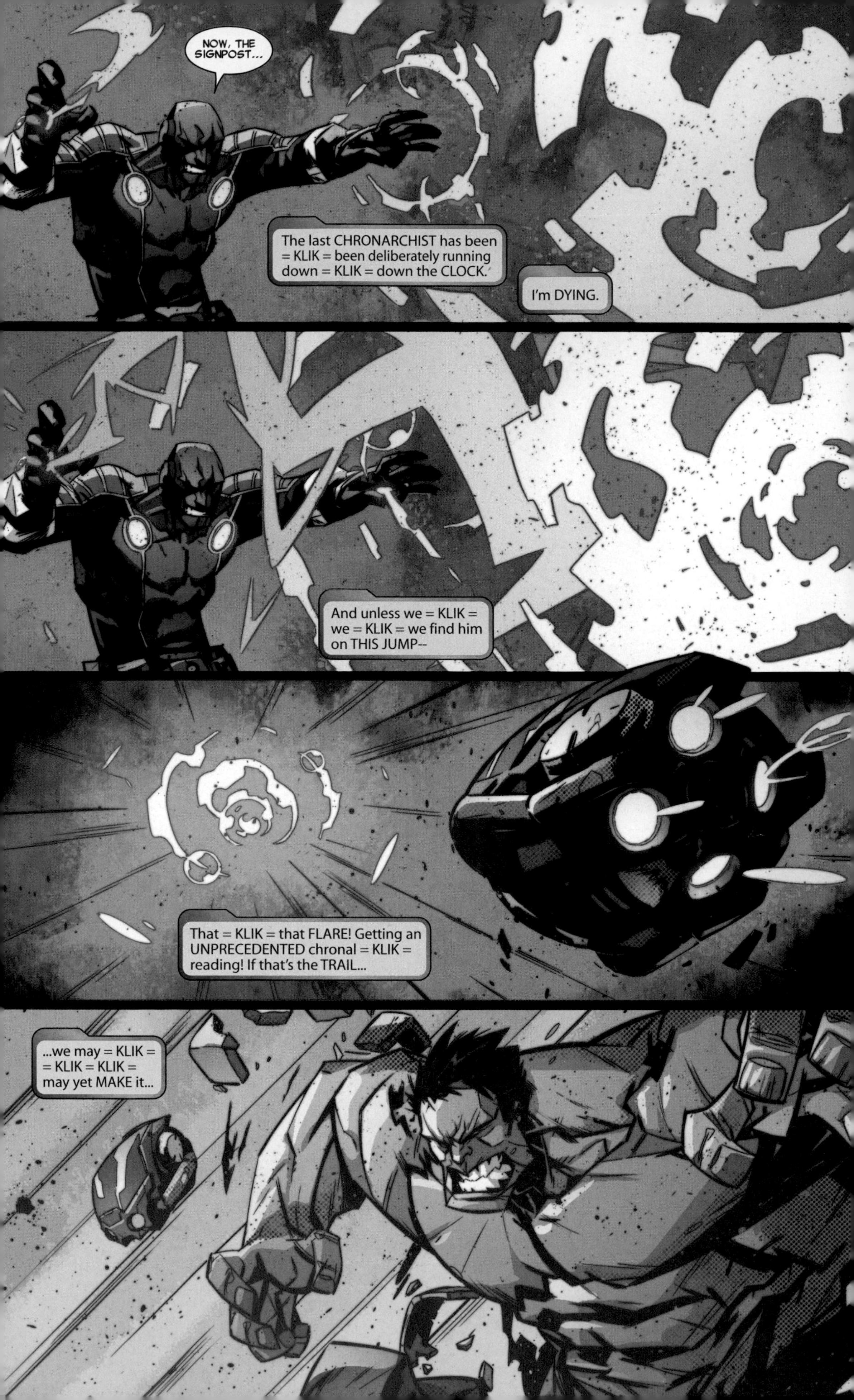
NOW, THE SIGNPOST...
The last CHRONARCHIST has been = KLIK = been deliberately running down = KLIK = down the CLOCK.
I'm DYING.
And unless we = KLIK = we = KLIK = we find him on THIS JUMP--
That = KLIK = that FLARE! Getting an UNPRECEDENTED chronal = KLIK = reading! If that's the TRAIL...
...we may = KLIK = = KLIK = KLIK = may yet MAKE it...

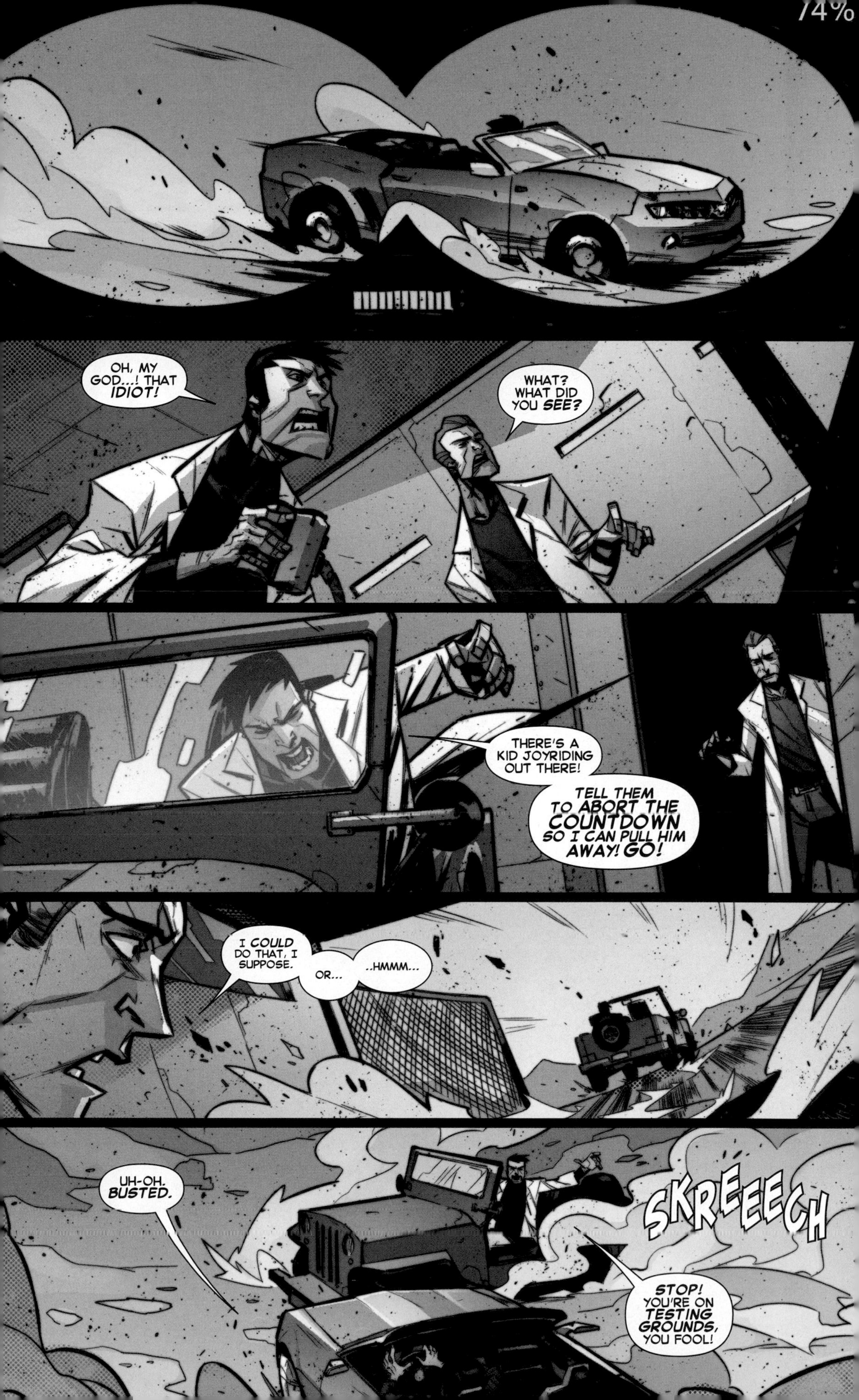

OH, MY GOD...! THAT IDIOT!
WHAT? WHAT DID YOU SEE?
THERE'S A KID JOYRIDING OUT THERE!
TELL THEM TO ABORT THE COUNTDOWN SO I CAN PULL HIM AWAY! GO!
I COULD DO THAT, I SUPPOSE.
OR...
..HMMM...
UH-OH. BUSTED.
SKREEEECH
STOP! YOU'RE ON TESTING GROUNDS, YOU FOOL!

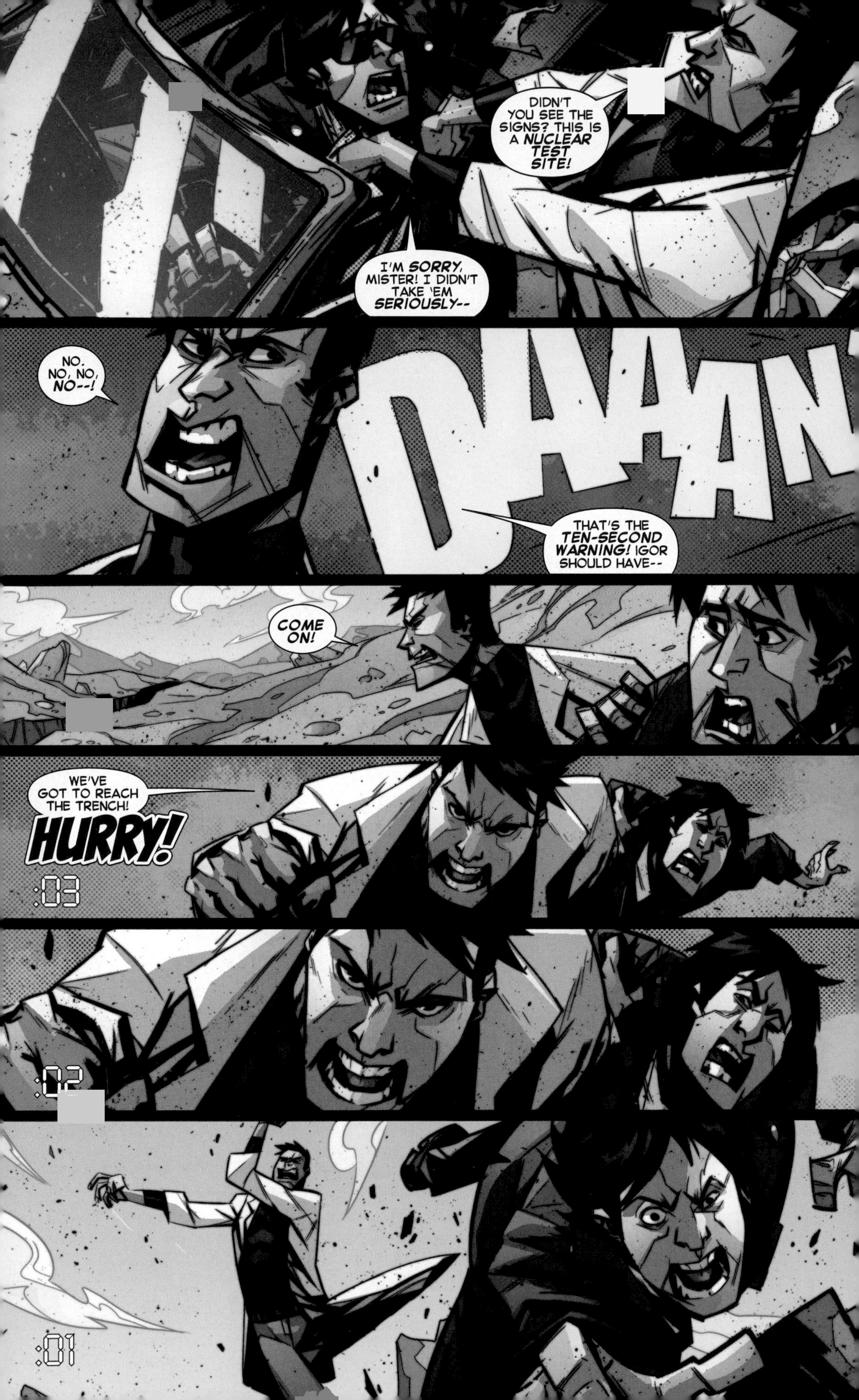
DIDN'T YOU SEE THE SIGNS? THIS IS A NUCLEAR TEST SITE!
I'M SORRY, MISTER! I DIDN'T TAKE 'EM SERIOUSLY--
NO. NO, NO, NO--!
DAAAN
THAT'S THE TEN-SECOND WARNING! IGOR SHOULD HAVE--
COME ON!
WE'VE GOT TO REACH THE TRENCH!
HURRY!
:03
:02
:01

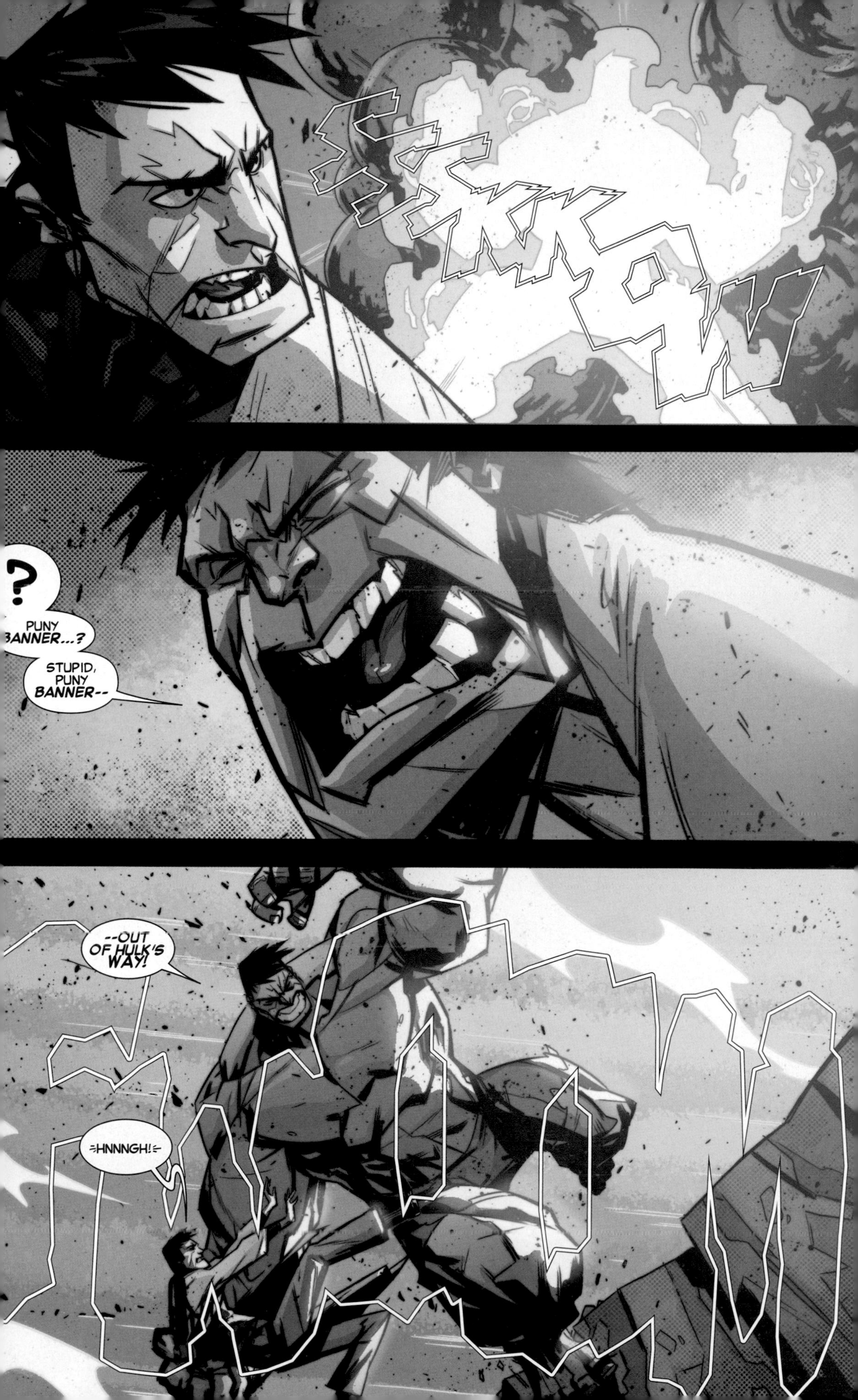
?
PUNY BANNER...?
STUPID, PUNY BANNER--
--OUT OF HULK'S WAY!
HNNNGH!

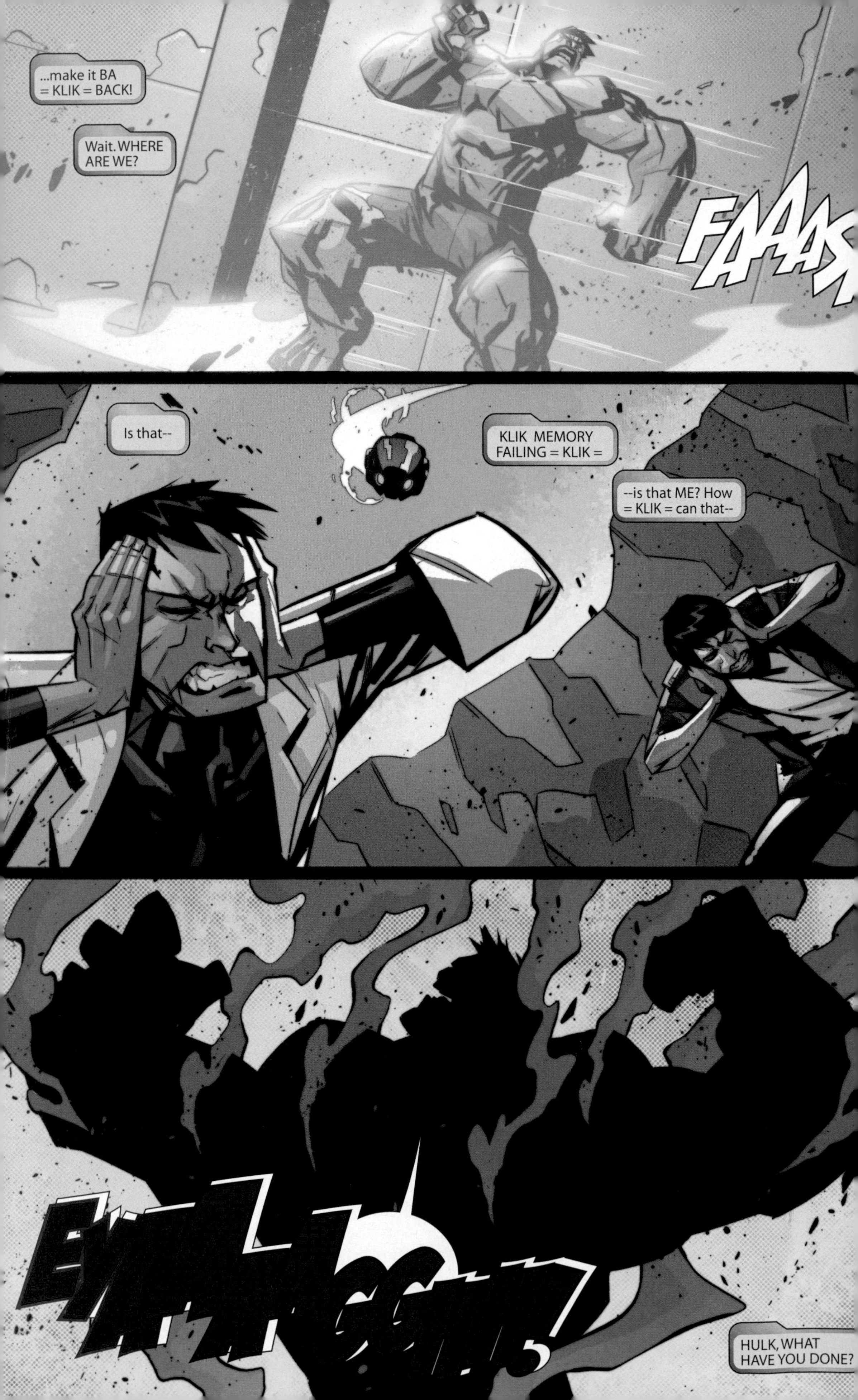

...make it BA = KLIK = BACK!
Wait. WHERE ARE WE?
FAAAS
Is that--
KLIK MEMORY FAILING = KLIK =
--is that ME? How = KLIK = can that--
HULK, WHAT HAVE YOU DONE?

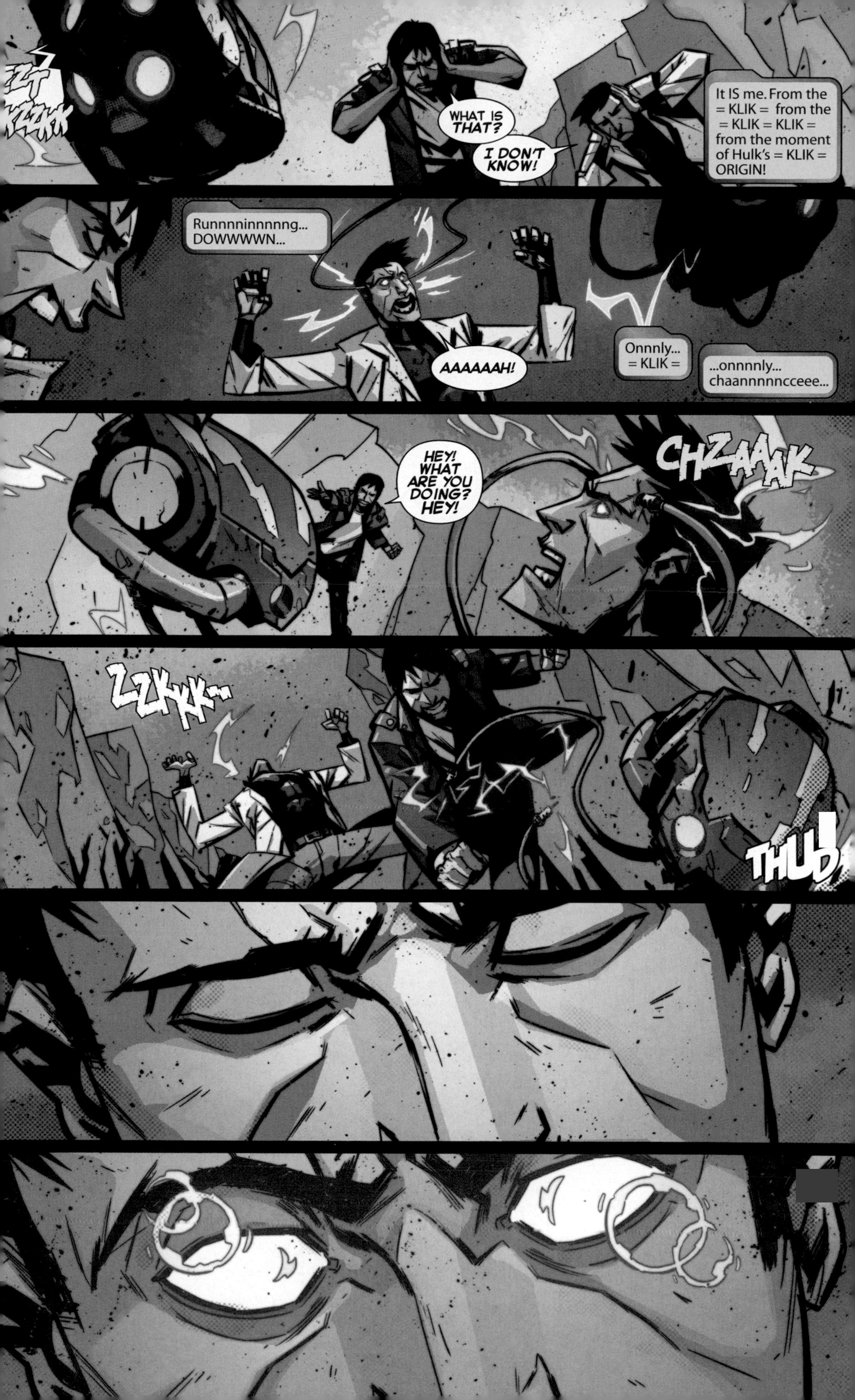
WHAT IS THAT?
I DON'T KNOW!
It IS me. From the = KLIK = from the = KLIK = KLIK = from the moment of Hulk's = KLIK = ORIGIN!
Runnnninnnnng... DOWWWWN...
AAAAAAH!
Onnnly... = KLIK =
...onnnnly... chaannnnnncceee...
HEY! WHAT ARE YOU DOING? HEY!
CHZAAAK
ZZKKK
THUD!

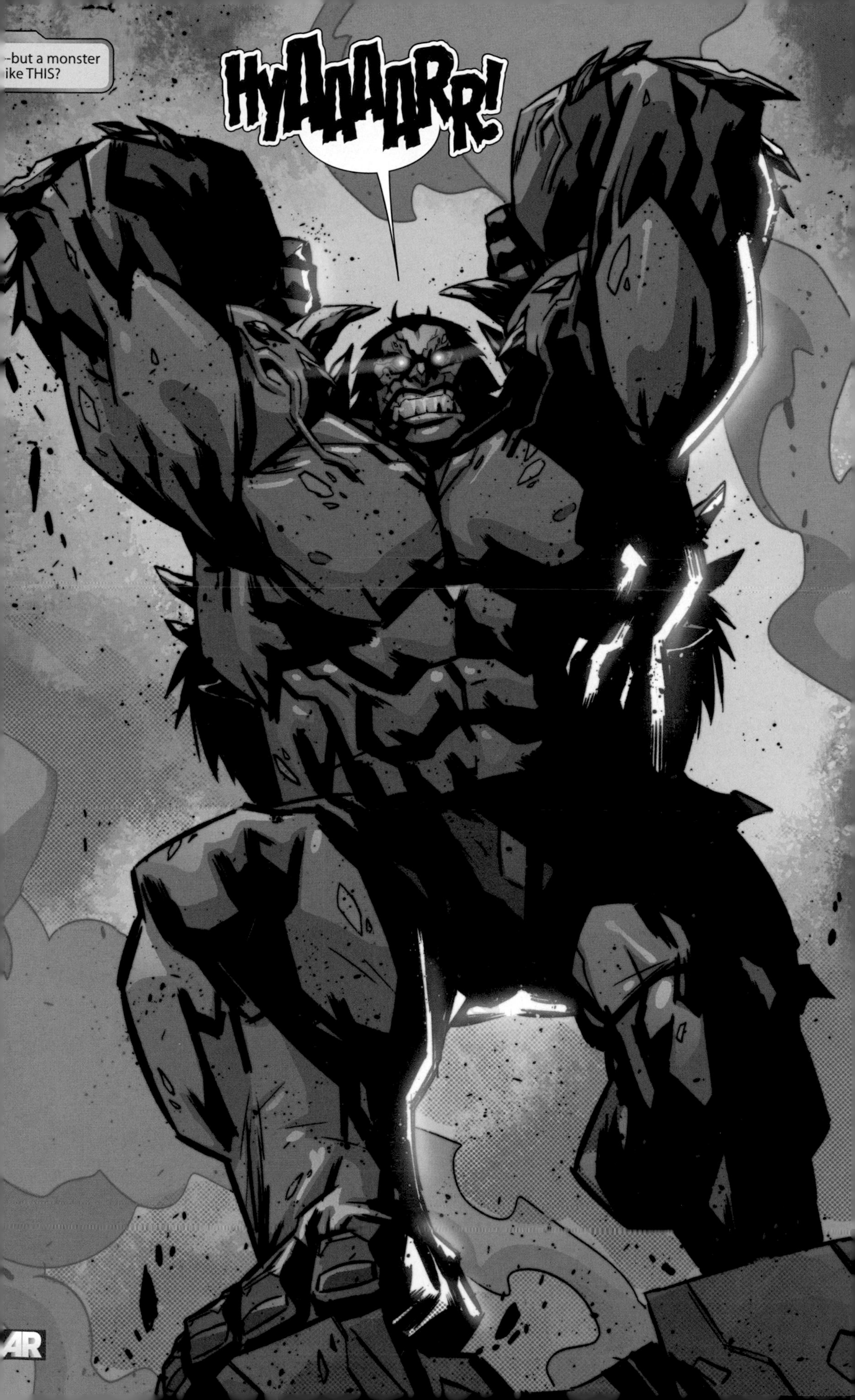
-but a monster
ike THIS?
HYAAAARR!

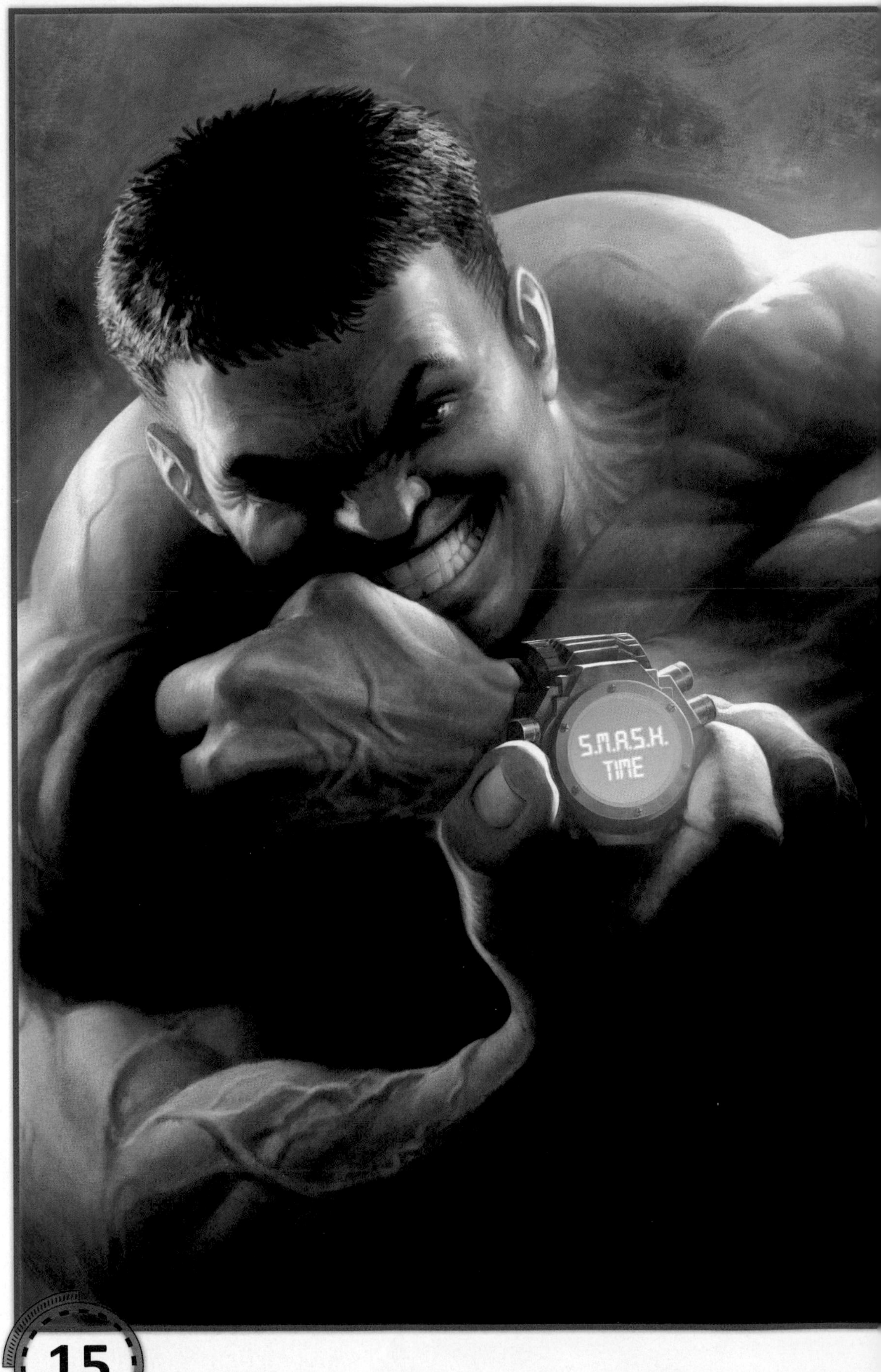
S.M.A.S.H.
TIME

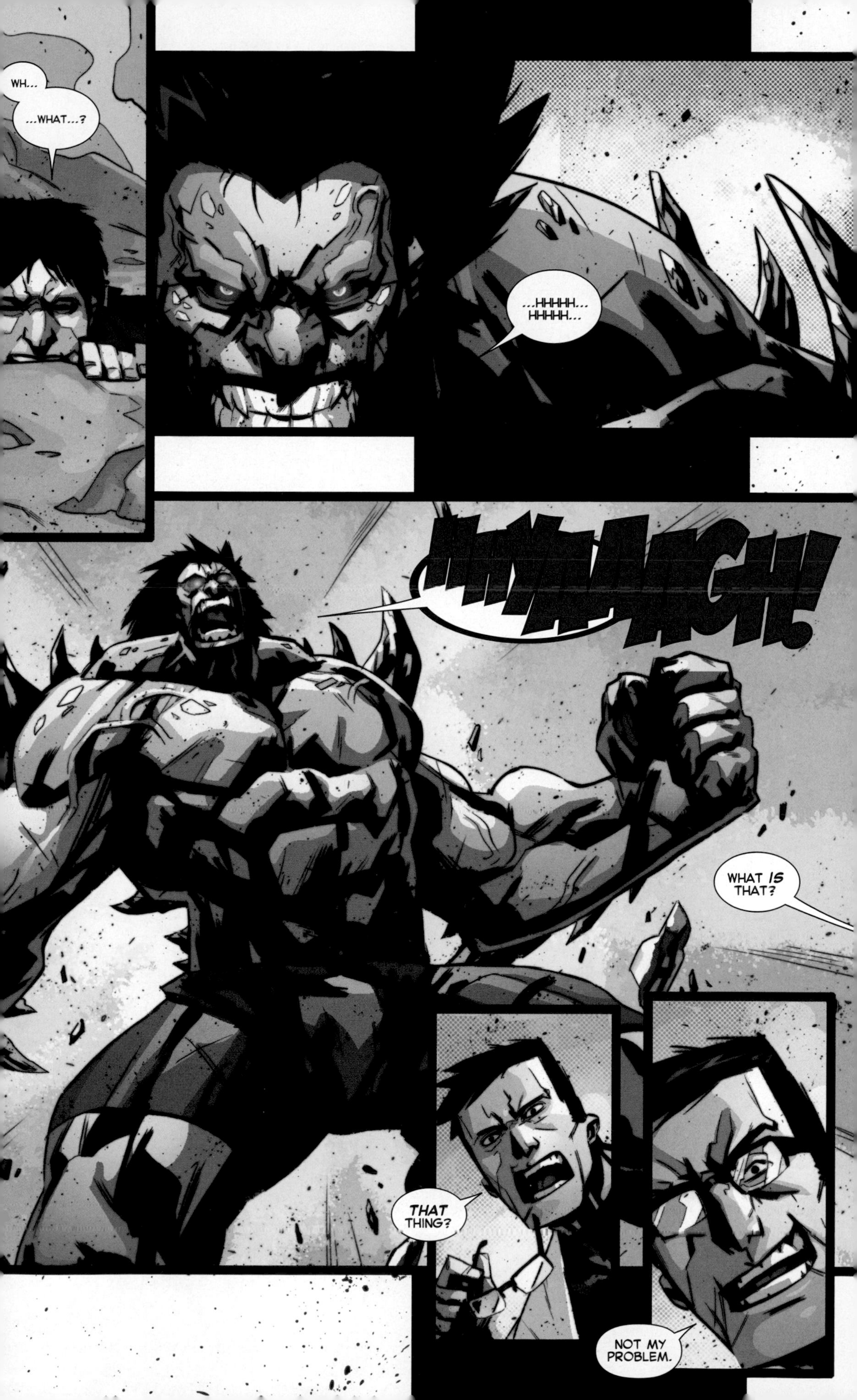
WH...
...WHAT...?
...HHHHH...
HHHHH...
WHAT IS THAT?
THAT THING?
NOT MY PROBLEM.

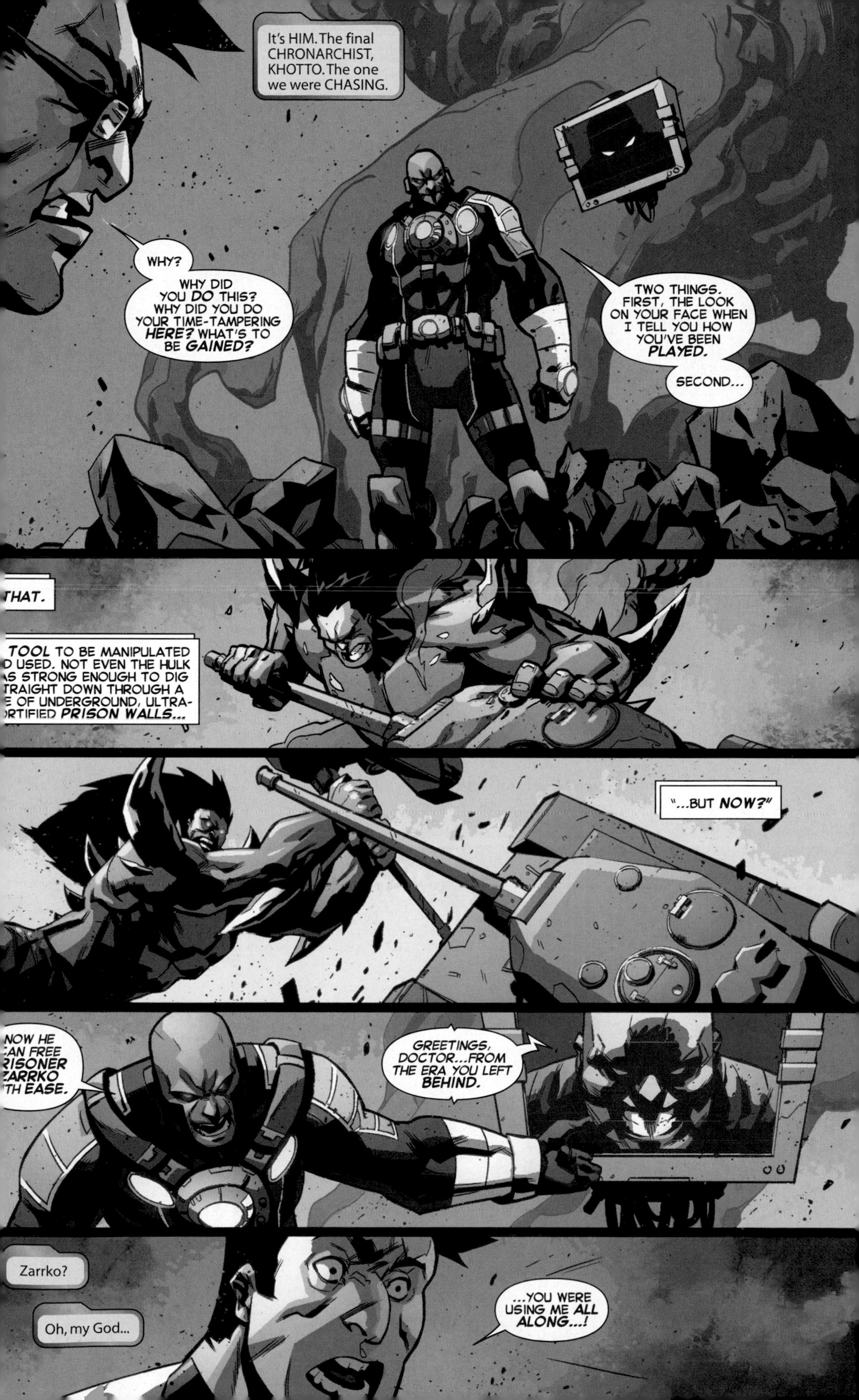
It's HIM. The final CHRONARCHIST, KHOTTO. The one we were CHASING.
WHY?
WHY DID YOU DO THIS? WHY DID YOU DO YOUR TIME-TAMPERING HERE? WHAT'S TO BE GAINED?
TWO THINGS. FIRST, THE LOOK ON YOUR FACE WHEN I TELL YOU HOW YOU'VE BEEN PLAYED.
SECOND...
THAT.
TOOL TO BE MANIPULATED
D USED. NOT EVEN THE HULK
AS STRONG ENOUGH TO DIG
TRAIGHT DOWN THROUGH A
E OF UNDERGROUND, ULTRA-
ORTIFIED PRISON WALLS...
"...BUT NOW?"
NOW HE
AN FREE
RISONER
ZARRKO
TH EASE.
GREETINGS, DOCTOR...FROM THE ERA YOU LEFT BEHIND.
Zarrko?
Oh, my God...
...YOU WERE USING ME ALL ALONG...!

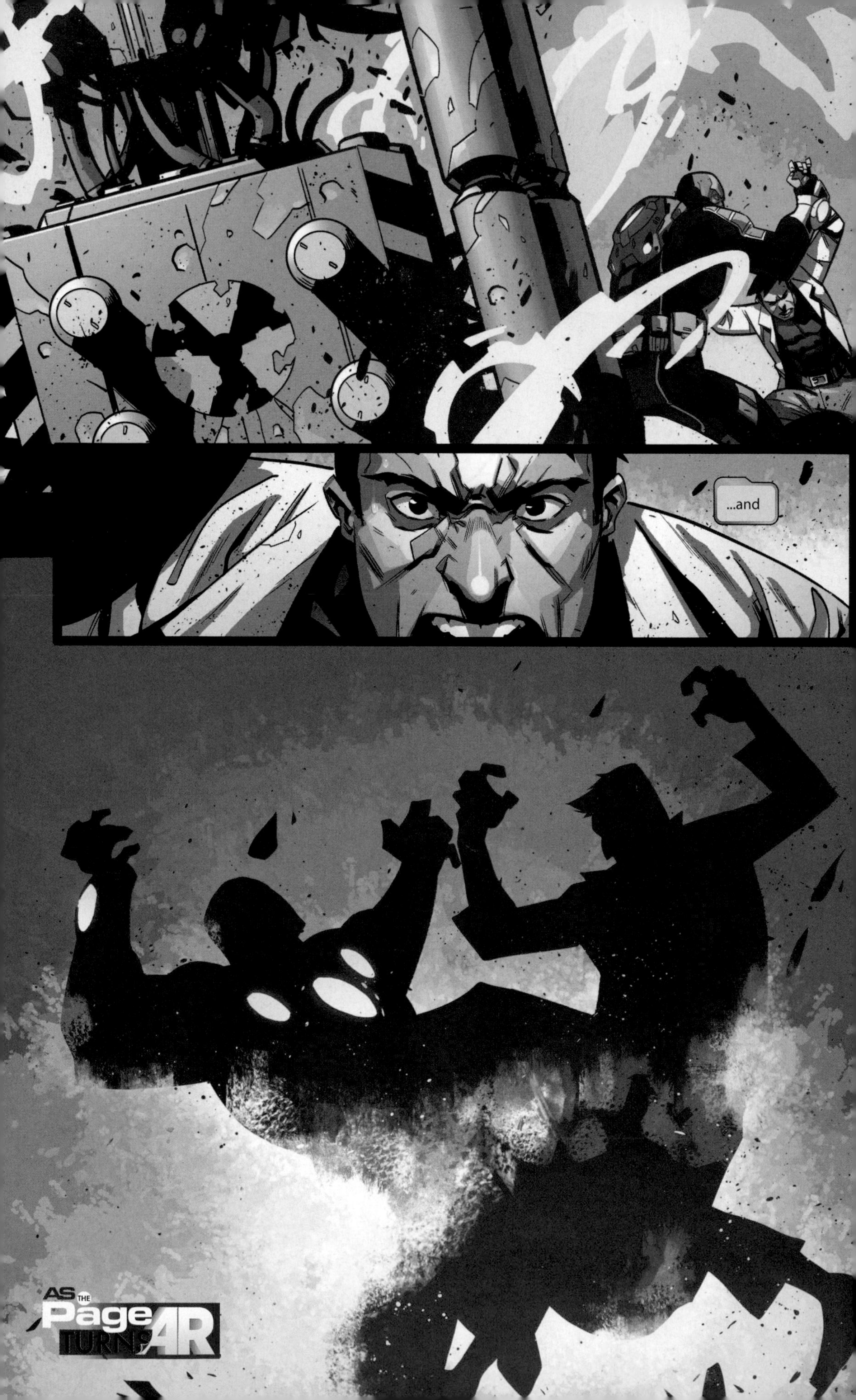
...and

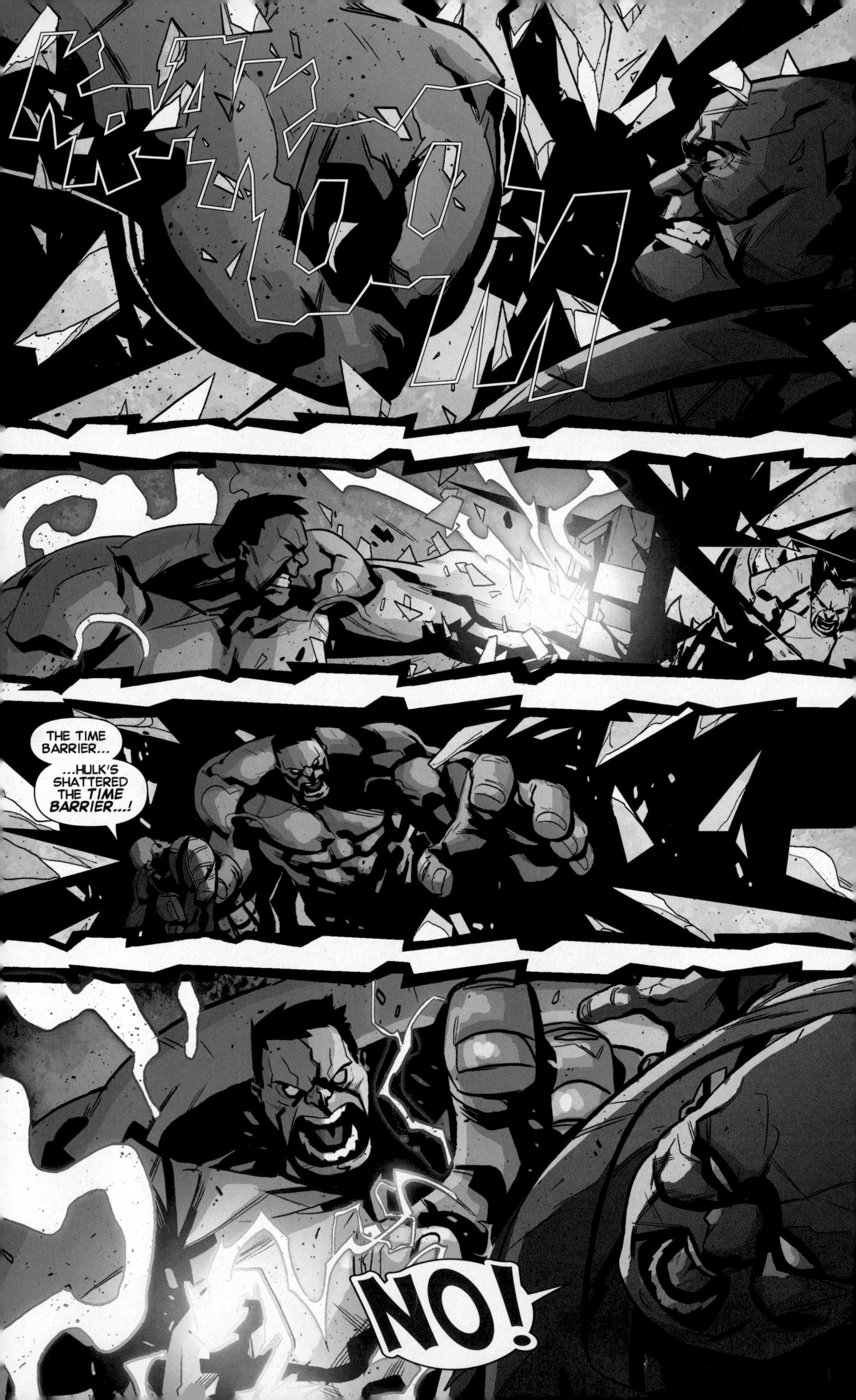
THE TIME BARRIER...
...HULK'S SHATTERED THE *TIME BARRIER*...!
NO!

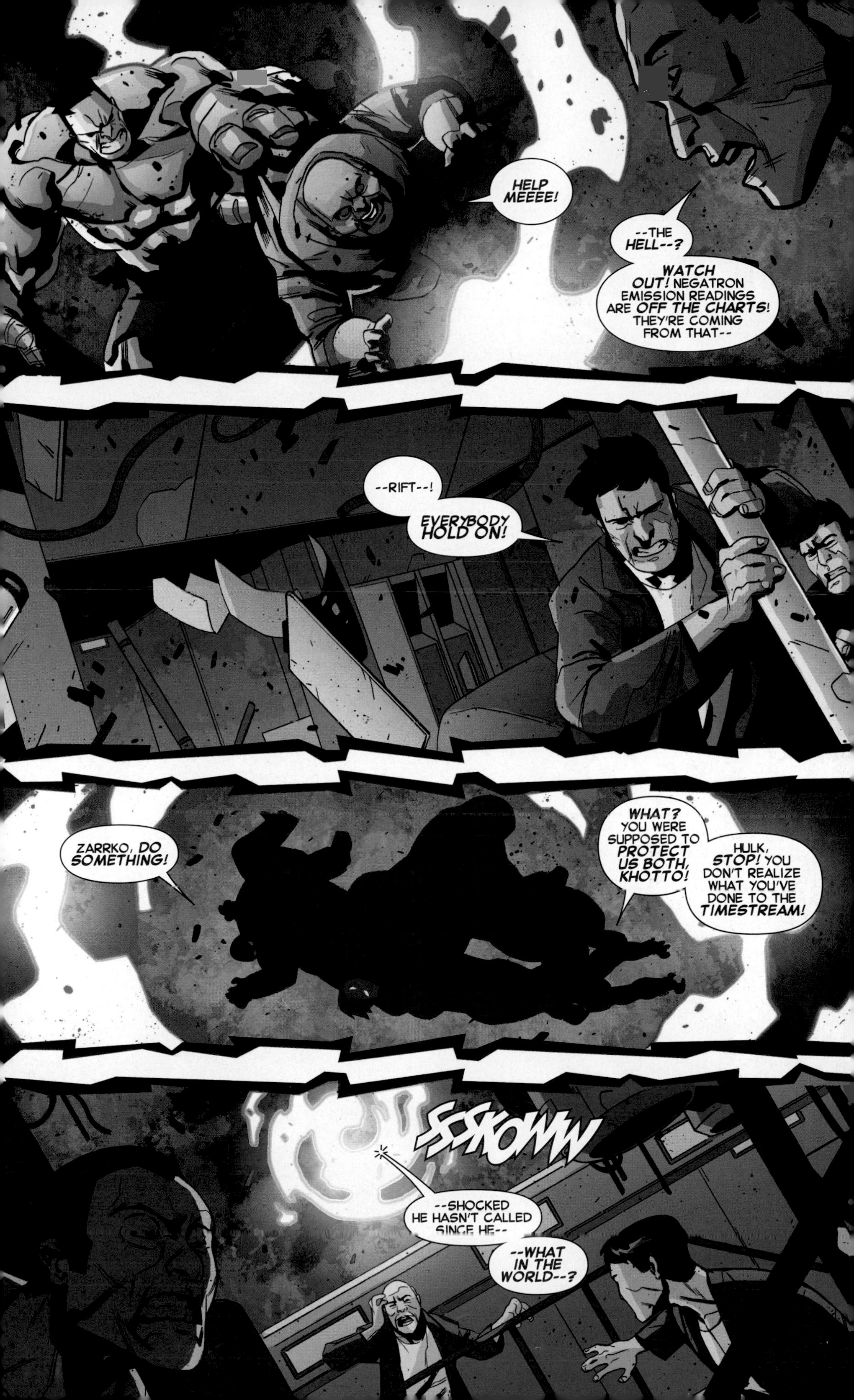
HELP MEEEE!
--THE HELL--?
WATCH OUT! NEGATRON EMISSION READINGS ARE OFF THE CHARTS! THEY'RE COMING FROM THAT--
--RIFT--!
EVERYBODY HOLD ON!
ZARRKO, DO SOMETHING!
WHAT? YOU WERE SUPPOSED TO PROTECT US BOTH, KHOTTO!
HULK, STOP! YOU DON'T REALIZE WHAT YOU'VE DONE TO THE TIMESTREAM!
SSKOWW
--SHOCKED HE HASN'T CALLED SINCE HE--
--WHAT IN THE WORLD--?

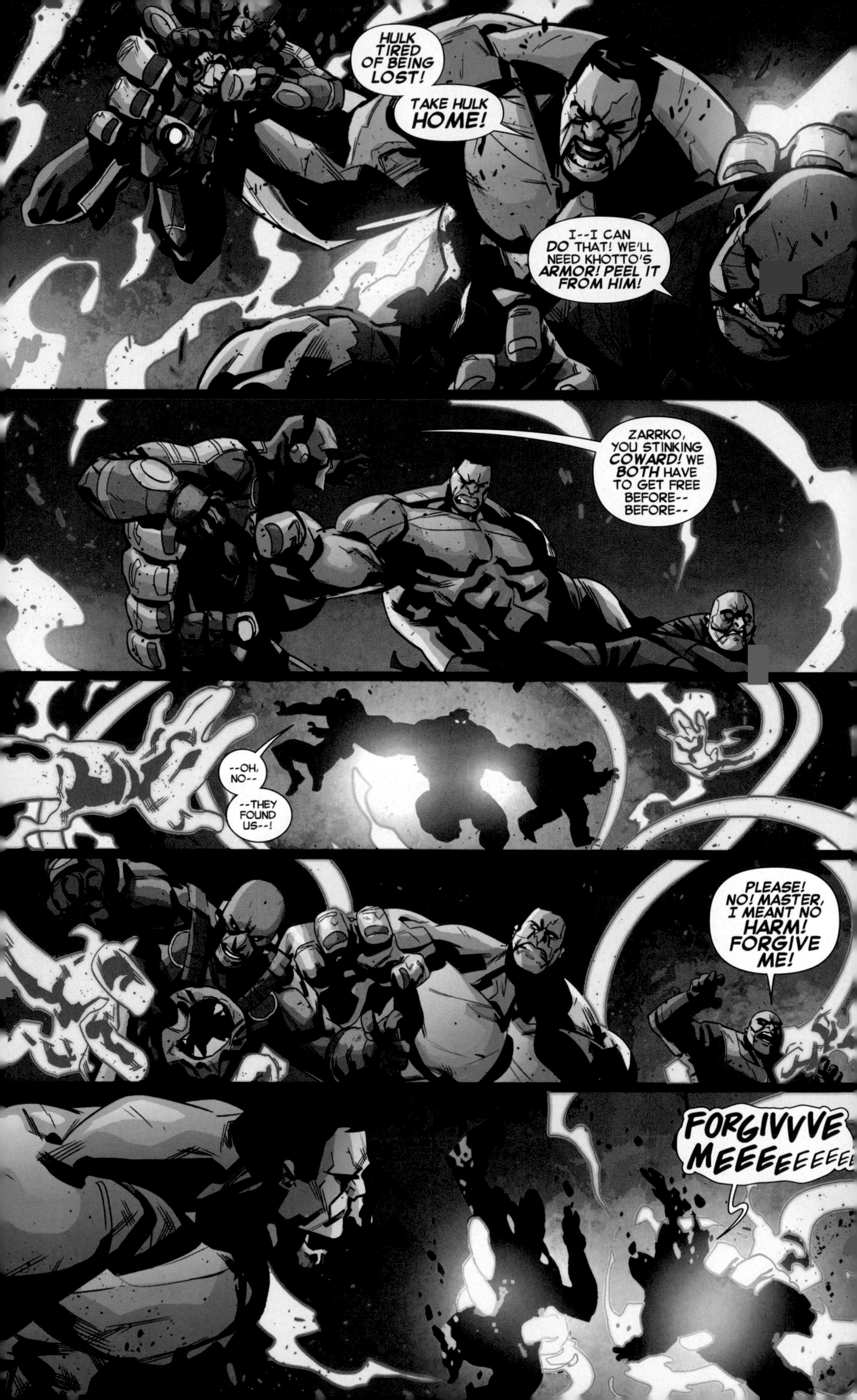
HULK TIRED OF BEING LOST!
TAKE HULK HOME!
I--I CAN DO THAT! WE'LL NEED KHOTTO'S ARMOR! PEEL IT FROM HIM!
ZARRKO, YOU STINKING COWARD! WE BOTH HAVE TO GET FREE BEFORE-- BEFORE--
--OH, NO--
--THEY FOUND US--!
PLEASE! NO! MASTER, I MEANT NO HARM! FORGIVE ME!
FORGIVVVE MEEEEEEEEE

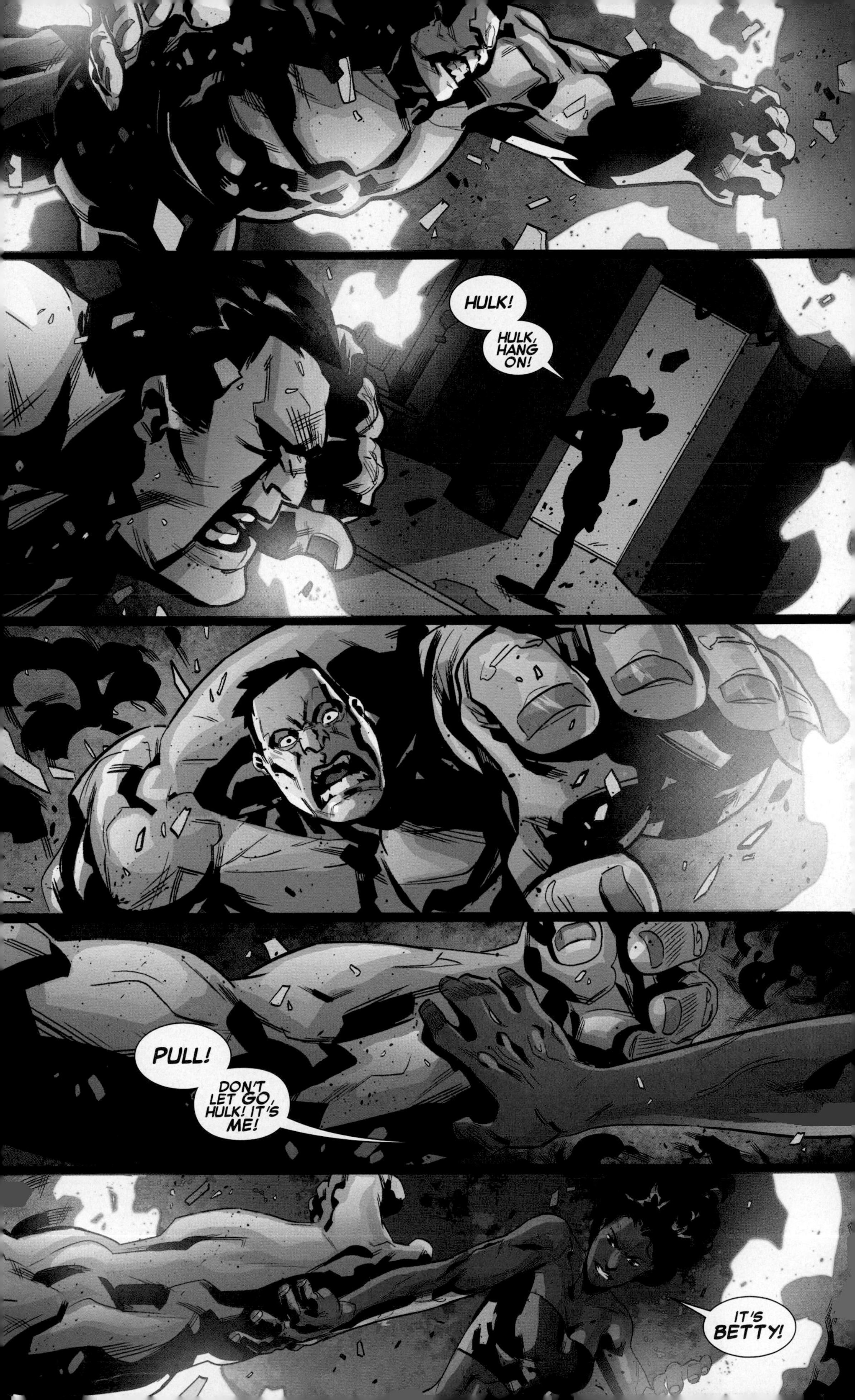
HULK!
HULK, HANG ON!
PULL!
DON'T LET GO, HULK! IT'S ME!
IT'S BETTY!

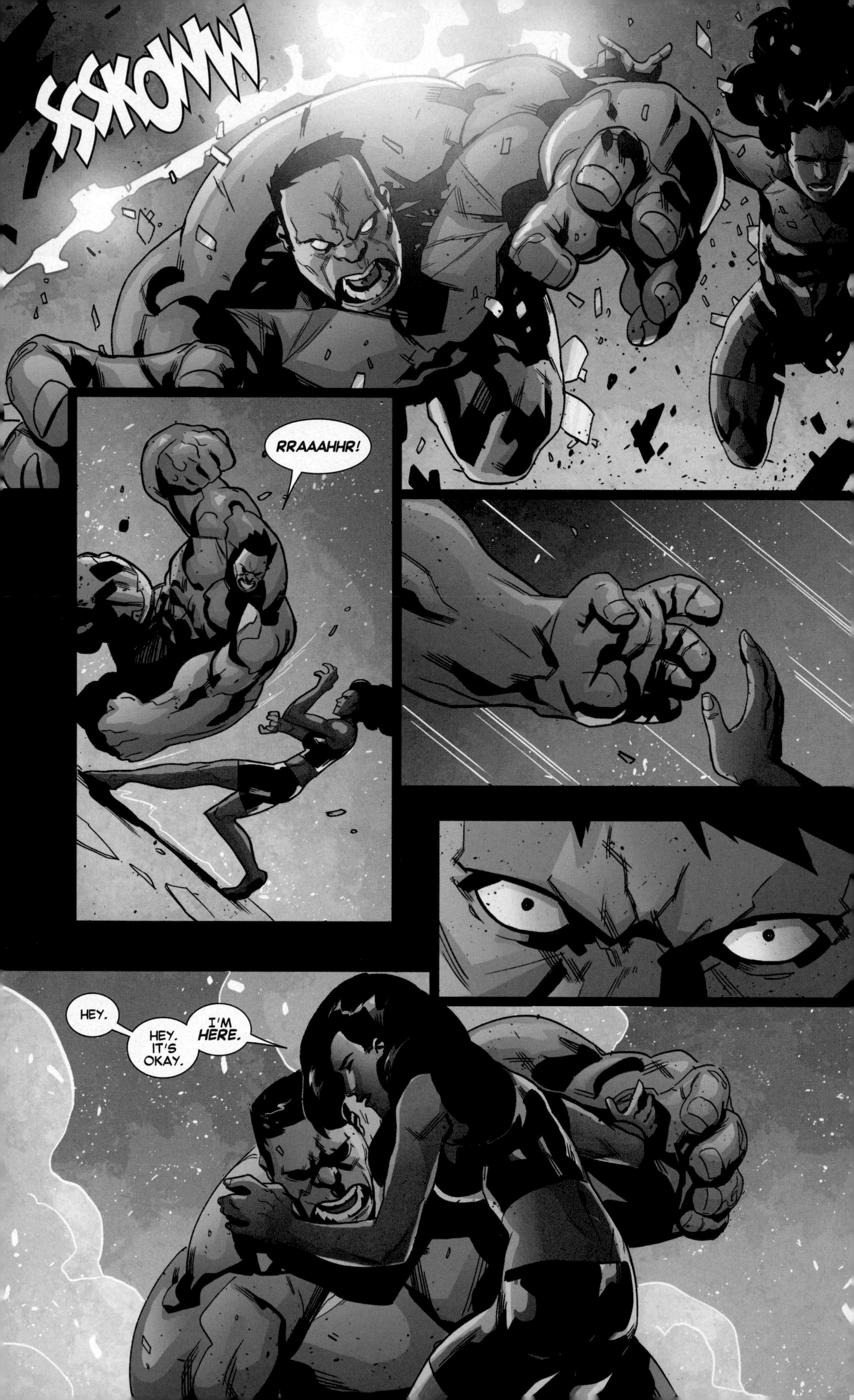
SSKOWW
RRAAAHHR!
HEY.
HEY. IT'S OKAY.
I'M HERE.

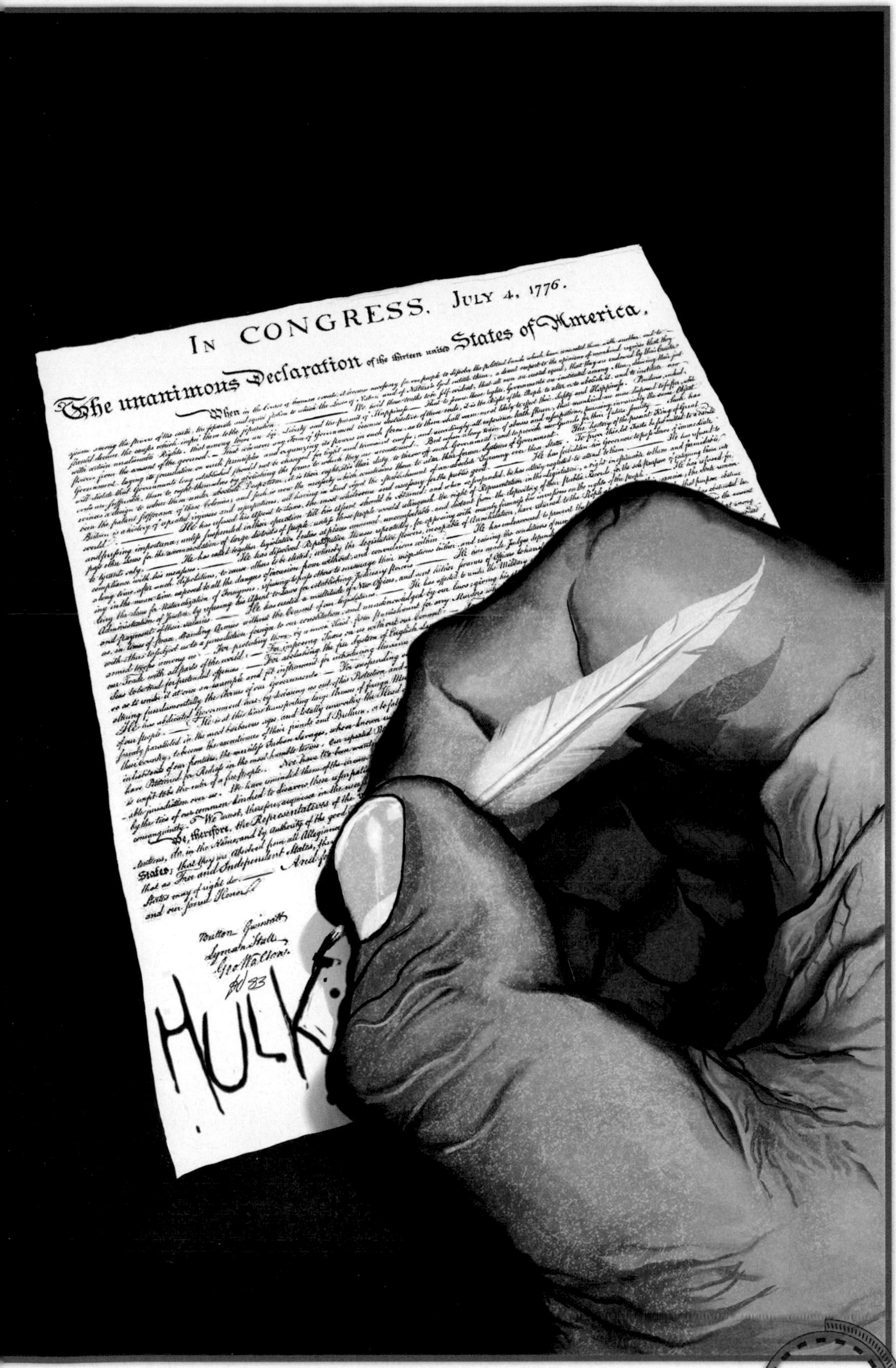
IN CONGRESS. JULY 4, 1776.
The unanimous Declaration of the thirteen united States of America,
HULK

VARIANT BY MICHAEL DEL MUNDO 11

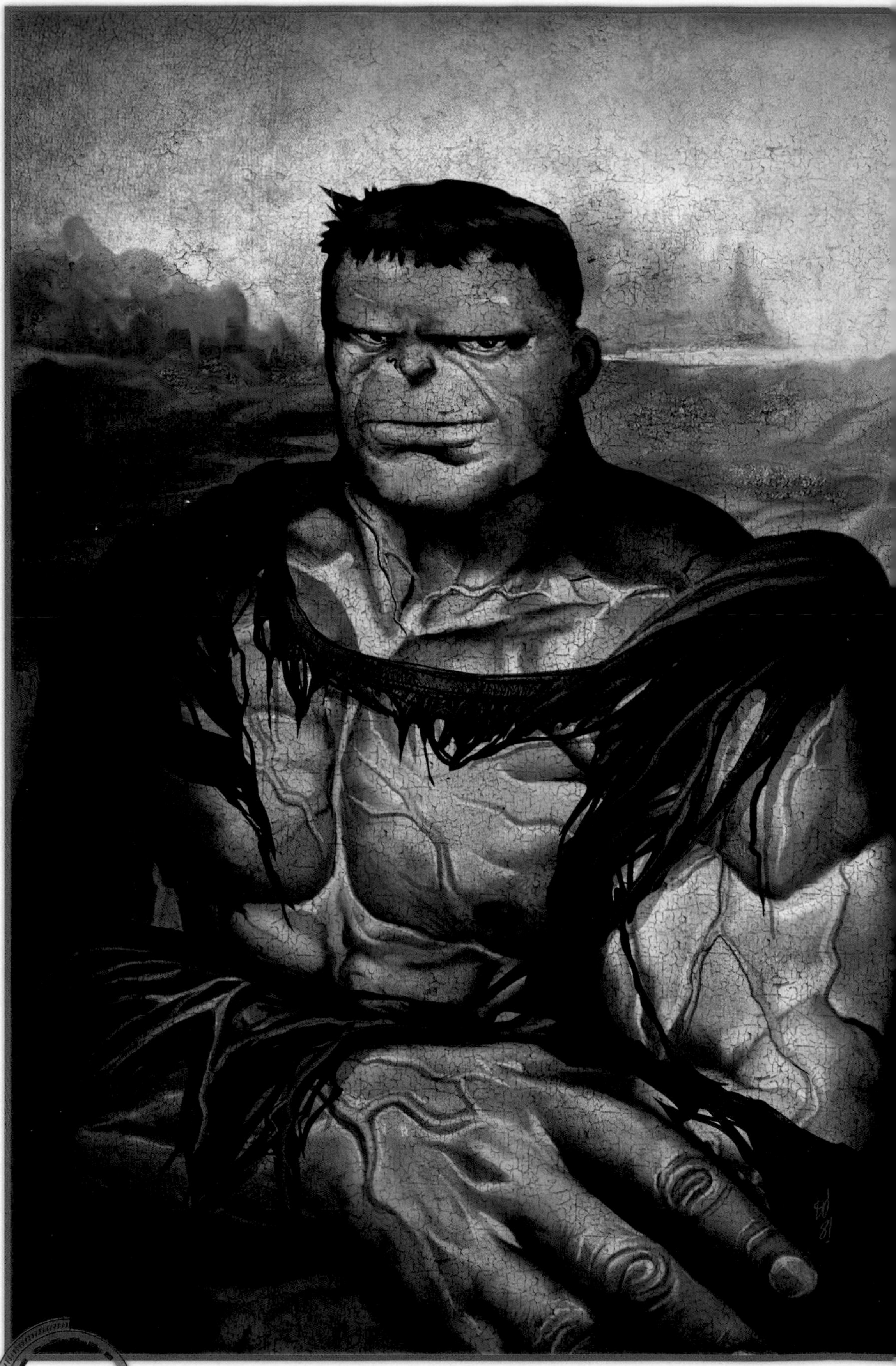

VARIANT BY MICHAEL DEL MUNDO

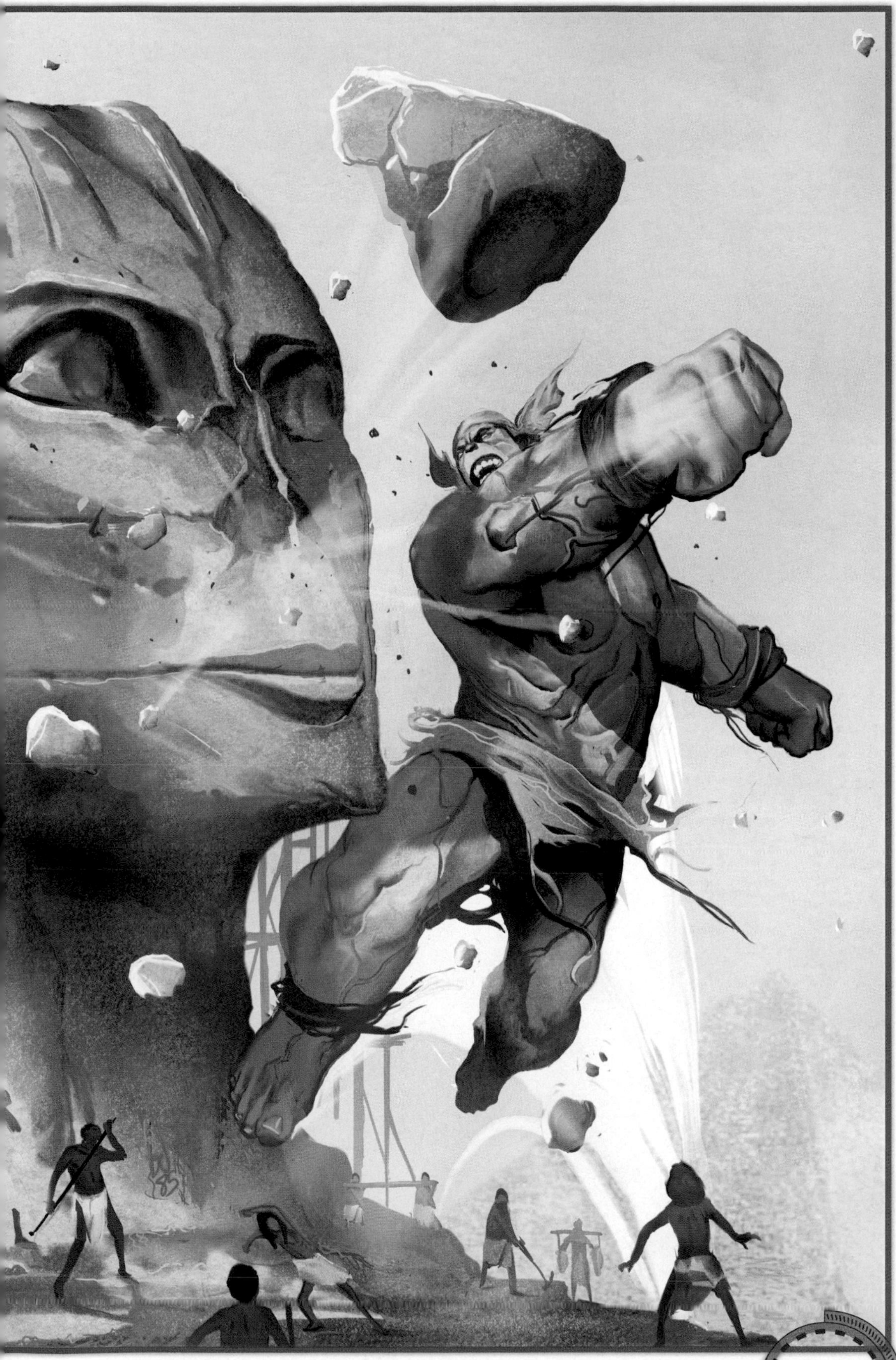

VARIANT BY MICHAEL DEL MUNDO

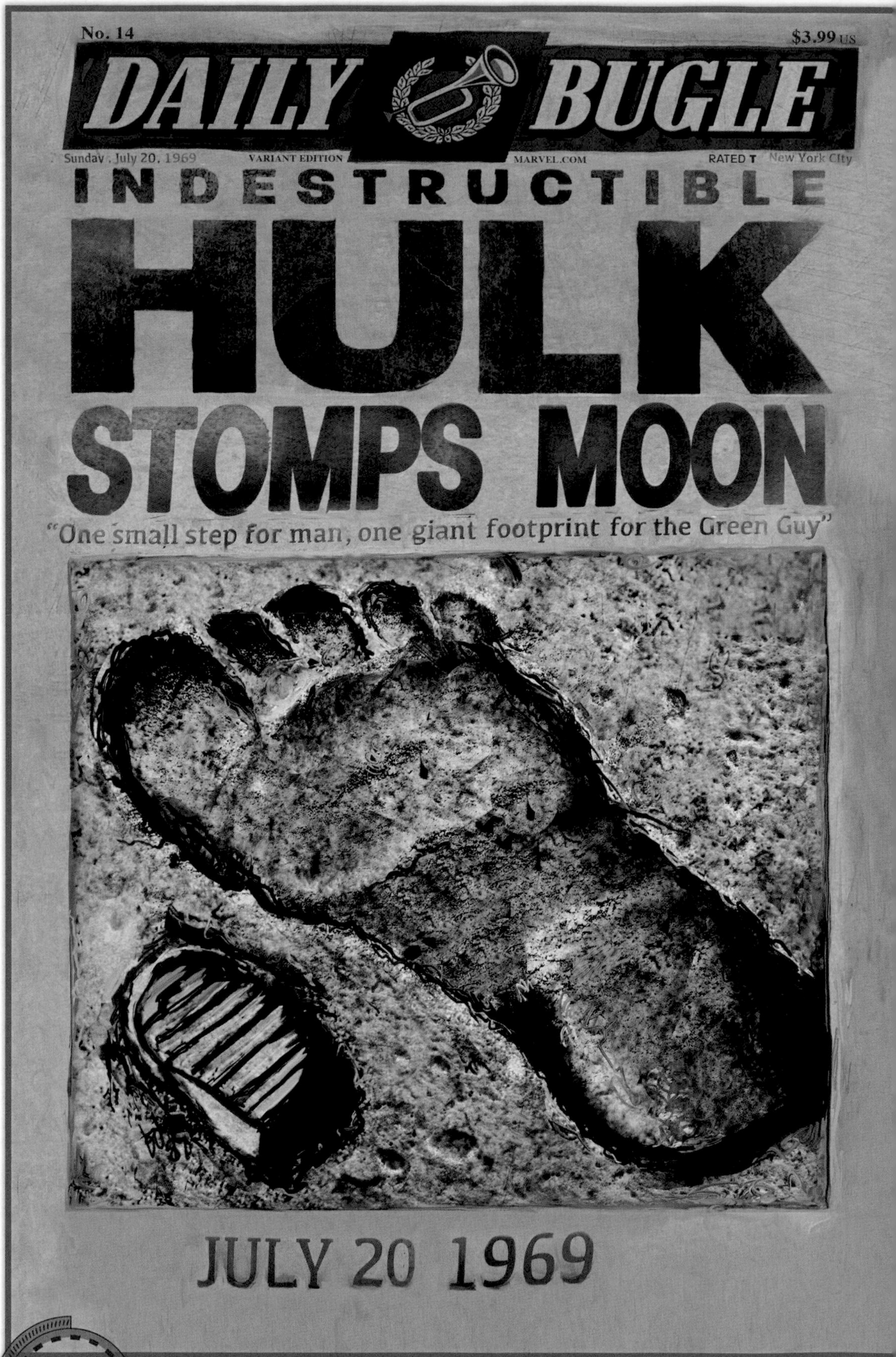
No. 14
$3.99 US
DAILY BUGLE
Sunday . July 20, 1969
VARIANT EDITION
MARVEL.COM
RATED T
New York City
INDESTRUCTIBLE
HULK
STOMPS MOON
"One small step for man, one giant footprint for the Green Guy"
JULY 20 1969

VARIANT BY MICHAEL DEL MUNDO

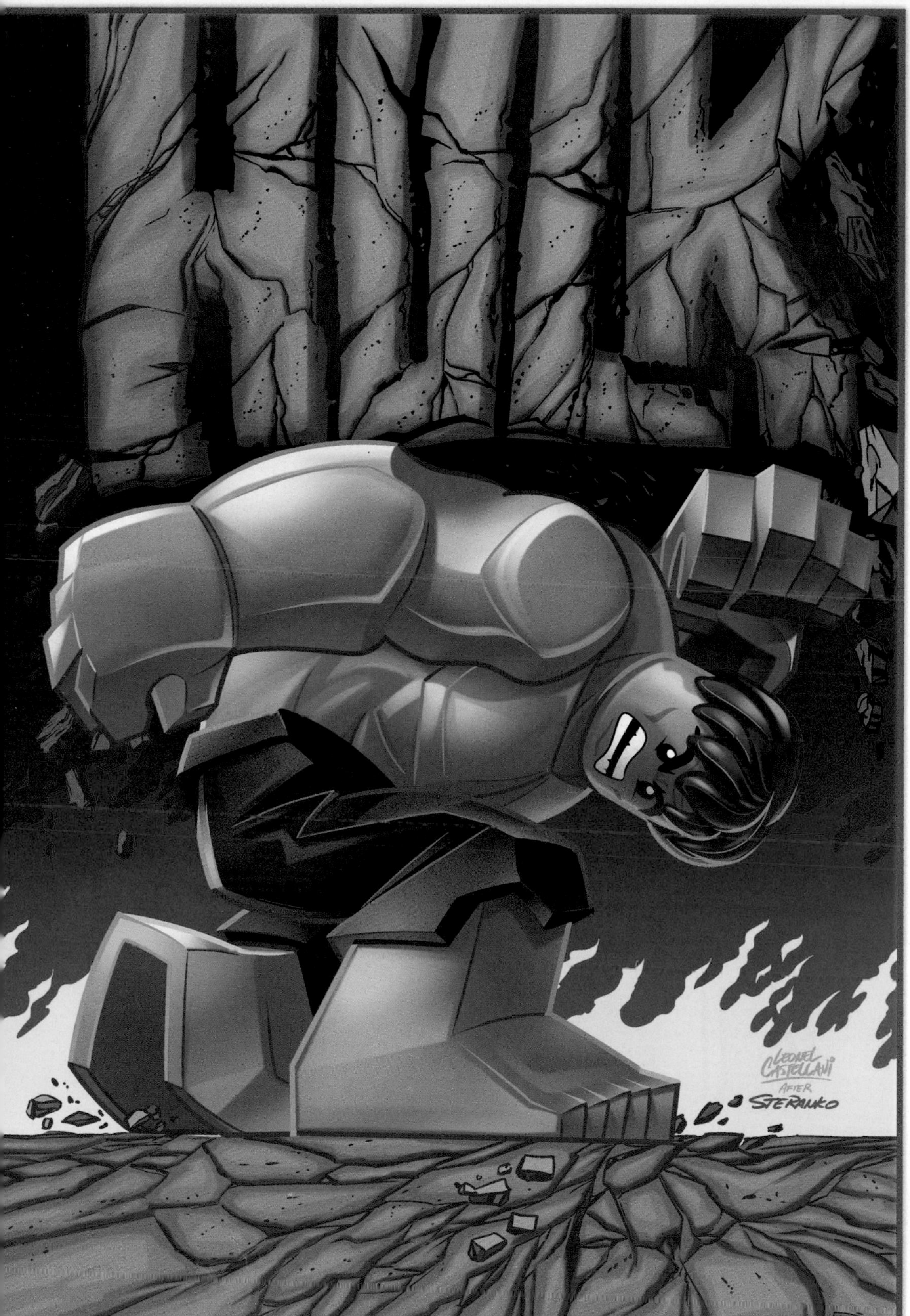
LEONEL CASTELLANI AFTER STERANKO

LEGO VARIANT BY LEONEL CASTELLANI

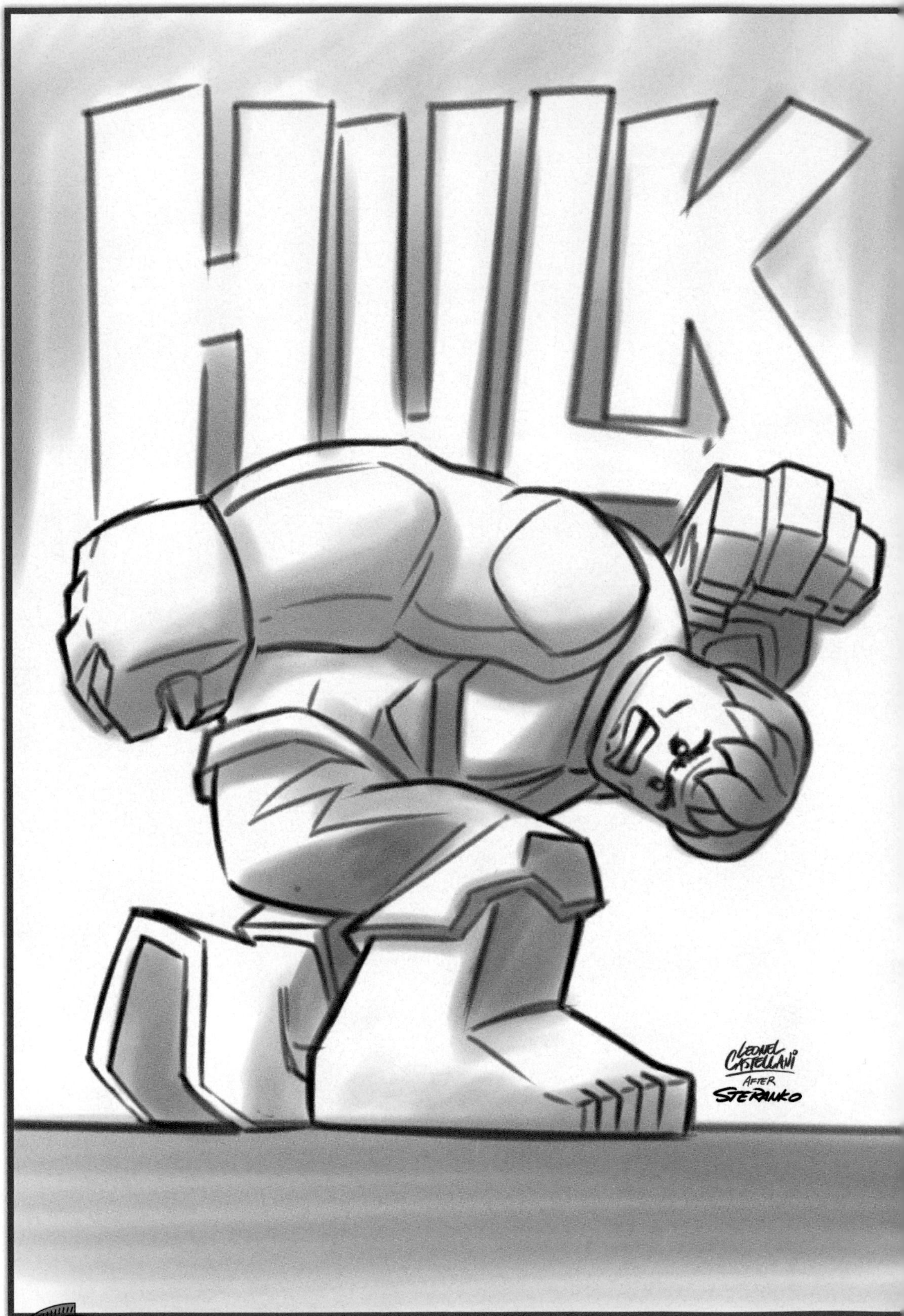
HULK
LEONEL CASTELLANI AFTER STERANKO

14

LEGO SKETCH VARIANT BY LEONEL CASTELLANI

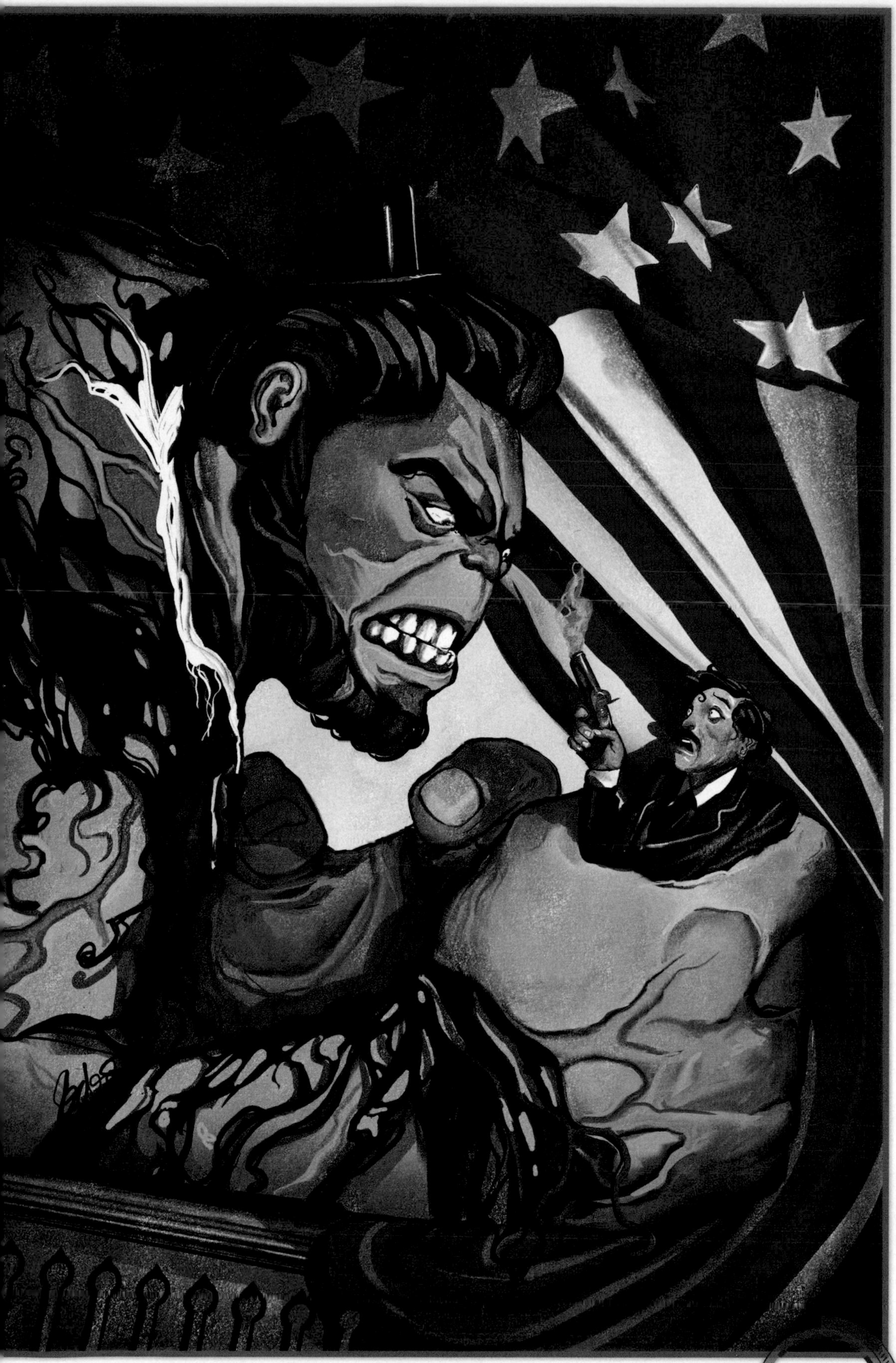

VARIANT BY MICHAEL DEL MUNDO

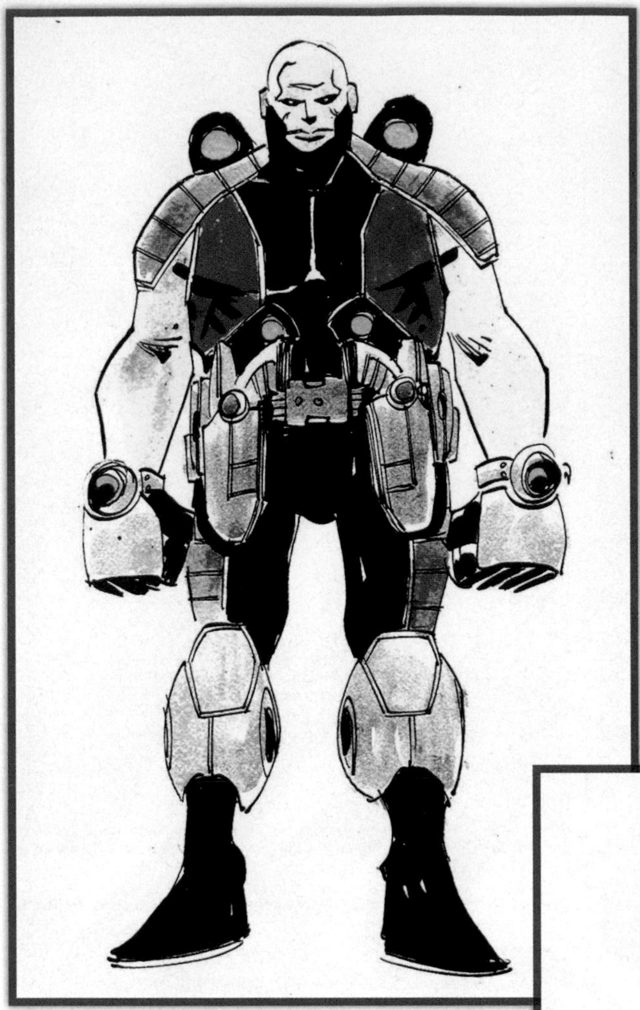

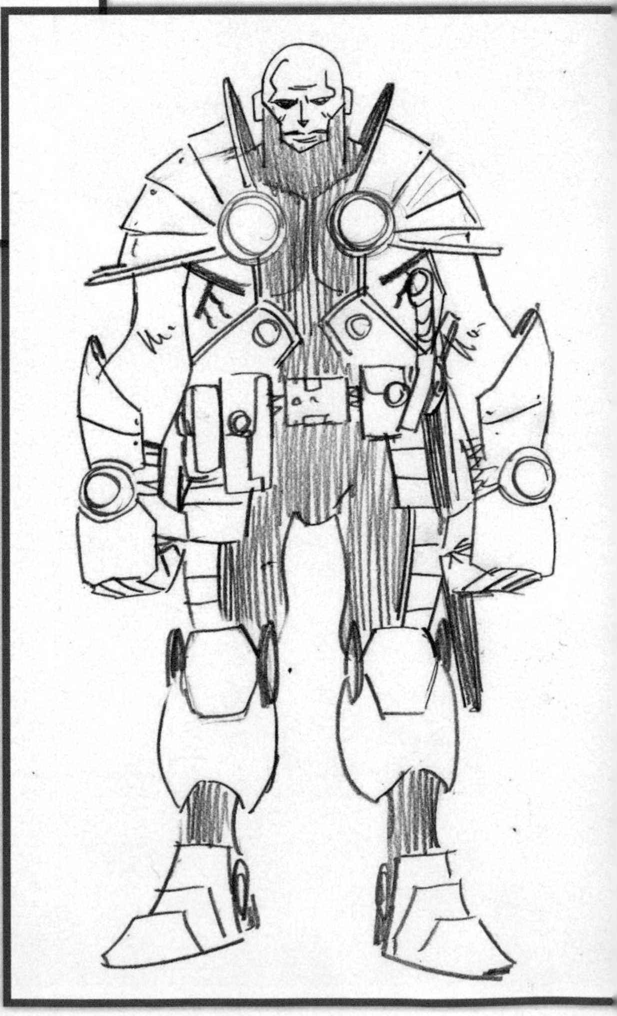

CHRONARCHIST CHARACTER DESIGNS BY MATTEO SCALERA

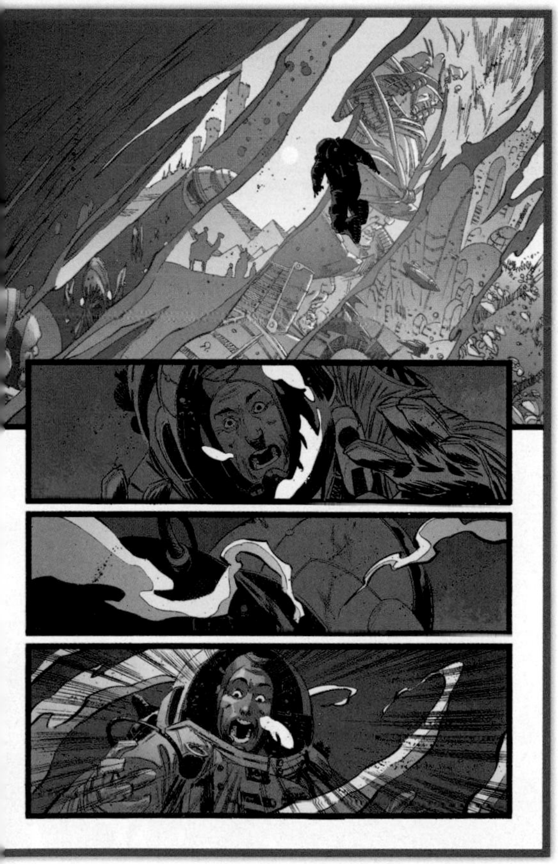

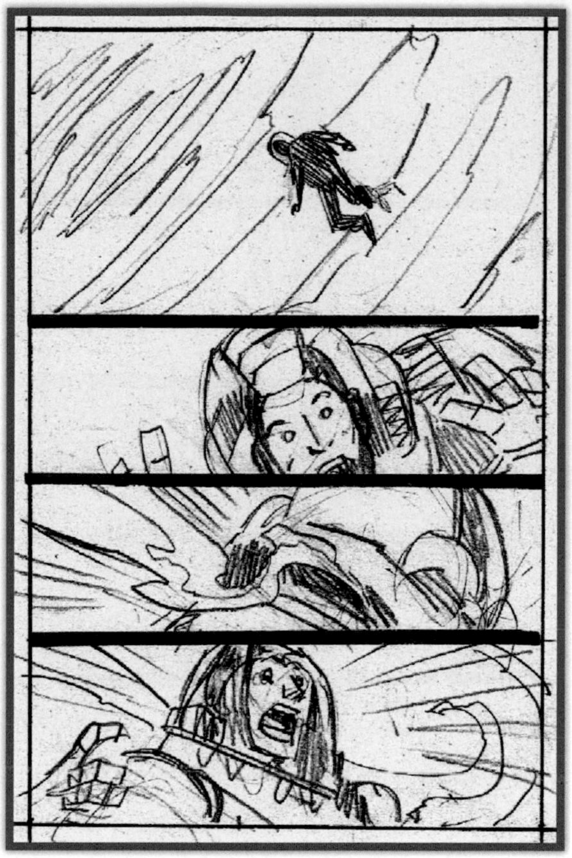

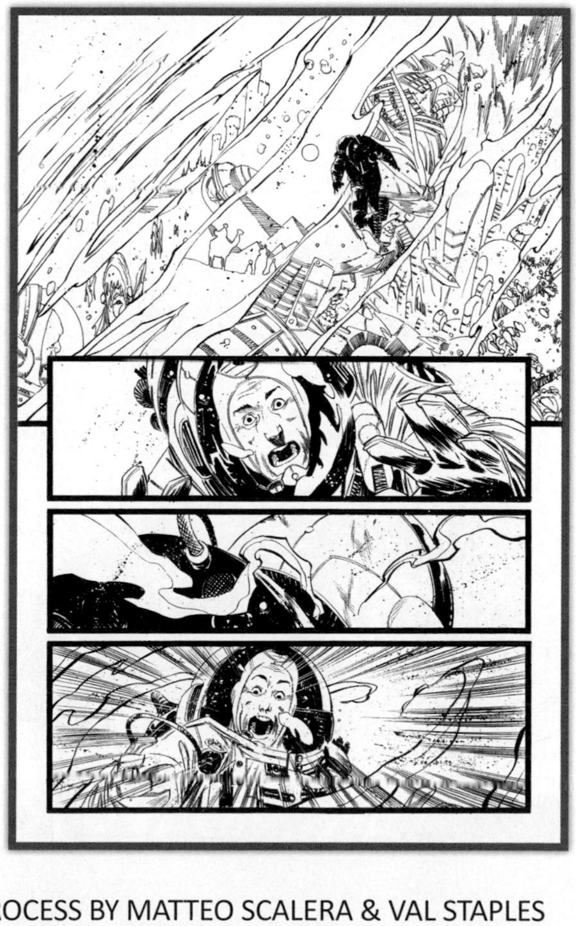

ISSUE #11, PAGES 1-16 ART PROCESS BY MATTEO SCALERA & VAL STAPLES

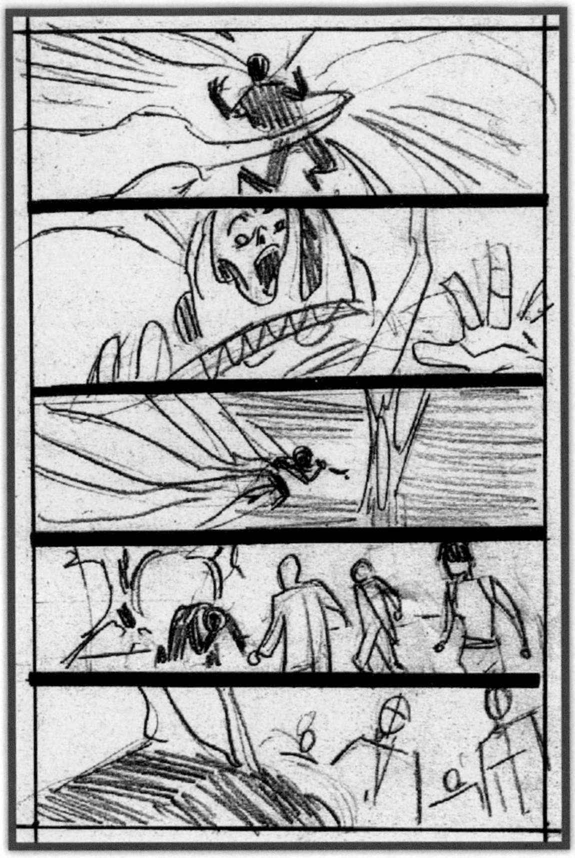

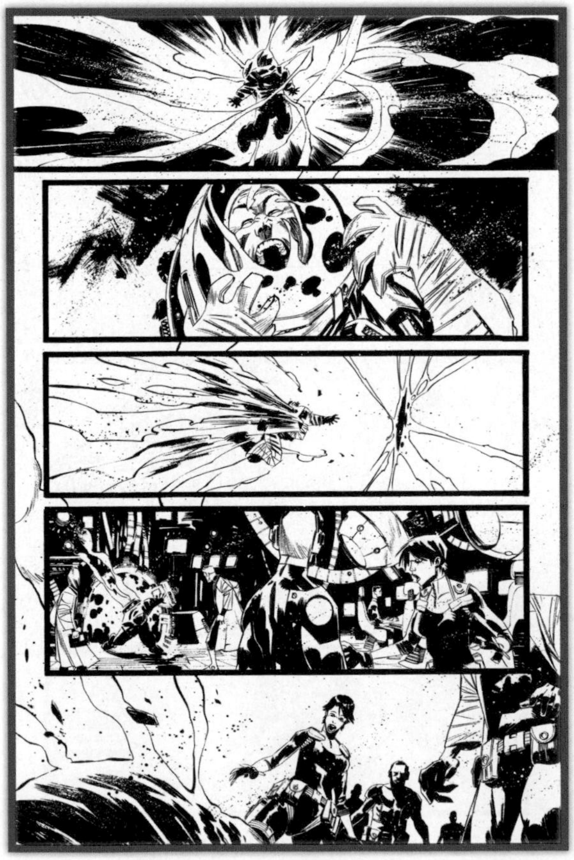

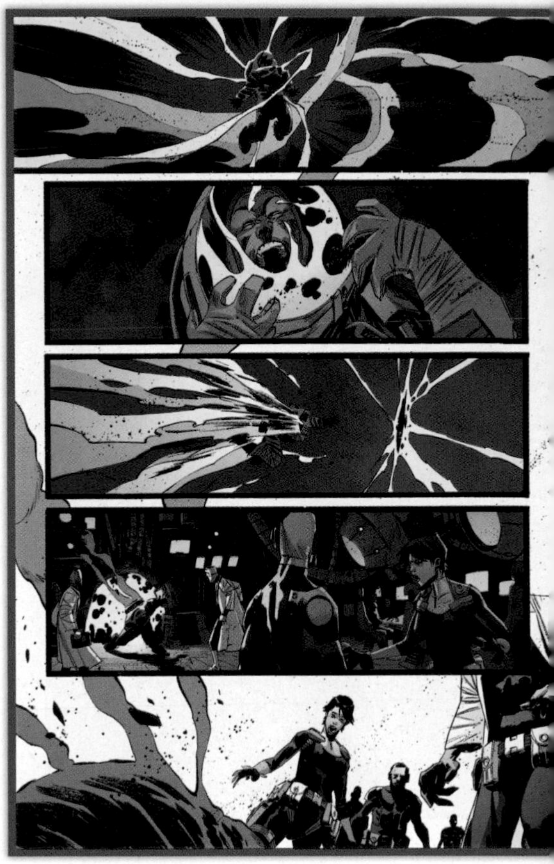

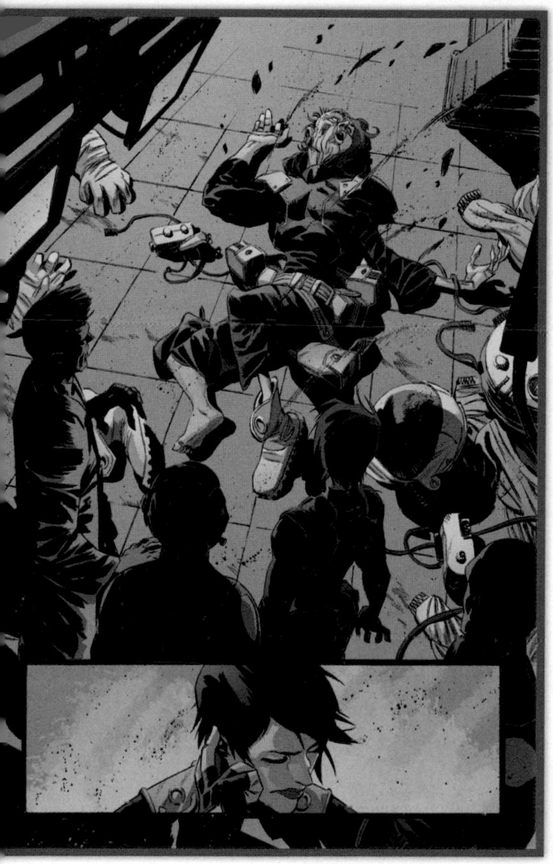

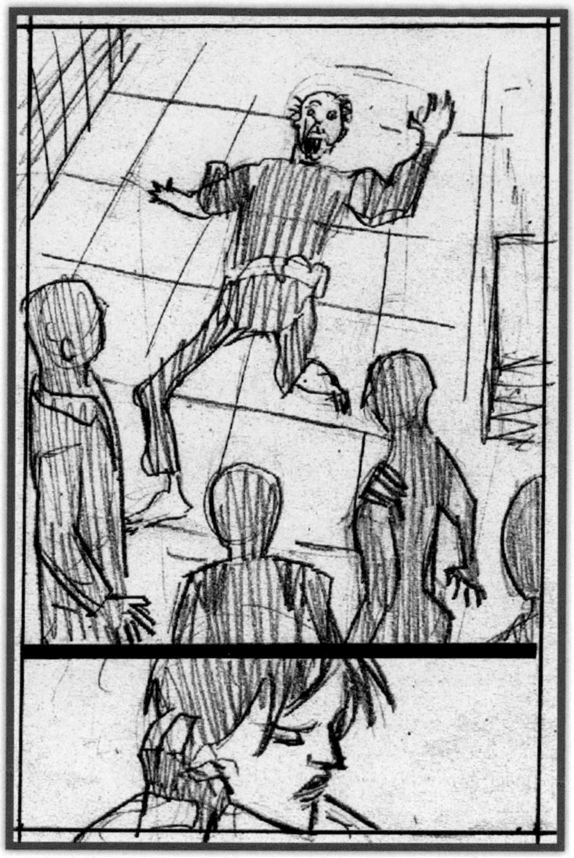

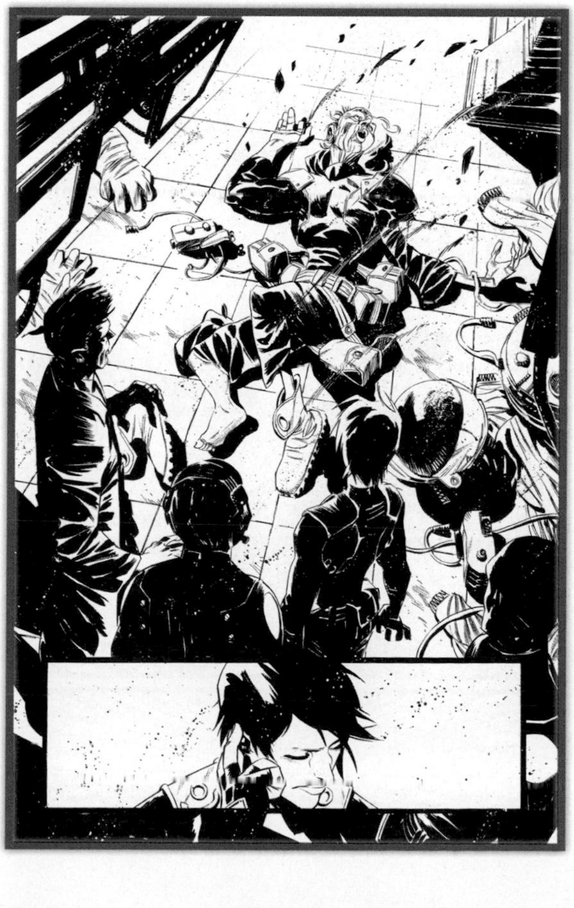

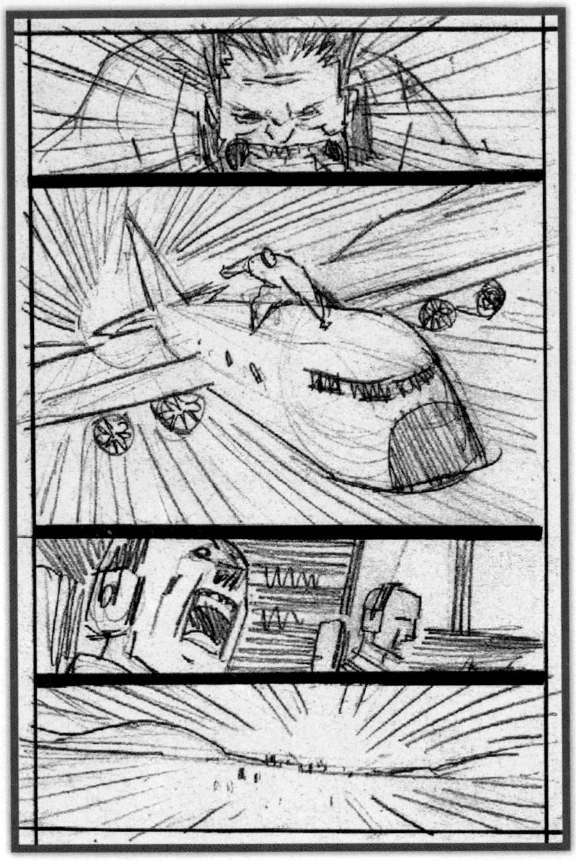

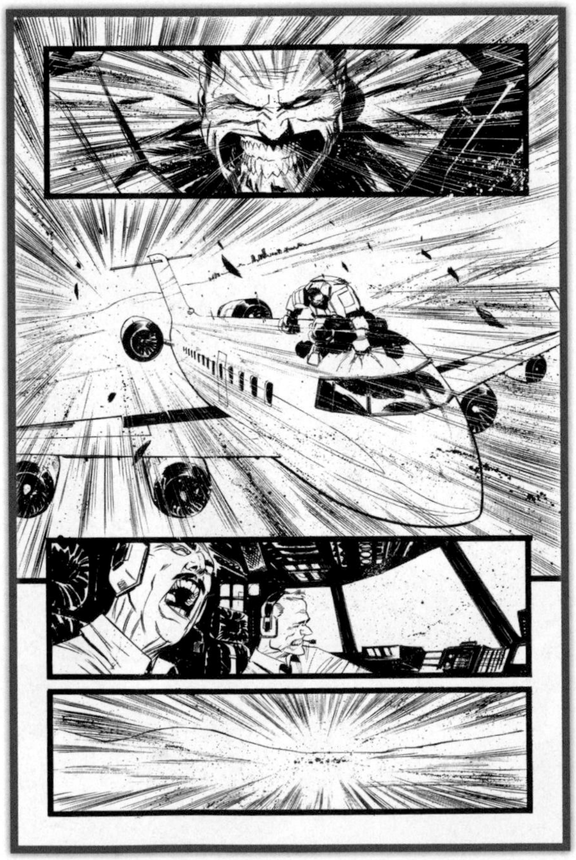

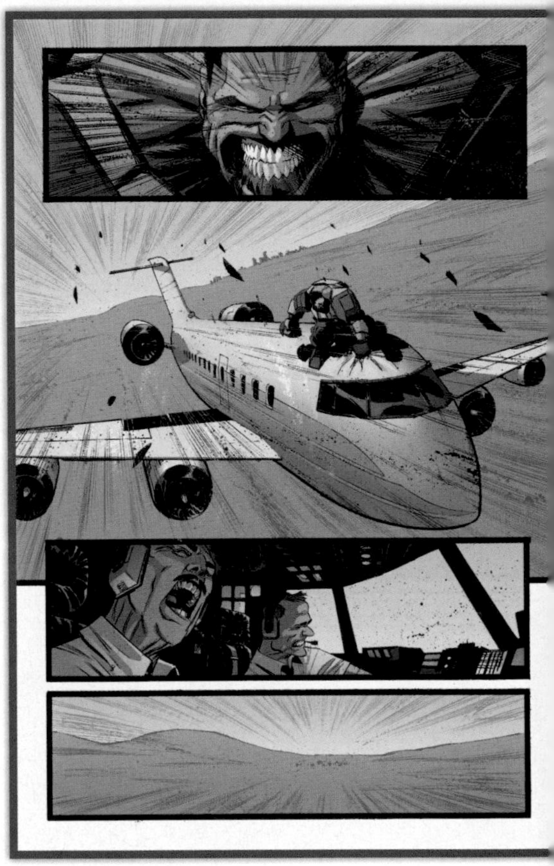

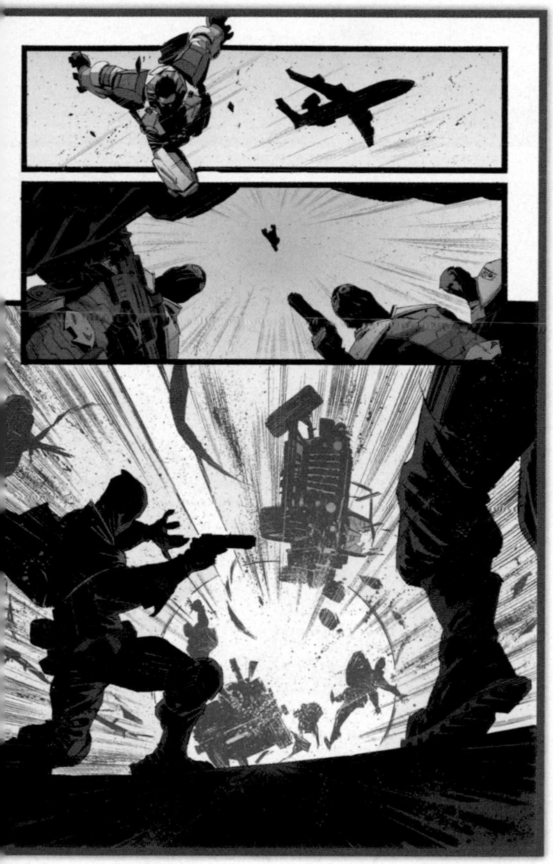

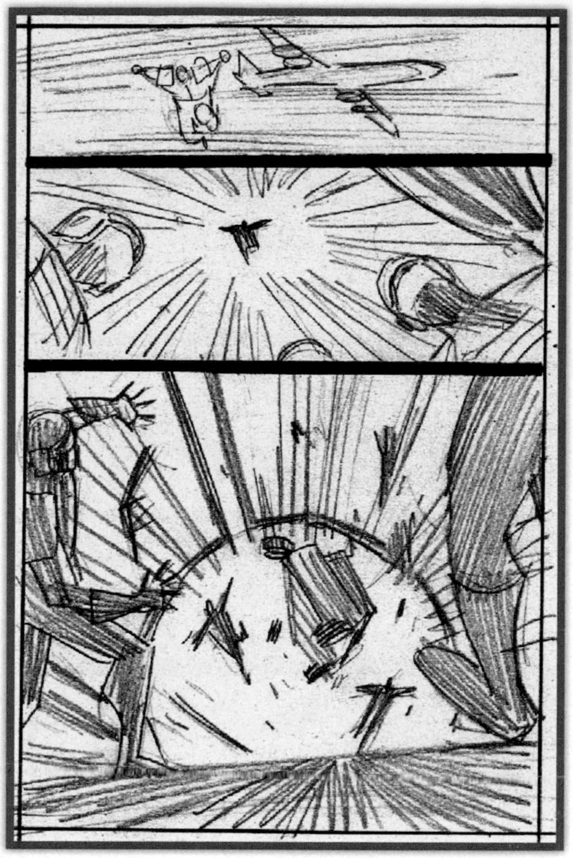

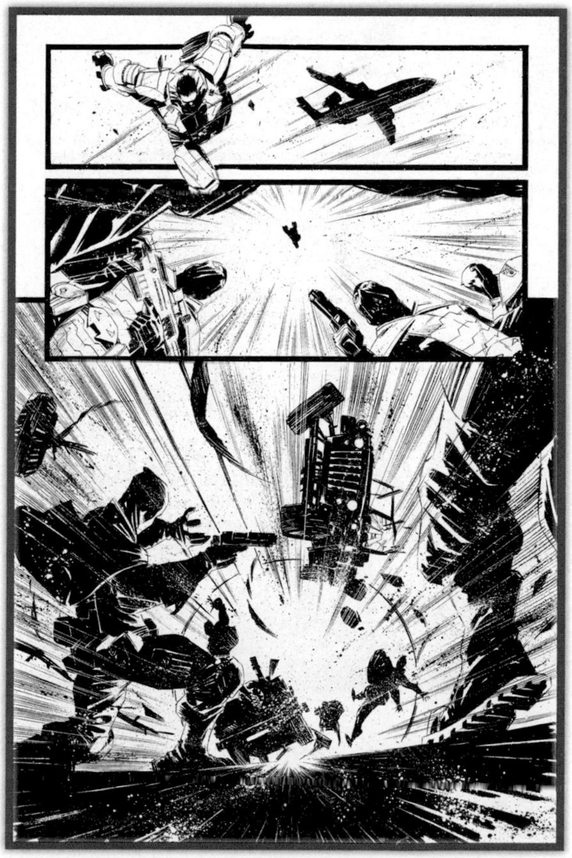

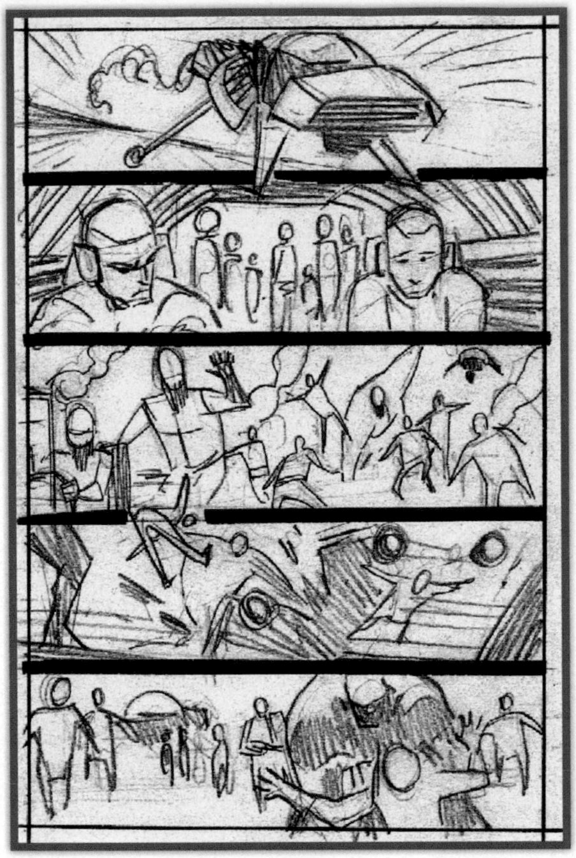

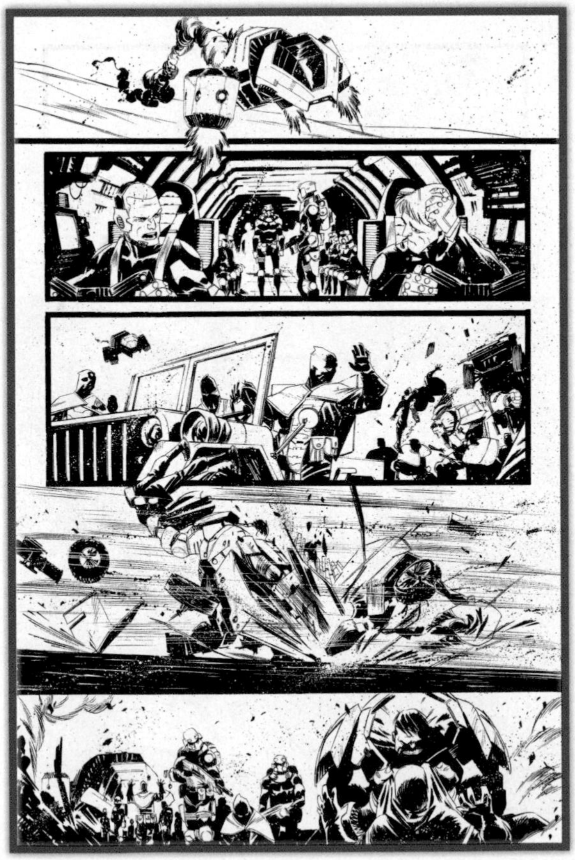

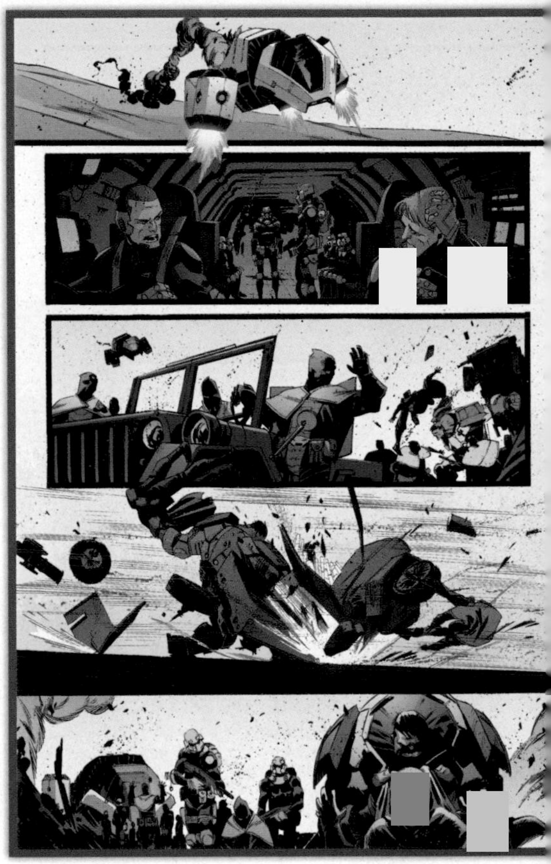

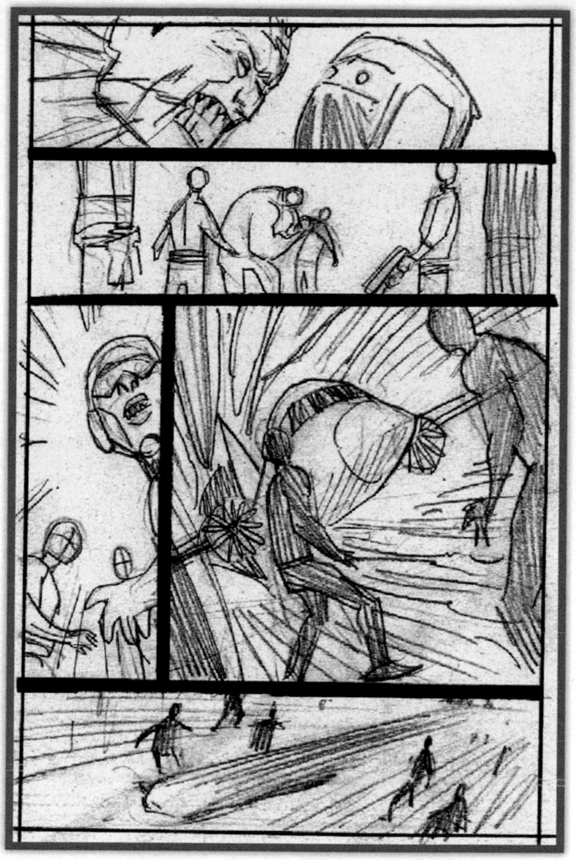

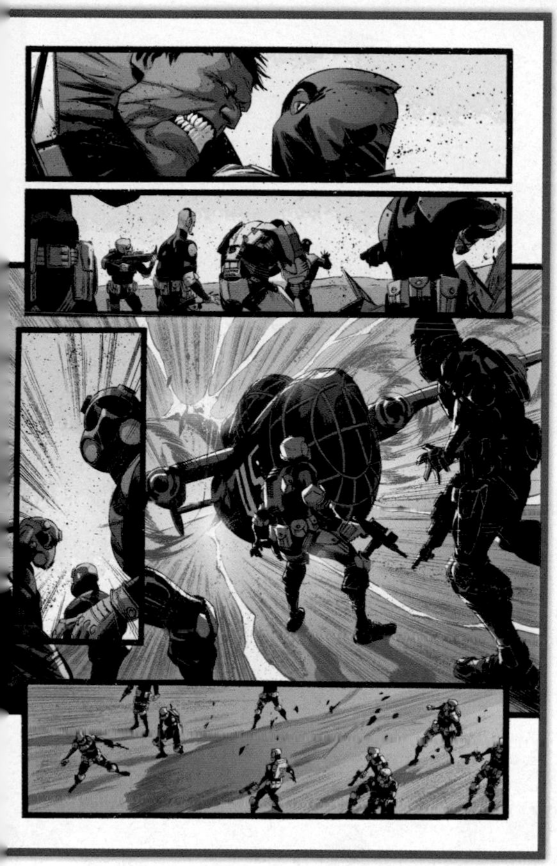

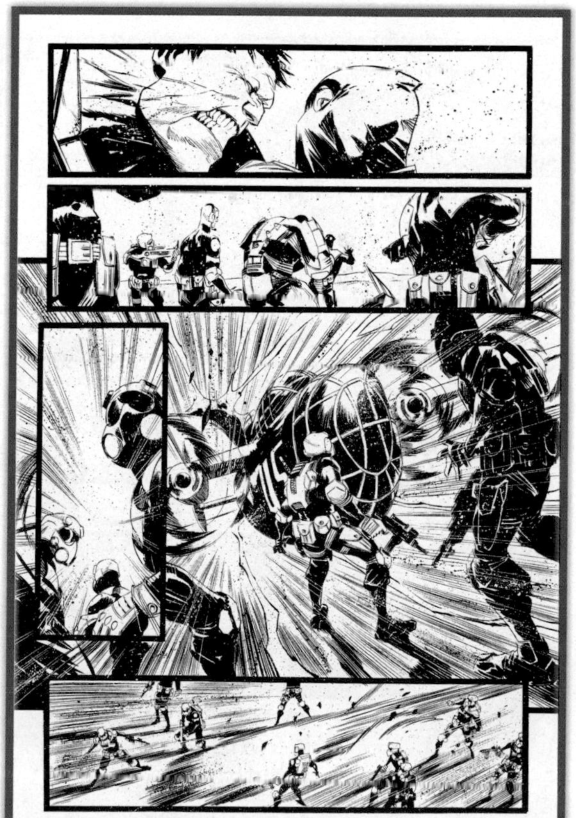

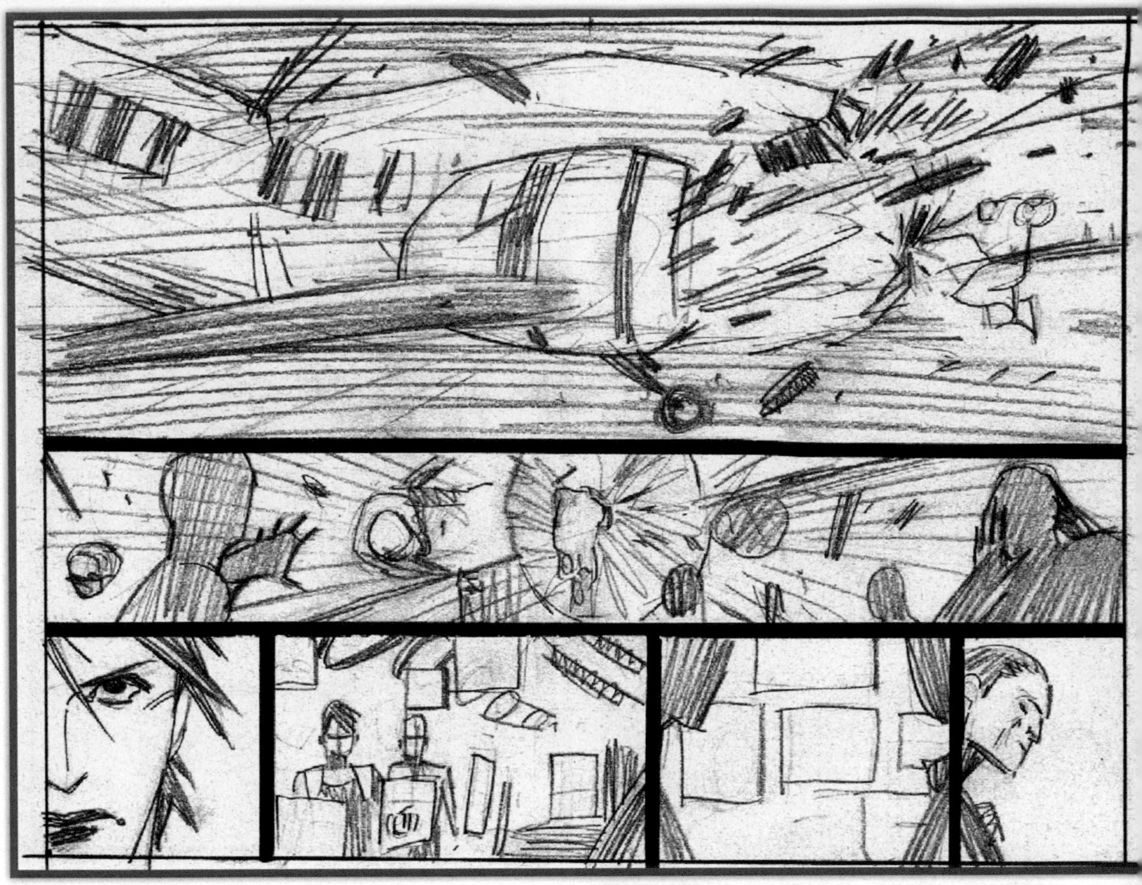

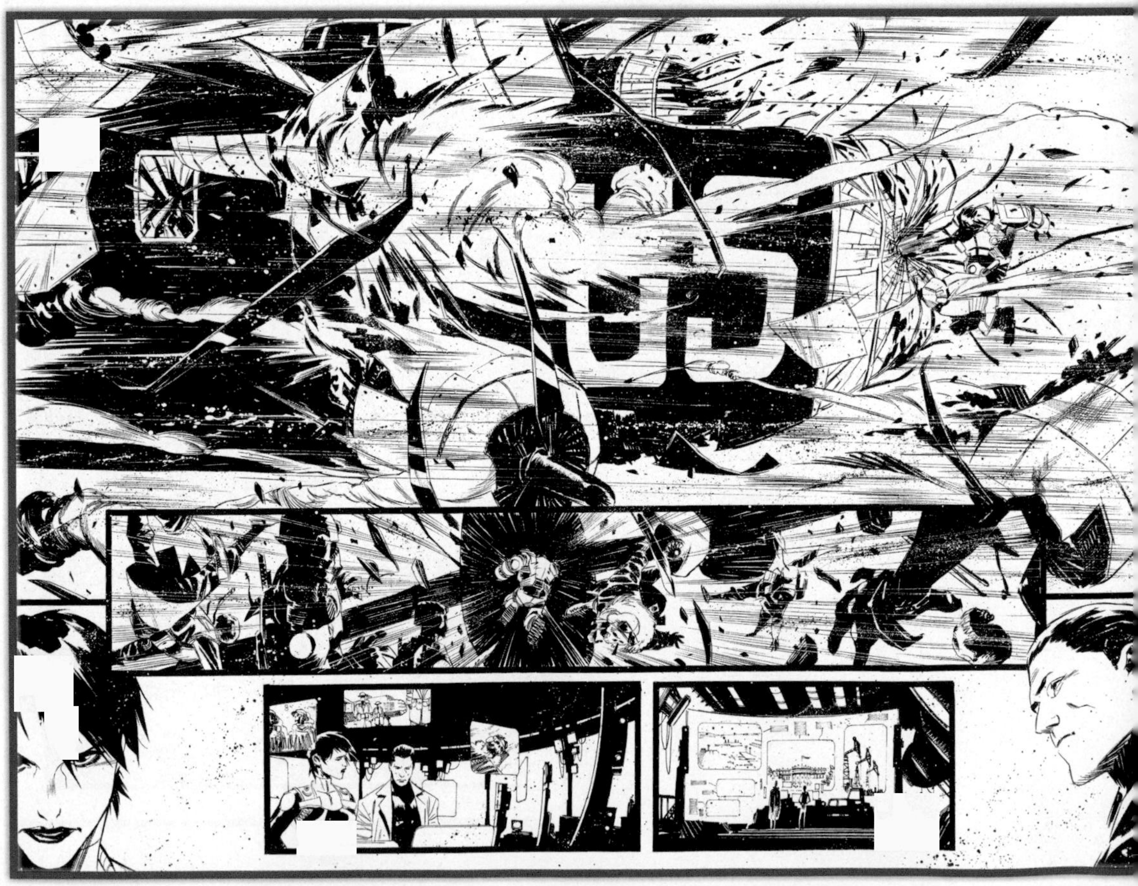

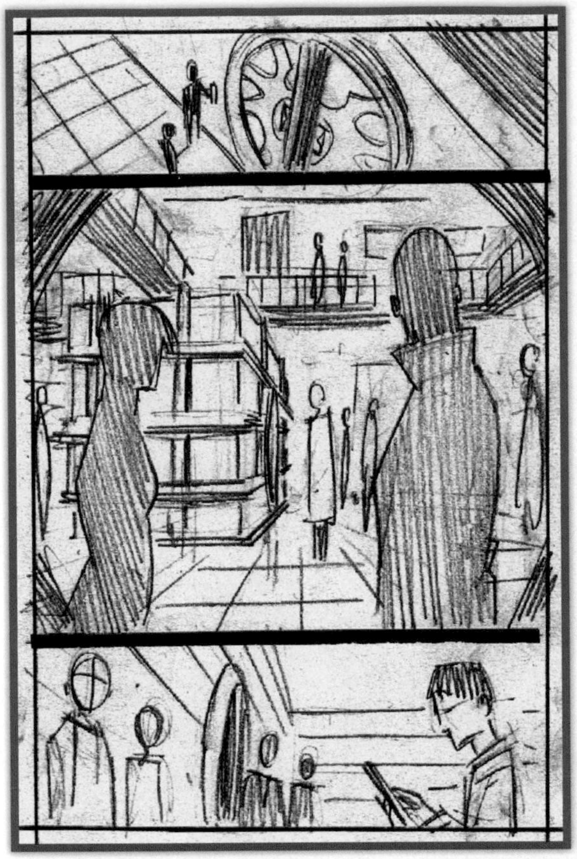

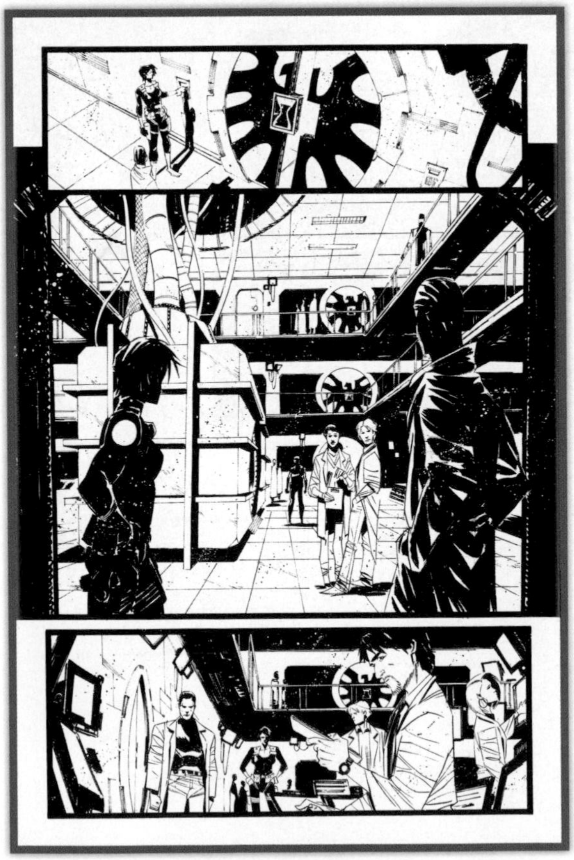

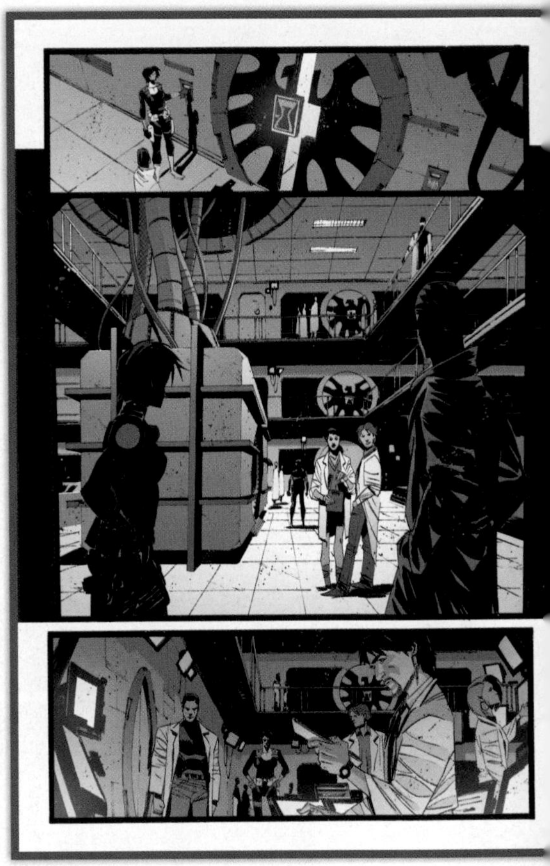

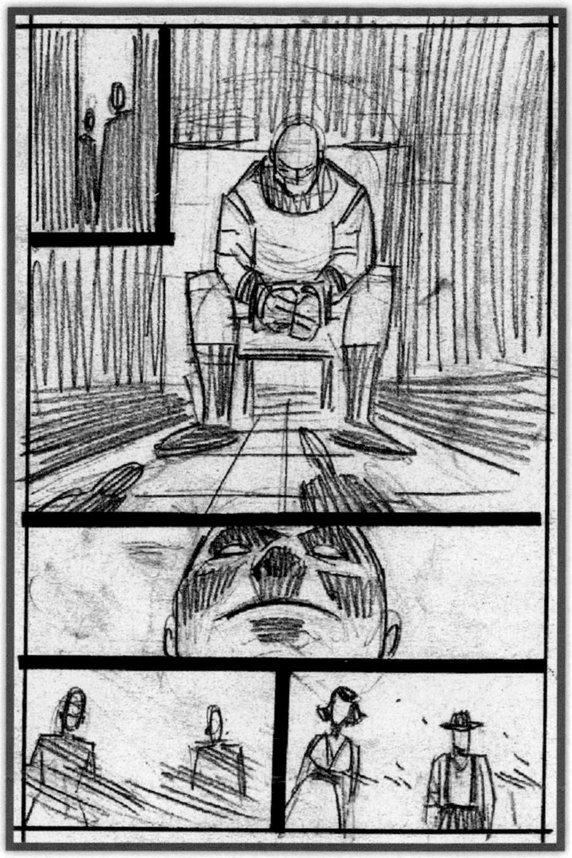

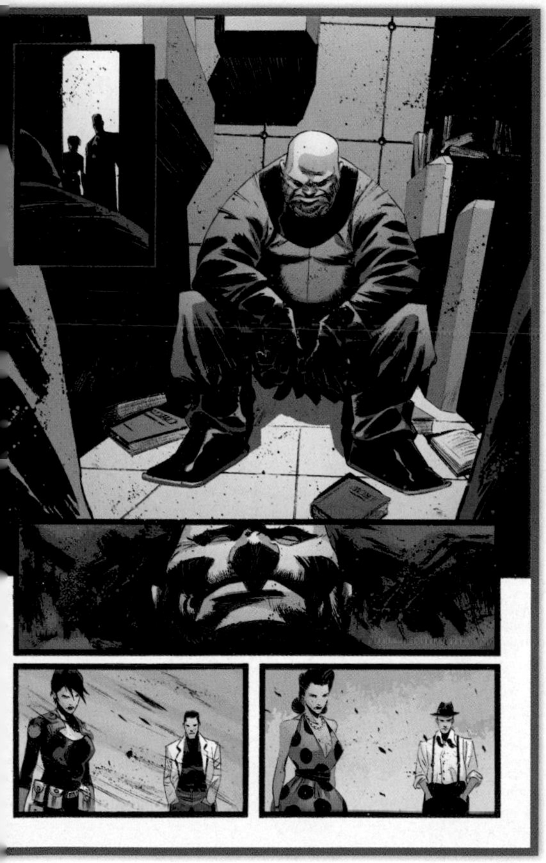

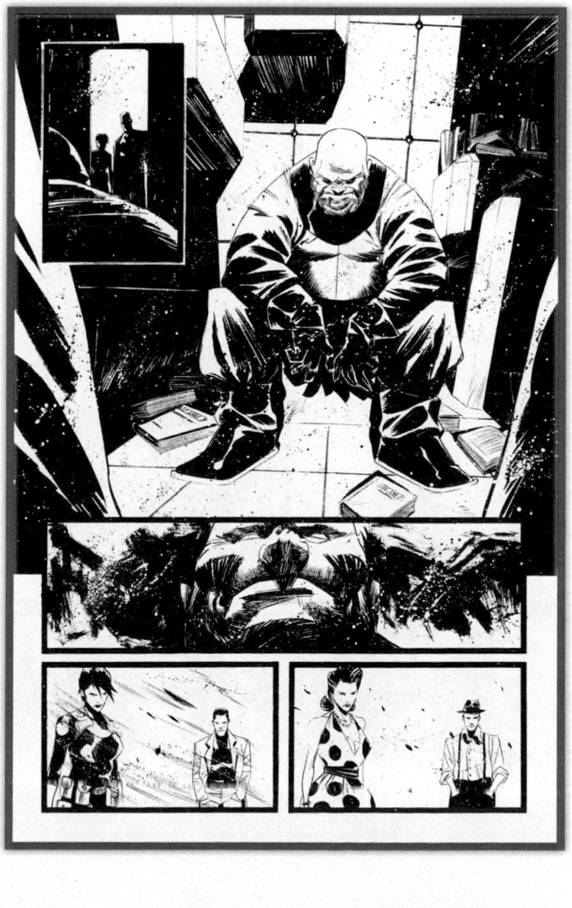

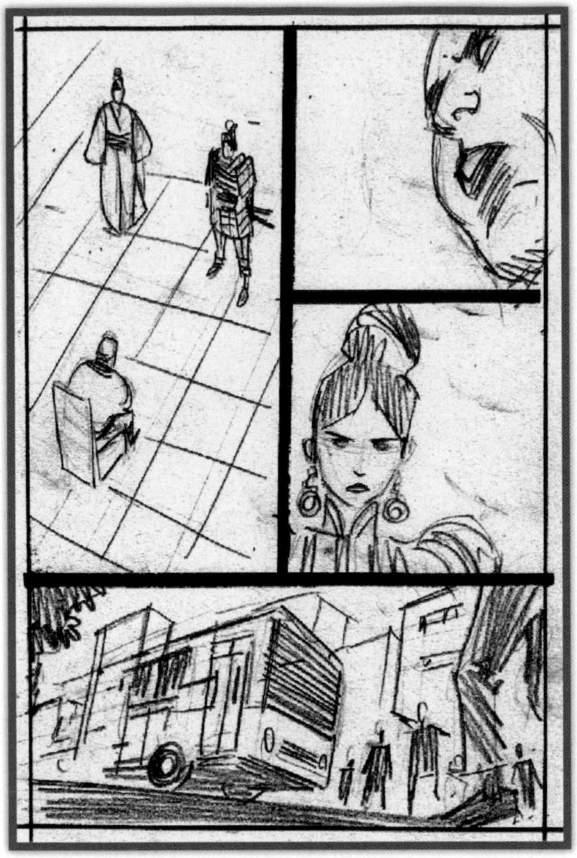

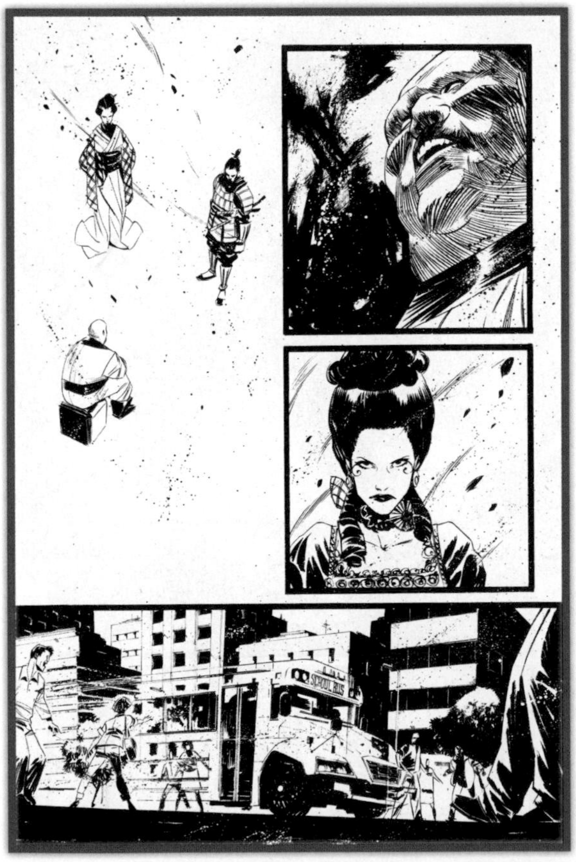
SCHOOL BUS

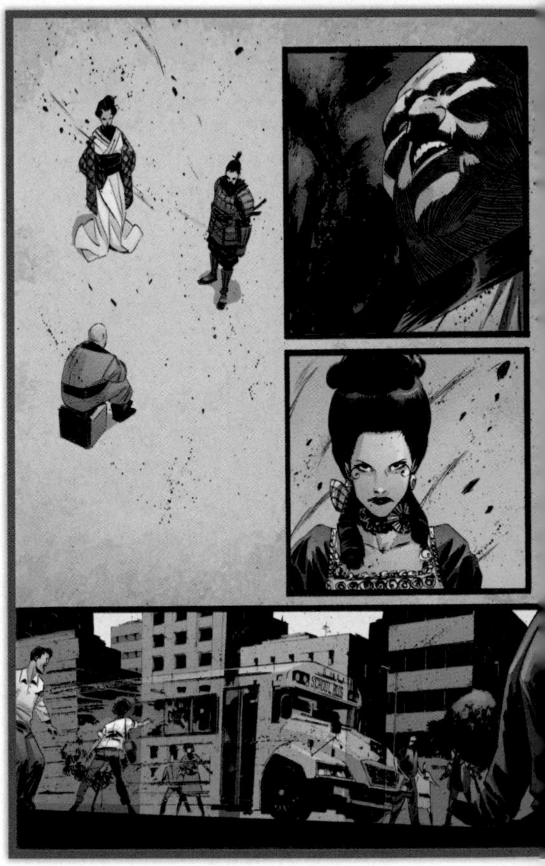
SCHOOL BUS

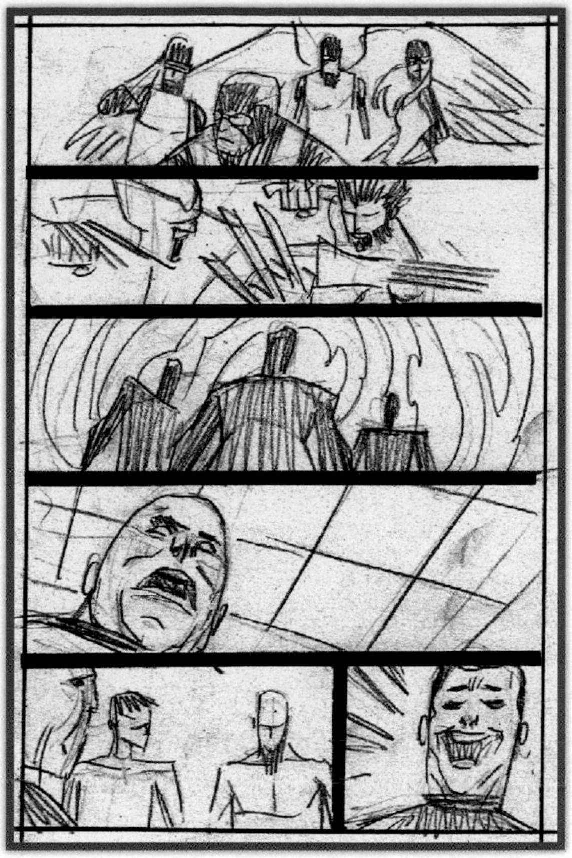

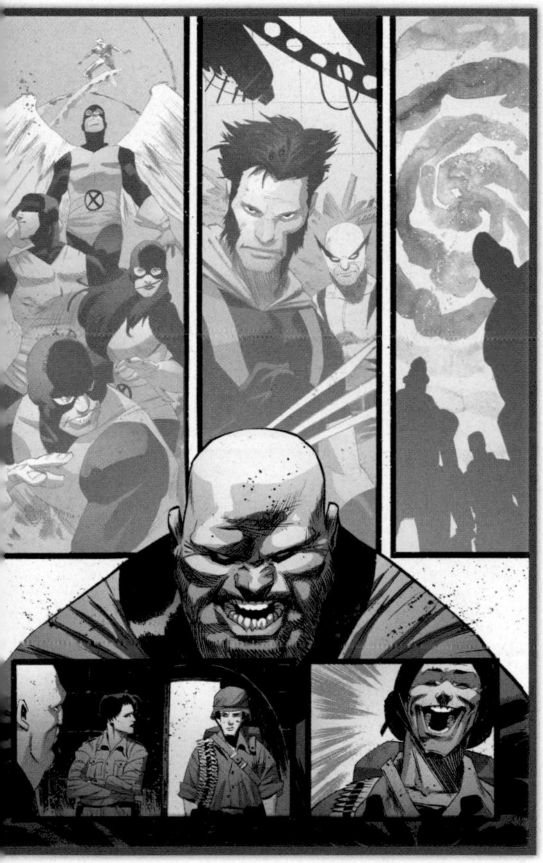

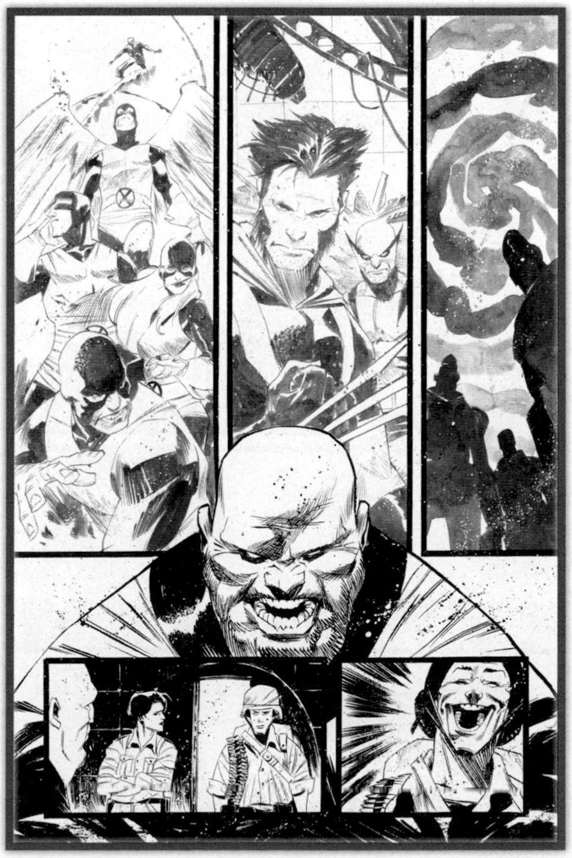

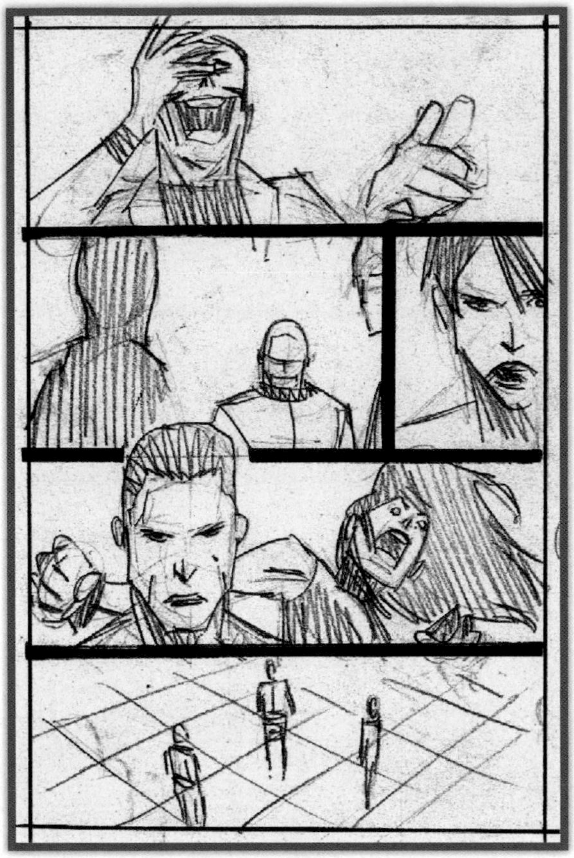

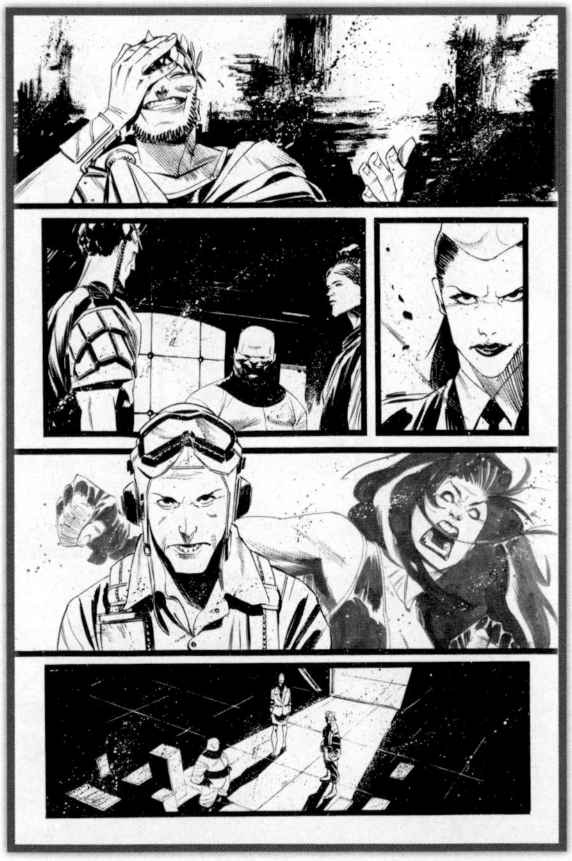

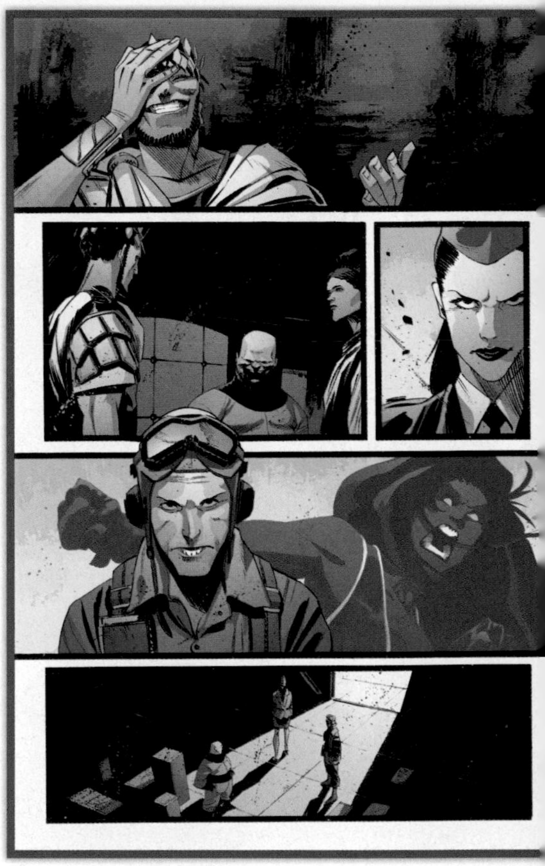

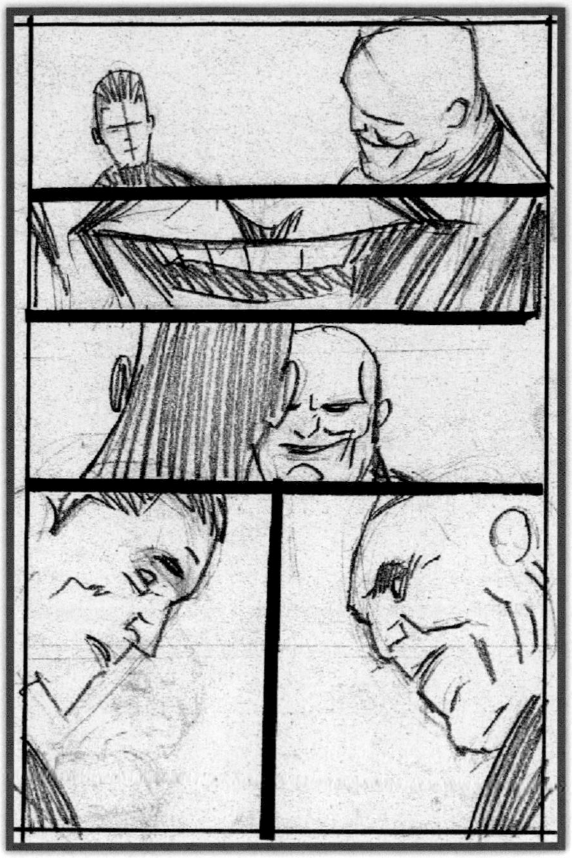

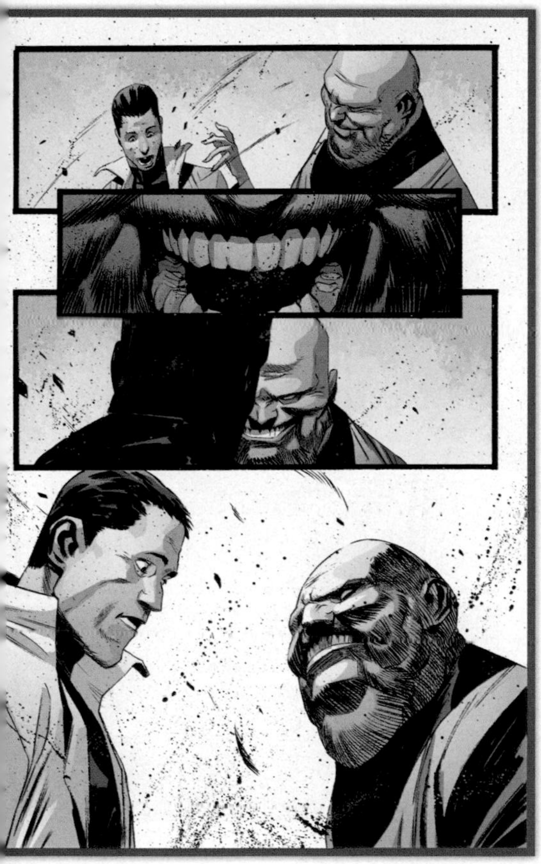

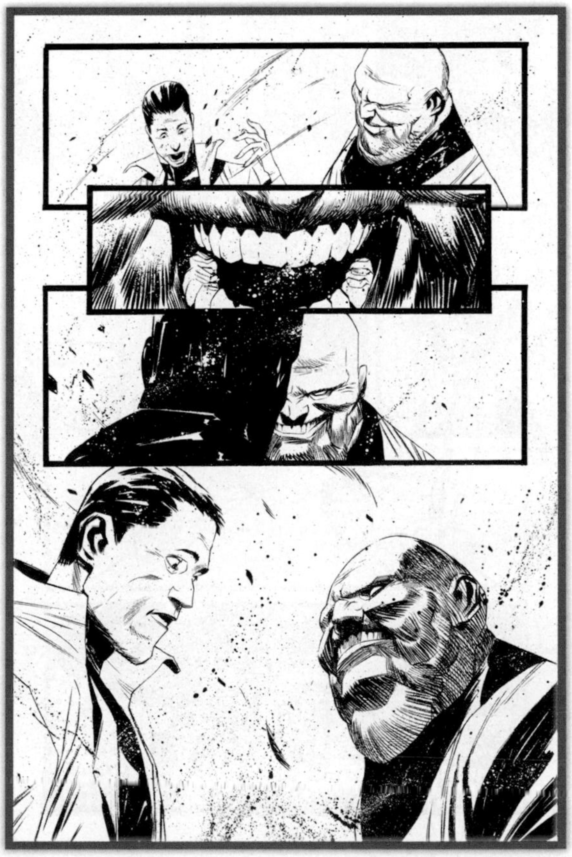

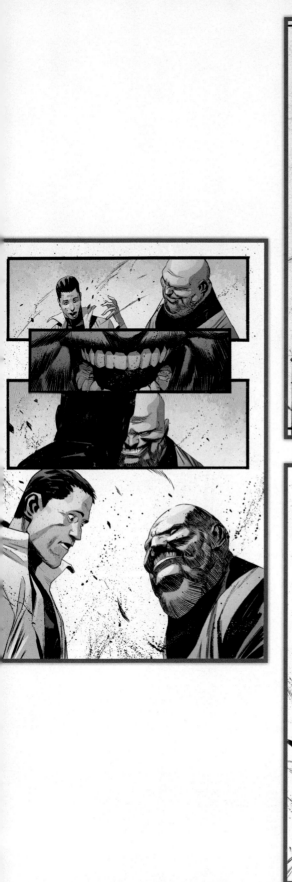

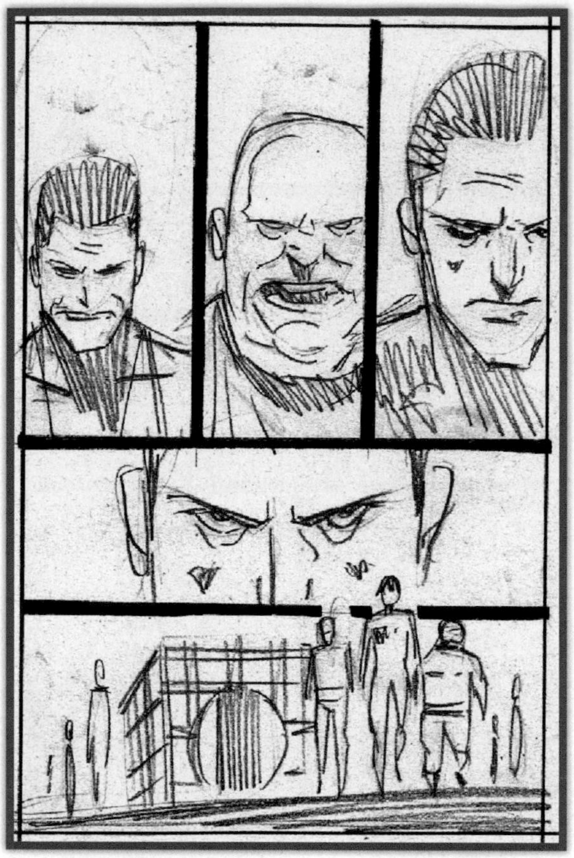

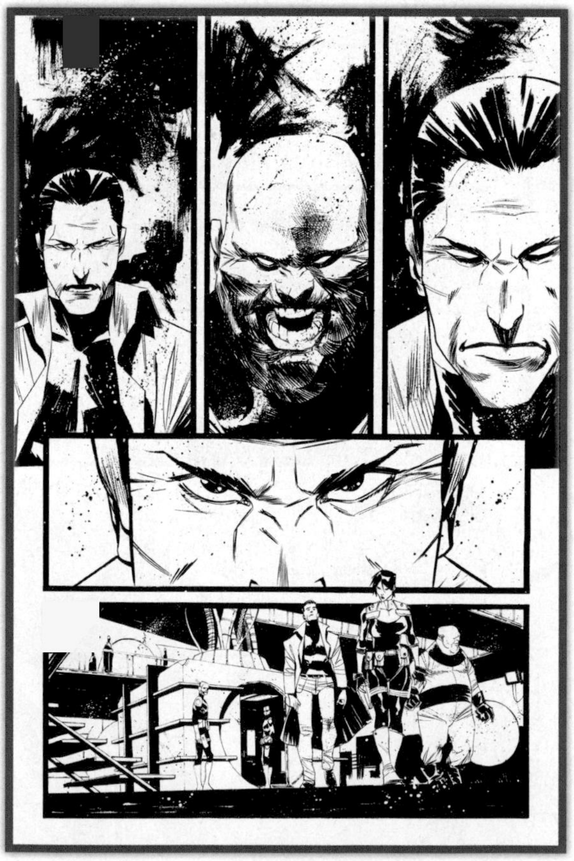

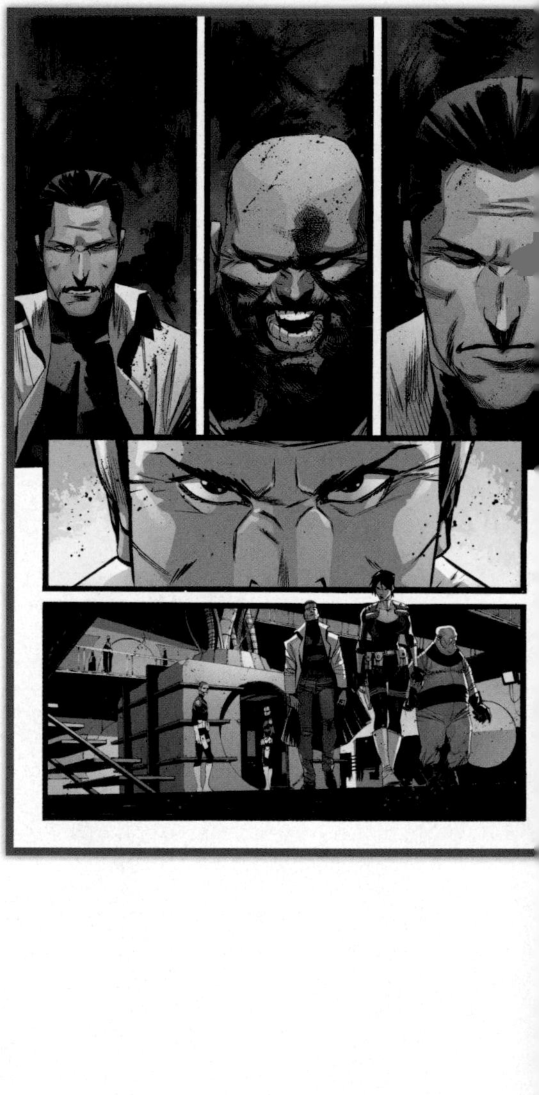

"I CAN'T REMEMBER A TIME THAT I WAS SO NTERTAINED BY A HULK COMIC." – *Weekly Comic Book Review*

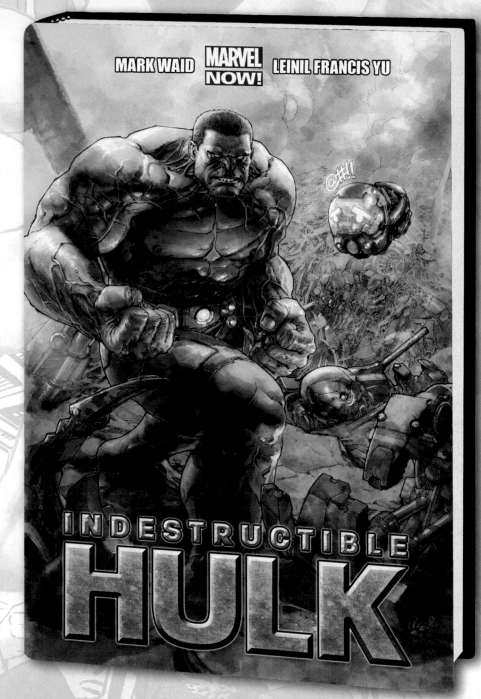

INDESTRUCTIBLE HULK VOL. 1: AGENT OF S.H.I.E.L.D. PREMIERE HC
978-0-7851-6831-7 • FEB130623

YOU EVER LIKED THE HULK, THIS IS THE BOOK TO PICK UP" – *Comic Booked*

© 2013 MARVEL

TO ACCESS THE FREE *MARVEL AUGMENTED REALITY APP*
THAT ENHANCES AND CHANGES THE WAY YOU EXPERIENCE COMIC

1. **Download the app for free via**
   marvel.com/ARapp
2. **Launch the app on your camera-enabled**
   Apple iOS® or Android™ device*

3. **Hold your mobile device's camera ov**
   any cover or panel with the AR grap
4. **Sit back and see the future of comics**
   in action!

*Available on most camera-enabled Apple iOS® and Android™ devices. Content subject to change and availability.

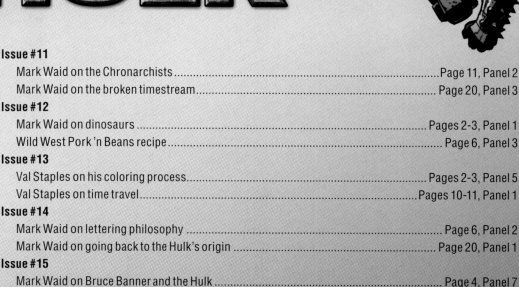

INDESTRUCTIBLE HULK

AR INDEX

TO REDEEM YOUR CODE
FOR A FREE DIGITAL COPY:

1. GO TO MARVEL.COM/REDEEM.
   OFFER EXPIRES ON 1/22/16.
2. FOLLOW THE ON-SCREEN INSTRUCTIONS
   TO REDEEM YOUR DIGITAL COPY.
3. LAUNCH THE MARVEL COMICS APP TO
   READ YOUR COMIC NOW!
4. YOUR DIGITAL COPY WILL BE FOUND
   UNDER THE *MY COMICS* TAB.
5. READ & ENJOY!

YOUR FREE DIGITAL COPY WILL BE AVAILABLE

| MARVEL COMICS APP | MARVEL COMICS AP |
| FOR APPLE® iOS DEVICES | FOR ANDROID™ DEVIC |

TMAX81DHXE9P